INTERN
SOCIA
A quarterly journ

.neory

Summer 1999
Contents

Editorial

John Rees   *The socialist revolution and the democratic revolution*   3

Mike Haynes   *Theses on the Balkan War*   85

Angus Calder   *Into slavery: the rise of imperialism*   133

Jim Wolfreys   *The physiology of barbarism*   147

John Newsinger   *Scenes from the class war: Ken Loach and socialist cinema*   155

Issue 83 of INTERNATIONAL SOCIALISM, quarterly journal of the Socialist Workers Party (Britain)

Published July 1999
Copyright © International Socialism
Distribution/subscriptions: International Socialism,
PO Box 82, London E3
American distribution: B de Boer, 113 East Center St, Nutley,
New Jersey 07110
Subscriptions and back copies: PO Box 16085, Chicago
Illinois 60616
Editorial and production: 0207 538 5821
Sales and subscriptions: 0207 531 9810
American sales: 773 665 7337

ISBN 1 898876 53 3

Printed by BPC Wheatons Ltd, Exeter, England
Typeset by East End Offset, London E3
Cover by Sherborne Design Ltd

For details of back copies see the end pages of this book

Subscription rates for one year (four issues) are:

Britain and overseas (surface):	individual	£14 ($30)
	institutional	£25
Air speeded supplement:	North America	£3
	Europe/South America	£3
	elsewhere	£4

Note to contributors
The deadline for articles intended for issue 85 of
International Socialism is 1 September 1999

All contributions should be double spaced with wide margins.
Please submit two copies. If you write your contribution
using a computer, please also supply a disk, together with
details of the computer and programme used.

INTERNATIONAL SOCIALISM ★

A quarterly journal of socialist theory

REVOLUTION, like war, was supposedly banished from the world scene a decade ago. In fact, social inequality and class conflict have become more marked in the last decade. But the major revolutionary challenges to the existing order in the last ten years—the revolutionary transformations in East Europe and South Africa and the still continuing Indonesian Revolution have so far resulted in the achievement of parliamentary regimes underpinned by capitalist economic structures. In 'The socialist revolution and the democratic revolution' John Rees looks back at the original democratic transformations, the classical bourgeois revolutions in England, America and France, and compares them with the upheavals of the last ten years. The comparison reveals that today more discriminating approaches are necessary in the field of strategy and organisation if workers' power is to be the outcome of contemporary revolutions.

THE WAR in the Balkans marks the most serious conflict in post-war European history. During the Cold War, military conflict was largely pushed to the margins of the system by the balance of power between the US and its Russian counterpart. But since the collapse of the Stalinist regimes a decade ago, NATO has expanded eastwards, creating a zone of instability from the Baltic states in the north, through East European and Balkan countries, to the Caspian and Black Sea states newly independent of Russia. Mike Haynes' 'Theses on the Balkan War' looks at the imperial interests at the heart of the new Balkan War and at the role of imperialism in past Balkan conflicts. He examines the forces within the Balkans which could begin to drive the curse of the major powers from the region and outlines the responsibilities of the left in the imperial centres.

ANGUS CALDER's timely review of *The New Oxford History of the British Empire* reminds us that the Balkan War, and excuses given for it, have a long and inglorious history behind them. And Jim Wolfreys' review of Donny Gluckstein's account of the rise of the Nazis reminds us that there are no easy comparisons with modern authoritarian heads of state. The ever popular socialist film maker Ken Loach is the subject of our final book review, in which John Newsinger looks at some new appraisals of Loach's life and work.

Editor: John Rees. Assistant editors: Alex Callinicos, Chris Harman, John Molyneux, Lindsey German, Colin Sparks, Mike Gonzalez, Peter Morgan, Mike Haynes, Judy Cox, Megan Trudell, Mark O'Brien, Rob Hoveman and Michael Lavalette.

The socialist revolution and the democratic revolution

JOHN REES

Revolutionary mass movements have challenged the existing order on three crucial occasions in the last decade. In 1989 the Stalinist regimes of Eastern Europe were demolished, in part by mass movements from below. At about the same time South African apartheid was destroyed by a mass movement, at the core of which stood the organised working class, led by the African National Congress. Most recently the 32 year old dictatorship of General Suharto was overthrown in Indonesia by a mass uprising spearheaded by a highly politicised student movement. But none of these revolutionary upheavals have been led by socialists and none have led to a challenge to capitalist social relations. Why? Is it because, as US State Department official Francis Fukuyama claimed after the revolutions of 1989, liberal democracy and capitalist economic relations are now the natural boundaries of historical change? Or are subjective factors, the strength and ideology of the left, the principal reasons why these movements failed to meet their potential?

This essay looks first at the period when the revolutionary challenge of the bourgeois revolution did indeed find its limit in the achievement of capitalist economic relations and a parliamentary republic. This is the era which runs from the English Revolution of 1649, through the American Revolution of 1776, to the French Revolution of 1789. Examination then turns to the great era when the organised working class made its appearance on the stage, raising the spectre of revolutionary change which could run beyond these boundaries and establish a socialist society. From

Marx and Engels' experience in the revolutions of 1848 to Lenin and
Trotsky's actions in 1917, an analysis is made of the way in which the
unfinished business of the democratic revolution became fused in theory
and in practice with the project of working class self emancipation.

But for all the great value that can be extracted from those occasions
when workers became the principal directors of their own destiny, there
have also been many occasions when they were not able to act in this
way. Defeat has often robbed workers of this capacity, but so have political leaders within the working class who did not possess a strategy
capable of releasing the potential for self liberation which working class
struggle generates. Under these circumstances the dynamic of capital
accumulation still produces great social crises which result in profound
social transformations. The unification of Italy and Germany in the
second half of the 19th century and the great wave of anti-colonial revolutions in the second half of the 20th century are examples. The role of a
key layer of the middle classes in these latter transformations is examined in order to shed light on the conflict between the competing
strategies of the socialist revolution and the democratic revolution, and
their differing relationships to the wider class formations and conditions
of capital accumulation in the revolutions of the last ten years.

The events of 1989 marked the end of an era in which Communist
parties internationally carried the notion that working class movements in
important parts of the world were excluded from the possibility of
socialist revolution until after they had completed the tasks of the democratic revolution. But similar arguments continue to be advanced even
without this agency promoting them, just as they arose in 1848 and 1917,
long before the rise of Stalinism. Nevertheless, the absence of powerful
Stalinist organisations reinforcing this ideological trend gives the socialist
alternative a greater possibility of winning adherents than at any time
since the early 1920s.

The classical bourgeois revolutions: England, America and France

The history of the great bourgeois revolutions can illuminate two crucial
aspects of the modern relationship between the democratic revolution
and the socialist revolution. Firstly, it can show with great force the rad-
icalising dynamic which works at the heart of all revolutions. In all these
revolutions those who made the revolution entered the conflict with a
consciousness far removed from the notion of forcibly overthrowing the
existing order. Only repeated internal crises in the revolutionary process
eventually brought them face to face with this necessity. During this
process of polarisation many individuals, indeed whole political organisations, moved dramatically from the left of the revolution to the right, or

even from the revolutionary camp to the camp of counter-revolution.

This dynamic of radicalisation is as marked in the great proletarian revolutions as it is in the bourgeois revolutions. It is in this aspect that the similarities between the two are the most striking. But in the second comparison between the two sorts of revolution it is the contrasts which are most obvious. This concerns the differences between the socio-economic conditions under which the two sorts of revolutions take place: the bourgeois revolutions against a pre-capitalist social structure, the proletarian against a developed industrial capitalism. This framework ultimately governs the limits of the revolutionary process, providing the practical barrier in which the most radical programmes of the revolutionary movement find their limit. Both aspects of this process are clearly expressed in the history of the first of the great bourgeois revolutions, the English Revolution.

The English Revolution 1640-1688: Alexis de Tocqueville once said that 'the most dangerous moment for a bad government is generally that in which it sets about reform'.[1] But the fate of Charles I shows that resistance to reform can be just as dangerous. It was Charles's determination to retain, indeed to strengthen, the absolutist cast of his regime in the face of social and economic change which was the immediate cause of the revolution. Marx, referring to John Hampden's refusal to pay the Ship Money with which Charles attempted to overcome the financial crisis of the state, put the point like this:

> It was not John Hampden...who brought Charles I to the scaffold, but only the latter's own obstinacy, his dependence on the feudal estates, and his presumptuous attempt to use force to suppress the urgent demands of the emerging society. The refusal to pay taxes is merely a sign of the dissidence that exists between the Crown and the people, merely evidence that the conflict between the government and the people has reached a menacing degree of intensity.[2]

In the initial phase of the revolution, from the summoning of the Long Parliament by Charles I in 1640 to the outbreak of civil war in 1642, the broad parliamentary opposition polarised into those willing to take their resistance to the king to the point of armed conflict and those who would rather side with the king than countenance the threat to the existing order which civil war represented. But even in this first stage the beginnings of further polarisation are evident. For it was the London crowd, composed of the lowest levels of the 'middling sort' of small craftsmen and traders bolstered by servants and labourers, which drove the parliamentary resistance forward. And, by repulsion, they also obliged the king and his supporters to define themselves clearly as a reactionary political force.[3] This tripartite division is characteristic of bourgeois revolutions. The revolution is fundamentally a conflict between 'the "rising" bourgeoisie and the established feudal or aristocratic class that it was seeking to displace from the levers of social and political control'. But, as George Rudé explains:

> there is more to it than that: in each of these revolutions...there was also an additional popular element that was also struggling for a place in the sun... In the English Revolution of the 17th century, there were not only the leaders of Parliament and the New Model Army, the Presbyterians and the Independents (all broadly representative of the 'bourgeois' challenge), but also the Levellers, Diggers and lower class sectaries, who offered some sort of challenge in the name of other, 'lower', social groups.[4]

The divisions between the king's supporters, the parliamentary leaders and the London crowd in the opening years of the revolution were the beginning of this process.

When civil war became a reality between 1642 and 1645 a further polarisation in the parliamentary ranks took place. This time it was between those who were willing to prosecute the war to the point of destroying the king and possibly the monarchy—the Independents grouped around Cromwell and Ireton—and, on the other side, the Presbyterians who only fought in order to weaken the king to the point where compromise once again became possible. Indeed, the Presbyterians claimed they were fighting for 'king and parliament'. To these moderates Cromwell replied, 'I will not cozen you with perplexed expressions in my commission about fighting for king and parliament. If the king happened to be in the body of the enemy, I would as soon discharge my pistol upon him as upon any private man'.[5] In this phase of the revolution the decisive act was Cromwell's creation of the New Model Army, based on the experience of creating his own regiment of Ironsides. This was only possible by mobilising the lower orders of society. 'I had rather have a plain russet coated captain that knows what he fights for and loves what he knows, than that which you call a gentleman and is nothing else', as Cromwell put it.[6] But, having raised such forces, Cromwell was less content when they developed a political programme and an organisation of their own.

The third and final phase of radicalisation involved a further division in the parliamentarian ranks—indeed in the New Model Army, which emerged victorious from the civil war. The army itself became the key political body in the country after it defeated Charles at Naseby in 1645. London, the bank and armoury of the army, was the other key focus of political development. In both elements from amongst the very lowest of the bourgeoisie, the artisans, shopkeepers and small businessmen, and the ordinary soldiers, now formed organisations which mounted a political challenge to the strategy of the Grandees, the leading, and previously most radical, elements on the parliamentary side. The Levellers in London and the agents, or 'agitators' to use the contemporary term, elected by the mutinous regiments of the New Model Army increasingly operated as one. They developed in *The Agreement of the People* the most democratic programme seen during the English Revolution. In the debates held in Putney Church in 1647 these forces directly confronted their military commanders and social superiors in the original of all such great revolutionary exchanges. The Levellers and the agitators won the ideological argument, but lost the power play. This was in part because the king's escape from captivity reunited the Grandees, the Levellers and the agitators in the second civil war.

Shortly before Charles's execution, Leveller John Lilburne was summoned before Cromwell and his Council of State to account for the Levellers' continued agitation in favour of their radical version of *The Agreement of the People*. Lilburne was, as ever, unyielding. He was told to retire, but from the next room he heard Cromwell say, 'I tell you, sir, you have no other way of dealing with these men but to break them, or they will break you...and so render you to all rational men in the world as the most contemptible generation of silly, low spirited men in the earth, to be broken and routed by such a despicable, contemptible generation of men as they are, and therefore, sir, I tell you again, you are necessitated to break them'.[7] Cromwell proceeded to do just as he promised, and a few months later the Leveller mutiny in the army was crushed by Cromwell at Burford churchyard in Oxfordshire.

Nevertheless, these same developments and the remaining challenge from the left also forced the Grandees to abandon compromise with the king and embark on the road which led through regicide to the establishment of a republic. And at this time there was one last attempt to radicalise the revolution further: the Diggers' dozen or so attempts, most famously at St George's Hill in Surrey, to found 'communist' communities. As expounded by their best known spokesman, Gerrard Winstanley, the Diggers' programme ran well beyond the democracy expounded by John Lilburne and the Levellers and raised the issue of social and economic equality. But if the social basis for the Levellers was shallow, the social basis for the Diggers was insufficient to sustain them as a movement, let alone underpin their programme and make it a viable project for the wider society. Certainly the moment was inauspicious: in 1649 the Levellers and agitators had been routed. But there was more to their rapid eviction by troopers and local gentry than bad timing. Even at the height of popular radicalisation there was no social class, because no underlying economic development had created such a class, which could provide a political actor capable of implementing the Diggers' radical dream. Their bequest to radicals who came after them, down to our own times, is the dream of political, social and economic freedom, even though they lacked the means to realise it in their own time.

History is full of such intimations of the future by social movements and individuals alike. Leonardo da Vinci's drawing of a 'helicopter' is one such magnificent presentiment of things to come, but hundreds of years of economic development were necessary before Leonardo's drawing could become a practical proposition. So it was with the Diggers. Nevertheless, we do not turn our back on the genius of Winstanley any more than we would on the genius of Leonardo. We look to combine their image of the future with what we now know to be the material means of making the image real.

The American Revolution 1776-1786: In the American Revolution of 1776 we see the same process of radicalisation taking hold during the course of the revolution, but the colonial relationship with Britain gave the forces and phases of revolutionary development a significantly different character. To begin with, the underlying economic causes of the American Revolution are partly to do with the economic development of the colonies, but the crisis itself cannot be understood in isolation from how this growth interacted with the imperial policy of Britain.

In 1763 Britain emerged victorious from its war with France for control of the North American colonies. But war debts concentrated the minds of the British ruling class on regaining full control of its colonial possessions and imposing new taxes. In 1764 the Currency Act and the Revenue (or Sugar) Act aimed to make colonial merchants pay in sterling rather than their own coin, and to slap duty on imported sugar even when, as had not previously been the case, it came from other parts of the British Empire. In 1765 the Stamp Act ruled that any transaction specified by the act was illegal unless the appropriate stamp was purchased. Legal, church, political and commercial documents, passports, dice and playing cards, books, newspapers and advertisements were all subject to taxation under the act. Furthermore, there was a directly political side to the act. Money raised under the act would stay in the colonies but would be directly under the control of Britain's appointed governors, not, as before, the colonial assemblies. Here was the origin of taxation without representation.

Even before the Stamp Act, a coalition of merchants, professionals and slaveowners together with artisans, labourers, farmers, servants and sailors had emerged to oppose Britain. At first their pamphlets and speeches were cautious, but they grew bolder—graduating from resistance to revolution and from protest to a war for independence—with each imperial crisis. Resistance to the Stamp Act was the first phase of radicalisation. A Stamp Act Congress brought nine colonial delegates to New York City to pass strongly worded resolutions and addresses to the king. But in the towns from which the delegates came, tax collectors were being tarred and feathered by angry crowds, protesters gathered at the foot of 'Liberty trees', and collective political organisations, the Sons of Liberty, sprang into being. The first of the various Sons of Liberty organisations were the Loyal Nine of Boston, and among their members were a printer, a brazier, a painter and a jeweller. These artisans were joined by men like Sam Adams and, later, Tom Paine, intellectuals whose lives were closely intertwined with those of the artisans, but who were able to command both the respect and fear of the merchants and slaveowners of the revolutionary coalition.

The popular movement in America emerged sooner and reached its peak earlier in the revolutionary process than in the English Revolution. Colonial society allowed far greater freedom to speak, write and organise than did Stuart England before the summoning of the Long Parliament. Loyalism to Britain was probably weaker than loyalism to Charles I, and American revolutionaries had the English Revolution on which they could model their movement. In the upper reaches of the revolutionary coalition John Locke's theories of representative government, and of the population's ultimate right to revolt against tyrannical authority, were invoked. But at the plebeian end of the spectrum thoughts also turned back a century or so. Many of the colonies were originally peopled by Puritan refugees from Stuart tyranny and later by Cromwell's troopers. In 1774 one 'Joyce, Jun' appeared as 'Captain' of the 'Committee for Tarring and Feathering' in Boston, where most inhabitants would have caught the reference to the officer who took Charles I prisoner in 1647. About the same time farm families were frequently calling their newborn boys Oliver, to make plain their admiration of Charles's nemesis.[8]

Popular mobilisation defeated the Stamp Act, which was repealed the year after it was introduced. But Britain was by no means finished with the American colonies. Just as the Stamp Act was repealed the Declaratory Act was passed, insisting that Britain could 'make laws…to bind the colonies and people of America…in all cases whatsoever'.[9] In 1767 the Chancellor of the Exchequer, Charles Townshend, passed acts taxing paint, paper, lead, glass and tea. Colonial America responded with a tax strike which ran until 1770. Throughout this period popular mobilisations continued. They culminated in the event which precipitated the repeal of the Townshend duties, the Boston massacre of 5 March 1770. British Redcoats opened fire on an angry crowd of protesters, killing five of them. The dead give an accurate social cross-section of the movement: an African-Indian sailor, a ship's mate, a leather maker, a rope maker and an ivory turner's apprentice. Their deaths helped to cement the lower levels of the revolutionary alliance to their leaders.

The movement deepened and radicalised. And it did so again after the Boston Tea Party in December 1773, when protesters disguised as Mohawk Indians dumped tea, the one remaining commodity subject to Townshend duties, from ships into Boston harbour. Even before the Continental Congress met in 1774, Committees of Correspondence staffed by the same sort of people—indeed often by the very same individuals—who had formed the Sons of Liberty to resist the Stamp Act a decade earlier, carried the newly revolutionary message throughout the colonies.

By 1775 the committees had replaced the ruins of royal government as the effective power in the colonies, transacting 'all such matters as they shall conceive may tend to the welfare of the American cause'. Committees raised militias, organised supplies, tried and jailed the revolution's enemies and began to control goods and prices. They called mass meetings to 'take the sense of citizens', and they frustrated Britain's plans to regain control by calling an election for a provincial assembly by ensuring that radicals won. In January 1776 Tom Paine published a revolutionary manifesto, *Common Sense*, which used the plain language of ordinary artisans and farmers to urge the movement on to a final break with Britain. It sold 150,000 copies and its arguments were repeated wherever revolutionaries met to convince others that establishment resistance must give way to independence.

This decade long radicalisation could not help but alarm the elite figures who tried to stay at the head of resistance to Britain, even as they realised that Britain could not be beaten without such popular agitation. The War of Independence helped them to keep this movement within bounds. Unlike the conflict of 1642-1645 in England, this was not a civil war but a colonial war for independence from Britain. Consequently, the effect of the war was not to further polarise the revolutionary camp, as it had done the New Model Army or would do during the French Revolution, but rather the opposite. In the decade of popular protest which preceded the American War of Independence, class antagonism against the rich of colonial America ran along the same courses as fury at Britain. Once war broke out, the Colonial Army under George Washington increasingly replaced the guerrilla methods of the first battle at Lexington with regular army discipline enforced by the rich and powerful who dominated the officer corps. By contrast, the creation of the New Model Army required the 'internal coup' of the self denying ordinance against the aristocrats who had stayed with parliament, and the fact that the war was fought against fellow Englishmen fuelled social radicalism.

Popular disaffection with the war was, if anything, greater in America than in England, although in both cases some felt, wrongly but understandably, that it was a 'rich man's war' which would change little regardless of who won. Daniel Shays, a poor farm hand and former soldier, led a rebellion in 1786 which briefly raised the spectre of renewed popular radicalism. The rebels used the same tactics that had proved so effective against Britain, gathering in arms to close the local court house. But now their allies of 1774, the Boston radicals, were divided. Some, allied with conservative merchants, ran the state government and sent loyal militiamen to scatter the Shaysites. Sam Adams was one such, helping to draw up a Riot Act and to suspend habeas corpus and so allow the authorities to keep prisoners in jail without bringing them to trial. One defeated Shays supporter pleaded, 'Tis true I have been a committeeman,' but, 'I am sincerely sorry ...and hope it will be overlooked and pardoned'.[10] Unmoved by such sentiments, Adams argued, 'In a monarchy the crime of treason may admit of being pardoned or lightly punished, but the man who dares rebel against the laws of a republic ought to suffer death'.[11] The Shays Rebellion never developed either the programmatic clarity of *The Agreement of the People* nor the political weight of Lilburne's organisation. Nevertheless, the parallel with the defeat of the Levellers at Burford is obvious.

The triumphant ruling class, led by the Federalists Alexander Hamilton and James Madison, moved to create a strong unitary state. They, like Cromwell, were successful for a decade before the restoration of the monarchy gave power back to the social centre of the ruling class. In Britain power came to an alliance of landowners and the bourgeoisie; in America to slaveholding landowners and, in a subordinate position, the predominately Northern bourgeoisie. But neither conservative dominated coalition would or could return to the pre-war settlement. And in both cases the bourgeoisie asserted itself within this more conducive framework in the longer run. In England in 1689 the ruling class frustrated renewed Stuart attempts at establishing monarchical power, and by 1832 the industrial bourgeoisie established complete hegemony over its old landowning partner. In America the epilogue was more dramatic than the prologue. The second American revolution, fought as the American Civil War, utterly crushed the power of the Southern landowning slaveocracy.

The French Revolution 1789: The French was the greatest and most complete of all the bourgeois revolutions, involving the mass of the population on a scale far greater than either the American or even the English Revolution.[12]

The Declaration of the Rights of Man...set forth human and national rights with a feeling for their universality far surpassing the empirical statement of liberties made by the English Revolution of the 17th century. Similarly the American Declaration of Independence, although couched in universal language and natural law, still contained limitations restricting the application of its principles. The bourgeoisie who formed the Constituent Assembly believed that their work was grounded in universal reason, and the Declaration expressed this clearly and forcefully.[13]

One reason for the unique depth and breadth of the French Revolution was that the bourgeoisie's cumulative experience of challenging the old order fed into French events. Thomas Jefferson was actually in Paris when the Declaration of the Rights of Man was written. Tom Paine and Lafayette, 'the hero of two continents', joined the revolution, although significantly both were on its moderate wing. More broadly, the French, like the Americans a decade or so before, drew on the political theory of John Locke and the Enlightenment tradition which owed so much to the impulse of the English Revolution.

But these direct and indirect ideological influences were not the main reason for the great reach of the French Revolution. The fundamental causes lay in the social and economic conditions under which the revolution took place. France was a much more economically advanced society at the time of its revolution than either England in the 1640s or America in the 1770s. Indeed, in 1789 in France the proportion of national product coming from industry and commerce (18 percent and 12 percent respectively) were similar to England and Wales at the same time. Even the proportion of national income coming from agriculture, at 49 percent, was only 9 percent higher than the figure for England and Wales.[14]

Yet this is only half the story. France's social and political development, unlike Britain's, stood diametrically opposed to its economic progress. France's class structure and the shape of its state remained caught in the long shadow of feudalism. The monarch's absolutist pretensions overawed most of the bourgeoisie (and even some of the aristocracy). But the most important dividing line ran between the aristocracy as a whole and the rest of society, whose leading non-noble element was the bourgeoisie. Abbé Sieyes' famous pamphlet *What Is The Third Estate?*, the initial manifesto and rallying call of the bourgeoisie, complained:

all the branches of the executive have been taken over by a caste that monopolises the Church, the judiciary and the army. A spirit of fellowship leads the nobles to favour one another in everything over the rest of the nation. Their usurpation is complete; they truly reign.[15]

This was no exaggeration: only nobles could be bishops or officers in the army. Nobles were exempt from taxes, which fell most heavily on a peasantry treated as little more than beasts of burden. Some historians have balked at describing French society before the revolution as feudal because some of the features of the high feudalism of the Middle Ages had already disappeared. But this is to miss the point made so clearly by de Tocqueville at the time:

> *Feudalism had remained the most important of our civil institutions even after it had ceased to be a political institution. In this form it aroused still greater hatred, and we should observe that the disappearance of part of the institutions of the Middle Ages only made what survived of them a hundred times more odious.*[16]

It was the intensity of the contradiction between the economic development of France and the unreconstructed nature of its social structures which underpinned the scale of the French Revolution. In the final analysis the bourgeoisie, often far from willingly or enthusiastically, found that the intransigence of the old regime was so great that they had to rouse far greater numbers of the small bourgeoisie, and the ordinary people and the peasants below them, if they were to be victorious. Yet in 1789 no leader of the French bourgeoisie realised how great a struggle would be needed to vanquish the old order, any more than Hampden or Adams had done before them. Once again, only successive crises and successive renewals of the revolutionary leadership revealed the full extent of what would be necessary to accomplish the revolution.

At first it even seemed as if sections of the aristocracy might be willing to participate in the work of reforming the old order. But by the time the king was forced to call the Estates General on 5 May 1789 the challenge of this 'aristocratic revolution' had run its course. In this first internal crisis the Third Estate nominally represented the whole of the non-noble, non-clerical nation. In fact they represented the bourgeoisie. Of the 610 delegates of the Third Estate, the biggest single element (25 percent) were, as in so many capitalist parliaments since, those professionally engaged in advocacy for the wealthy: lawyers. Some 13 percent were actually manufacturers; another 5 percent were from the professions; only 7 to 9 percent were agriculturalists.[17]

The Third Estate declared itself the leadership of what, at this stage, remained an attempt to force the king into reform without destroying the entire ruling institutions of society. The first radicalisation of the revolution took place as a minority of the Third Estate joined the majority of the clergy and the aristocracy to work for compromise. And, despite the fall of the Bastille and the first eruption of the peasant struggle which

deepened the revolution at every turn, the remaining majority of the
Third Estate, now renamed the Constituent Assembly, still searched for
agreement with its enemies.

The king's flight to Varennes on 21 June 1791 made it clear to even
the most ardent compromiser that no such agreement was possible. The
nobility now fomented open counter-revolution at home and conspired
with the crowned heads of Europe to wage war from abroad, hoping that
the experience of war would unite the nation behind the traditional ruling
class. 'Instead of civil war, we shall have war abroad, and things will be
much better', wrote Louis XVI.[18]

The popular response to this threat took not only the aristocracy but
also the existing leadership of the revolution by surprise. In 1792 the
popular mobilisation against the threat of counter-revolution within and
without sealed the fate of the monarchy and marked a further radicalisation of the revolution. The Girondins, named after the region of France
they came from, insisted that the 'passive citizens', the lower orders of
ordinary people, now be called upon to defend the nation and the revolution. But the mobilisation of the popular masses under the banner of the
sans culottes and the *enragés* brought with it demands which the
Girondins could not countenance. In Paris in May 1792 the 'red priest'
Jacques Roux demanded the death penalty for hoarders of grain; a year
later he was insisting, 'Equality is no more than an empty shadow so
long as monopolies give the rich the power of life and death over their
fellow human beings'.[19] This message was carried through Paris by
means of direct democracy: the assemblies and meetings of administrative 'sections' of the city, the associated political clubs and left wing
newspapers.

Under pressure from the aroused small bourgeoisie, journeymen and
labourers, and the continued peasant risings, divisions emerged between
the Girondins and the Mountain, the left wing deputies led by the
Jacobins, so called because they occupied the upper tiers in the National
Assembly. Fearful of the movement they had called into existence, the
Girondins stood aside from the revolutionary movement of 10 August
1792 which overthrew the monarchy and the restrictive electoral system.
It was a fatal abstention, and the fate of Girondins was sealed along with
that of the king.

The Jacobins were the recipients of the laurels of 10 August. But
the Jacobins themselves relied on the support of two different class
fractions, the small bourgeoisie and the artisans on the one hand, and
the day labourers and journeymen whom they employed, the *sans
culottes*, on the other. The *sans culottes* had their own organs of
mobilisation in the Paris sections which only in part overlapped with
those organisations, like the Jacobin Club and its affiliates, which

were more or less fully under the control of the bourgeoisie. This alliance, and the popular mobilisation which underlay it, reached its high point in 1793-1794.

By 1793 the Jacobin revolutionary government finally constructed itself in such a way that it was capable of effectively and definitively dealing with its aristocratic enemy, in part by granting the popular demand for a law setting maximum prices for essentials (and also for wages). But at the very moment of victory the alliance between the Jacobins and the *sans culottes*, which made victory possible, fell apart. On the 22 June 1793 Jacques Roux spoke at the radical Cordeliers Club, demanding the punishment of speculators:

> *If that article was not in the constitution...we could say to the Mountain; You have done nothing for the **sans culottes**, because it was not for the rich that they fight, it is for liberty...We adore liberty, but we do not want to die of hunger. Suppress speculation and we have nothing more to ask.*

At the same meeting another *enragé*, Jean Varlet, added:

> *The **sans culottes** of Paris, Lyons, Marseilles and Bordeaux...**alone comprise the people**; we must thus establish a line of demarcation between the shop-keeper, the aristocrat and the artisan; the first two classes must be disarmed...tomorrow the people must triumph, tomorrow we must finish our work.*[20]

Even the Jacobins could not allow either an economic programme which limited the bourgeoisie in this way, or a redefinition of 'the people' which rested on *sans culottes* alone and thereby excluded the section of the bourgeoisie on which the Jacobins predominately relied. 'It is hardly surprising,' notes George Rudé, 'that the political ideas and social aspirations of such men should differ in important respects from those of proprietors, lawyers, doctors, teachers and businessmen who sat in the Convention or even from those of the smaller lawyers, tradesmen, and civil servants who predominated in the provincial Jacobin clubs and societies'.[21]

The *sans culottes* posed a danger to the French bourgeoisie greater than that posed by the Levellers to Ireton and Cromwell. The Levellers spoke of a radical form of petty bourgeois democracy, and so did the *sans culottes*. But the *sans culottes* raised the spectre of economic equality far more consistently and insistently, even if in a backward looking form. There was no equivalent of the laws of the maximum prices in the English Revolution. But even this was not the main distinction between the Levellers and the *sans culottes*. The differences lay not in the demands or the programmes of the Levellers and the *sans culottes,* but in the social forces which these political designations represented.

The Levellers were an organisation of the petty bourgeoisie in fact as well as in aspiration. Their leaders were never much troubled by any distinctive element contributed by those of the lower classes who chose to follow their banner. Nor had larger capitalists developed to the degree that they had in France, and therefore the distinction of interest between these different layers of the bourgeoisie was not so sharp.

Not so the *sans culottes.* They united petty bourgeois and craft workers in one organisation at a time when these layers found themselves pitted against a more developed layer of bigger capitalists. The *sans culottes* could not form a working class organisation, because this class did not yet have the capacity to frame its own demands and form its own movements. But they were an organisation which channelled the economic desperation of the common people, the wage labourers, journeymen and artisans who did not own the capital, even in the small amounts, which would have allowed them to count amongst the humblest of the bourgeoisie. Albert Soboul writes:

> *Falling under the province of the popular classes through their conditions of existence and often their poverty, the artisans nonetheless possessed their own workshops, their little sets of tools and were looked on as independent producers. Having journeymen and apprentices under them and under their discipline accentuated their bourgeois mentality. But the attachment to the system of small production and direct sale opposed them irredeemably to the bourgeoisie. Thus among the artisans and shopkeepers who formed the bulk of the **sans culottes** movement and with whom the bourgeois revolution must end, there arose a social ideal in contradiction with economic necessities.*[22]

The *sans culottes* wanted restrictions on capitalist wealth and a republic of small proprietors; but they were small capitalists themselves (or under the influence of small capitalists) and could hardly constrain the accumulation of capital with any consistency. They demanded that they be kept in work and their wages be protected; but this only gave confidence to the journeymen whom they employed. Thus 'the demands of this class of artisans and shopkeepers were sublimated in passionate complaints, in spurts of revolt, without ever specifying a coherent programme'.[23]

As yet there was no class developed enough to provide the social base on which a coherent anti-capitalist programme could rest. The journeymen and wage workers were still mainly dispersed in small workshops with little division of labour, not clearly differentiated from the peasantry from which they sprang. Strikes predated the revolution, but no wider political programme was yet developed from this experience.

Certainly journeymen and wage workers participated in the revolution as part of its most radical wing, but they did so under the political programme of their masters:

> *The revolutionary vanguard was not composed of factory workers but...an alliance of small employers and the journeymen who lived and worked with them. This mixed social composition gave the popular movement...a series of contradictions that derived from its inherent ambiguity. The workers' view of the world was dominated by that of the petty bourgeois craftsman, which was ultimately that of the bourgeoisie. Thus workers did not form an independent group either in the realm of thought or action. They failed to realise the connection between the value of their labour and the level of their wages...they had not fully realised the social function of labour.*[24]

The leadership of the Jacobins, who perhaps form a more accurate French counterpart to the Levellers, found in the *sans culottes* a force they could employ in a way which their forerunners in 1647 did not, as a result of the greater economic development of France. And they also found greater need to make use of such a force as a result of the entrenched and determined resistance of their aristocratic enemy, less weakened by partial integration into capitalist economic development than the English aristocracy of the previous century. But, even for the most radical bourgeois democrats, the alliance with the *sans culottes* was a pact with the devil. And they reacted against it, even more furiously than Cromwell reacted against the Levellers, as soon as its necessity had passed.

The effect was similar in both cases, but the consequences followed more swiftly and decisively in the French case. Deprived of its most radical support, the revolutionary government became prey to its enemies on the right. Cromwell had ten years, and the full term of his life, before counter-revolution repaid him for the suppression of the Levellers. Robespierre survived a matter of months before Thermidor (as the month was called in the new revolutionary calendar, 27 July 1794 in the old calendar) repaid him for the suppression of the *sans culottes*. The Thermidorians introduced their new constitution with a familiar cry, first heard from Henry Ireton in the Putney Debates and later theorised by Thomas Hobbes, now uttered by 'the champion of the new rich', Boissy d'Anglas:

> *We must be governed by the best men; those most suited to govern are men of good education and endowed with a great concern for the maintenance of order. You will rarely find such men outside the ranks of the propertied... A country governed by men of property belongs to 'the social order' whereas*

one governed by men of no property reverts to a 'state of nature'.[25]

The radical left once again enjoyed a bright but brief Indian summer. In the footsteps of Winstanley and Shays came Babeuf. But this 'revolution after the revolution' was, again, different to its forerunners. If the *sans culottes'* programme ultimately expressed a nostalgic reaction of a half emerged artisan working class to the contradictions of capitalism, then Babeuf's Conspiracy of Equals came close to connecting a utopian vision of communism, which gave it some continuity with the Diggers, with a class of wage workers far more developed than that in 17th century England. Moreover, in the Conspirators' organisation, despite the misleading indications of their title, the first dim outlines of modern working class political organisation can be traced.[26]

What changed in 1848?

Even before the outbreak of the 1848 revolutions Marx and Engels were clear on two points. The first was that the coming revolution would be a bourgeois revolution; that is, it would herald a capitalist state, hopefully democratic and republican in form. The second was that the bourgeoisie would have to be pushed to a decisive settling of accounts with the old order, since the growing strength of the working class made them fearful that unleashing the full power of the revolution would sweep them aside along with the feudal state. For Marx and Engels the revolution in Germany would be 'carried out under far more advanced conditions of European civilisation, and with a much more developed proletariat, than that of England in the 17th, and of France in the 18th century', and would therefore be 'the prelude to an immediately following proletarian revolution'.[27]

Thus in the early stages of the revolution Marx and Engels fought as the furthest left wing of the democratic revolution. But even *The Communist Manifesto*, written before the outbreak of the revolution, urged that although the working class should 'fight with the bourgeoisie whenever it acts in a revolutionary way', socialists should also 'instil into the working class the clearest possible recognition of the hostile antagonism between the bourgeoisie and the proletariat'.[28] Marx and Engels' approach at the start of the revolution was 'to spur on the bourgeoisie from an independent base on the left, organising the plebeian classes separately from the bourgeoisie in order to strike together at the old regime, and to prepare this democratic bloc of proletariat, petty bourgeoisie and peasantry to step temporarily into the vanguard should the bourgeoisie shows signs of cold feet, by analogy with the Jacobin government in France of 1793-1794'.[29]

But this position was significantly altered by Marx and Engels as the 1848 revolutions developed. For the first three months of the German revolution it looked as though the bourgeoisie, though irresolute, might be pushed into decisive action. But the longer the revolution went on, the more timid and paralysed the bourgeoisie became. By the time of the 'June Days' all the exploiting classes, including the bourgeoisie and most of their democratic spokesmen, were ranged on the side of reaction. Marx and Engels were increasingly driven to the conclusion that only the exploited classes, the workers and the peasants, could drive the revolution forward. As Marx wrote in his paper, *Neue Rheinische Zeitung*, whose bourgeois backers were abandoning it because of its radical stance:

> *The German bourgeoisie developed so sluggishly, so pusillanimously and so slowly, that it saw itself threateningly confronted by the proletariat, and all those sections of the urban population related to the proletariat...at the very moment of its own threatening confrontation with feudalism and absolutism... The Prussian bourgeoisie was not, like the French bourgeoisie of 1789, the class which represented the whole of modern society... It had sunk to the level of a type of estate...inclined from the outset to treachery against the people.*[30]

Faced with far greater treachery on the part of the bourgeoisie than they had at first expected, Marx and Engels altered their strategic position. Marx and Engels now concluded that independent action on the part of the working class and a more critical stance, on tactical issues as well as theoretical ones, toward the bourgeois democrats was essential. Marx's explanation of the attitude of the workers to the democrats is of great relevance:

> *The workers must drive the proposals of the democrats to their logical extreme (the democrats will in any case act in a reformist and not a revolutionary manner) and transform these proposals into direct attacks on private property. If, for instance, the petty bourgeoisie proposes the purchase of the railways and factories, the workers must demand that these railways and factories simply be confiscated without compensation as the property of reactionaries. If the democrats propose a proportional tax, then the workers must demand a progressive tax; if the democrats themselves propose a moderate progressive tax, then the workers must insist on a tax whose rates rise so steeply that big capital will be ruined by it; if the democrats themselves demand the regulation of state debt, then the workers must demand national bankruptcy. The demands of the workers thus have to be adjusted according to the measures and concessions of the democrats.*[31]

As the revolution developed, political divisions within the revolutionary camp based on underlying class differences began to harden:

> *It is the fate of all revolutions that this union of different classes, which in*
> *some degree is always the necessary condition of any revolution, cannot*
> *subsist long. No sooner is the victory gained against the common enemy than*
> *the victors become divided amongst themselves into different camps and turn*
> *their weapons against each other. It is this rapid and passionate development*
> *of class antagonism which, in old and complicated social organisms, makes*
> *revolution such a powerful agent of social and political progress.*[32]

In response to this polarisation Marx urged revolutionaries to concentrate on the independent political organisation of the working class,
confident that the more powerful this became the more it would push the
bourgeois democrats to the left whether they are in government or not.
Marx hoped the movement of workers could become so strong that it
could result in a revolution against the liberal democrats. Marx now
believed, as he did not clearly believe before the 1848 revolutions, that
this would be a socialist revolution.

It was this new perspective which led him to conclude that, since the
state apparatus is not a neutral body that can simply be passed from one
class to another, the working class must concentrate on building up its
own state apparatus alongside and in opposition to that of the propertied
classes. Organisations such as strike committees, local delegate bodies of
workers and mass meetings will emerge from the struggle against the old
regime. Where conditions of struggle allow, these will involve the formation of workers' militias, armed with what they are able to find or to
take from the armed forces of the state. Marx described these 'counter-
state' organisations as 'revolutionary local councils' or 'revolutionary
workers' governments', and they cannot coexist with the bourgeois state
for long without a decisive settling of accounts in which either the
workers will smash the state or the state will smash the organs of
workers' power:

> *The German workers...must contribute most to their final victory, by*
> *informing themselves of their own class interests, by taking up their indepen-*
> *dent political position as soon as possible, by not allowing themselves to be*
> *misled by the hypocritical phrases of the democratic petty bourgeoisie into*
> *doubting for one minute the necessity of an independently organised party of*
> *the proletariat. Their battle-cry must be: the Permanent Revolution.*[33]

Thus we see that the perspective of permanent revolution did not origi-
nate with Trotsky in 1906, but with Marx in 1850. Here is the origin of the

idea that there should be, from the beginning of the revolution and even while a workers' party is supporting 'democratic demands', a strategic perspective of independent working class socialist organisation, aiming first at the creation of dual power and then at a socialist revolution.

The bourgeois revolution from above

The 1848 revolutions definitively brought to a close the epoch in which the bourgeoisie were willing and able to act as a revolutionary class. After this date there were no more attempts by the bourgeoisie to lead the mass of the people in open revolution against the old order. But this did not mean that the bourgeoisie were now the effective political power, even in all the economically most developed countries. Nor did it mean that the dynamic process of capital accumulation came to a halt—far from it. Rather the effect of the bourgeois revolutions was to increase the tempo of capital accumulation and forge a world market, and therefore increase the competition between nation states, more completely than had previously been the case. Neither did the unwillingness of the bourgeoisie to provide political leadership for the mass of the population mean that popular revolts against the old order were a thing of the past.

Instead, there were two broad lines of causality which originated in 1848 and ran on through the 19th century. One was the element of continuing popular revolt, increasingly involving self conscious working class activity and organisation. The high tide of this current was reached in 1871 when the first successful workers' revolution flowered briefly in the Paris Commune. But even where such peaks were not scaled, popular and working class action could be seen—for instance, in the New Unionism of the 1880s in Britain and the growth of Marxist influenced unions and social democratic parties throughout Europe towards the end of the century.

The second process of change which followed 1848 was the bourgeoisie's continuing attempt to develop political and state forms adequate for the new conditions under which capital accumulation was now taking place. National unity and the attendant reshaping of the state machine to meet capitalist needs, a key prize won by the English, American and French revolutions, was now a pressing necessity for every capitalist class, especially since the competitive advantage which the forerunners gained from their revolutions was increasingly obvious to the laggards.

In the American Civil War, Lincoln sublimated popular mobilisation to the military struggle against the South, thus recasting American capitalism as a whole in the image of the Northern bourgeoisie. In so doing he forcibly unified the ruling class and enabled it to pursue its 'manifest destiny' of

conquering the land to its west as far as the Pacific. In Italy, national unification and the creation of a bourgeois state involved popular mobilisation
around the figures of Garibaldi and Mazzini, but this was kept within the
limits of Cavour's constitutionalism. In Germany, Napoleon's armies had
done much to clear the ground for Bismarck's state building enterprise. The
defeat of 1848 allowed this process to surge forward with little popular
impediment until the rise of the Social Democratic Party and the organised
working class.

The importance of briefly signposting this process is to demonstrate
that the bourgeoisie did not cease to pursue its own political goals,
including those which involved major social transformations, when it
renounced revolutionary methods of action. Neither did it wholly dis-
pense with the desire to utilise the energies of social classes beneath it. It
merely refused to give such classes revolutionary leadership. The bourgeoisie feared their action, and yet at the same time sought to profit from
the upheavals which popular movements created.[34]

Lenin and Trotsky on the socialist revolution and the democratic revolution

Lenin's initial estimation of the forces involved in the Russian Revolution
is contained in his *Two Tactics of Social Democracy in the Democratic
Revolution*. This work obviously predates the experience of 1917; in fact
it even predates his full absorption of the lessons of the 1905 Revolution.
In some important respects it is a regression to a point less politically
developed than that of Marx and Engels in 1850. In *Two Tactics,* Lenin
argued that the economic and social conditions in Russia were not sufficiently advanced for the coming revolution to be a socialist revolution.
The revolution would be bourgeois democratic in content:

> The degree of Russia's economic development (an objective condition), and
> the degree of class consciousness and organisation of the broad masses of the
> proletariat (a subjective condition inseparably bound up with the objective
> condition) make the immediate and complete emancipation of the working
> class impossible. Only the most ignorant people can close their eyes to the
> bourgeois nature of the revolution which is now taking place.[35]

Lenin thought the Russian bourgeoisie was too weak to lead the
democratic revolution in the way that the English bourgeoisie had done
in the 1640s, or the French bourgeoisie had done in the 1790s. The
working class would therefore have to lead an insurrection which would
overthrow tsarism and establish a democratic republic. But for the
working class to be able to perform this task it would have to be led by a

revolutionary party which insisted on a political strategy free of compromises with the vacillating bourgeois democrats and their fellow travellers inside the organisations of the working class, the Mensheviks.

This position clearly had a number of strengths. The greatest of these was the assertion of the leading role of the working class in the democratic revolution and the insistence on the building of a revolutionary party carrying out socialist propaganda, even though socialism was not the immediate aim of the revolution. Such a strategy required sharp criticism of and political independence from both the bourgeois democrats, the emerging Cadet party, and the Mensheviks.

But for all Lenin's insistence on these crucial elements, his position in *Two Tactics* contains a weakness which allows for constant backsliding, especially by those who claimed to be Lenin's supporters but who did not share his revolutionary intransigence. For, if the revolution is to result in a bourgeois democratic settlement, if a 'democratic dictatorship' is the furthest stage to which the revolution can advance, then the working class is reduced to being the furthest left wing, the most consistent element, in the democratic revolution. Its political representatives would play the role of the Levellers in the English Revolution or the *sans culottes* in the French Revolution. This situation contains the inherent danger that the revolutionary party will underestimate the consciousness and activity of the working class, tailoring its slogans to the democratic tasks of the day and forgoing independent socialist agitation. If such a situation arises the party can become a force retarding the development of the working class by failing to formulate a strategy which crystallises its aspirations. Instead the party can channel the energies of the class into fighting for goals far short of those which workers are capable of attaining.

The crucial advance made by Trotsky in his 1906 work *Results and Prospects* was to point out that if one looked at Russian society in isolation from the world economy it seemed true that it was too economically backward to support a socialist society. Yet capitalist industry had developed to the point where tsarism was in a terminal crisis. Although industry had not developed on the scale of, say, Britain or Germany, where it did exist in Russia it existed in a very advanced form. So it was that St Petersburg's Putilov works (destined to become a 'citadel of Bolshevism' in 1917) was the largest and one of the most technologically advanced factories of its kind anywhere in the world. This is what Trotsky called 'combined and uneven development': the most advanced forms of capitalist development are transplanted, often by international investment, into the heart of underdeveloped countries.[36]

Trotsky went on to agree with Lenin that the Russian bourgeoisie was too timid to lead a democratic revolution, largely because the working class which had grown up around the new industries frightened the bourgeoisie with the spectre of a revolution which could sweep both tsarism and the bourgeoisie away in a single blow. Consequently, the working class would not limit itself to bourgeois democratic demands. When the working class fought it could only do so using working class methods: strikes, general strikes, workers' councils and so on. But these methods of struggle were as much directed against the bourgeoisie as they were against tsarism. They raised the question, 'Who will run the factory?' as well as the question, 'Who will run the state?' The revolution would therefore be a social revolution (ie an economic and political revolution), not simply a political (ie democratic) revolution.

Trotsky completed his analysis by showing that the socialist revolution would be able to sustain itself, despite Russia's backwardness, because Russia was part of the world economy, because the crisis of capitalism was international and, therefore, because the revolution could spread to the advanced capitalist societies of the West. In so doing it could provide the material base to develop a socialist society, making the revolution permanent. In other words, the democratic revolution, by virtue of its dependence on the working class as its leading force and by virtue of its international dimension, would immediately grow over into the socialist revolution.

This is, of course, exactly what happened in 1917. But in 1917 the Bolshevik Party was still operating the perspective of *Two Tactics*. This is why it tailed the provisional government and the Mensheviks between February and April 1917. This is why the entire leadership of the Bolsheviks thought Lenin was mad when he returned to Russia and, at the Finland station, made a speech calling for a second, socialist revolution. This is why Lenin's *April Theses* at first found virtually no support among the Bolshevik leadership. Lenin had, in essence, accepted Trotsky's theory of permanent revolution.

The Russian Revolution

The main novelty which the Russian Revolution of 1917 added to this scene was that some socialists were, from the first, the willing assistants of the petty bourgeois democrats in their efforts to contain the revolution. The Mensheviks and the Social Revolutionaries (SRs) and, until Lenin's return to Russia in March 1917, a sizeable section of the Bolsheviks including Stalin and other leaders of the party, were willing supporters of the provisional government. The Mensheviks and the SRs at first performed this service from their seats in the Petrograd Soviet, but in April they formally joined the government. The Bolsheviks, despite the misgivings of some party members, supported the government without joining it. Only Lenin's *April Theses* rearmed the party by adopting the substance of Trotsky's (and Marx's) perspective of permanent revolution. From that point on the Bolsheviks were in opposition to the provisional government and solely concerned with strengthening the soviets, the independent organisations of the working class. As Trotsky wrote:

> In all past revolutions those who fought on the barricades were workers, apprentices, in part students, and the soldiers came over to their side. But afterwards the solid bourgeoisie, having cautiously watched the barricades from their windows, gathered up the power. But the February Revolution of 1917 was distinguished from former revolutions by the incomparably higher social character and political level of the revolutionary class, by the hostile distrust of the insurrectionists towards the liberal bourgeoisie, and the consequent formation at the very moment of victory of a new organ of revolutionary power, the soviet, based on the armed strength of the masses.[37]

It was by strengthening the power of the soviets that the Bolsheviks both managed to defeat the Kornilov coup against the provisional government and lead a successful socialist revolution in October 1917. But victory did not go uncontested, and nor did the strategy of permanent revolution.

The great division between revolutionary socialism and Stalinism was fought over precisely this issue. Stalinism was a counter-revolutionary movement. To understand why, we have to look at the condition of Russia in the early 1920s. Internationalism was at the core of the October Revolution, not as an abstract moral injunction but as the very means of the revolution's survival. Lenin repeated again and again, both before October and afterwards, that the Russian Revolution could only survive if the revolution spread to the West:

> It is not open to the slightest doubt that the final victory of our revolution, if it were to remain alone, if there were no revolutionary movement in other countries, would be hopeless... Our salvation from all these difficulties, I repeat, is an all European revolution.[38]

Trotsky repeatedly made the same argument.[39] It became the common coin of the Bolshevik party.[40] Most of all, Lenin and Trotsky hoped the revolution would spread to Germany. Had it done so it would not only have altered the whole international balance of class forces, making it impossible for the imperialist powers to continue their wars of intervention and unnecessary for the revolutionary government to cede the huge territories it lost in the peace of Brest-Litovsk. It would also have transformed the domestic situation of the revolution. Industry, and with it the numbers and confidence of the working class, could have been restored.

The crucial alliance with the peasantry, on which the revolution depended, could have been maintained as manufactured goods were sent to the country to be exchanged for grain to feed the starving cities.

But without such an international victory, the Russian Revolution remained isolated. The working class, decimated by the civil war, the wars of intervention and the starvation and famine which followed, recovered at a snail's pace, if at all. Grain had to be requisitioned from the peasantry at the point of a gun. Eventually the regime introduced a partial restoration of the market—the New Economic Policy—which gave rise to a profiteering layer of bureaucrats and richer peasants. Indeed, the bureaucracy remained the only stable element in a society whose revolutionary institutions had been undermined by the terrible price the working class had to pay in the fight to defend them.

These are the conditions under which the Stalinist trend in the bureaucracy began to assert itself. It came to represent a class which set its face against the whole idea of internationalism: Stalin's slogan was 'Socialism in One Country'. As we have seen, Trotsky and Lenin had realised that if the revolution was to be a socialist revolution, rather than simply a democratic revolution which at best would issue in a capitalist economy and a parliamentary republic, it must spread to the advanced industrialised countries. This was the whole theoretical basis on which the Third International was formed. Trotsky defended the principle on which the October Revolution had been, and could only have been, won: internationalism.

Once Stalinism broke the link between the possibility of socialist revolution at home and the fight to maintain it by spreading it internationally, the whole basis of the Bolsheviks' revolutionary policy in October collapsed. Stalin's 'Socialism in One Country' insisted that the Russian state could 'go it alone', and castigated Trotsky for 'underestimating the peasantry'. In the international arena this returned Bolshevik policy to the Menshevik position in 1917. The alternative model of revolution which Stalin propagated throughout the Third World was the 'two stage' revolution. The first stage was the democratic revolution, in which the working class should subordinate specifically socialist aspirations to a broad alliance aimed at achieving a democratic revolution. Only after this stage had been completed could socialist demands be raised. Stalin's approach meant that the revolution did not need the international working class to ensure victory, since a 'democratic revolution' could be achieved by a cross-class alliance of progressive forces acting within a purely national arena. Thus it became acceptable for socialists to argue that the working class should ally itself with the peasantry and 'progressive sections of the bourgeoisie' in future revolutions. In China in 1927 and in Spain in 1936 this led to disaster, because it subordinated working class revolution to bourgeois nationalists (Chiang Kai-shek) or bourgeois parliamentarians (the Republican parties in Spain). The result was counter-revolution and dictatorship in both cases.

The bourgeois revolution after the defeat of the Russian Revolution

The counter-revolution led by Stalin was, of course, not the only defeat suffered by the working class movement in the inter-war period. The rise of fascism centrally entailed a crushing series of working class reverses. In Italy, the 'two red years' of revolutionary struggle immediately following the Russian Revolution were ended by Mussolini's rise and the consolidation of fascism in the 1920s. The charge of the German Revolution took longer to dissipate, but ultimately the failure of the Stalinist dominated German Communist Party to resolve the crisis of the Weimar Republic in the working class's favour paved the way for Hitler to take power in 1933. The following year a belated workers' rising in 'Red Vienna' was crushed as the fascists took power. In 1936 the Spanish Revolution and the rising struggles around the election of the Popular Front government in France briefly raised the hope of turning the Nazi tide, but again the conduct of Stalin's Comintern destroyed the opportunity. The scene was set for world war.

The destruction engendered by the war, and the further demobilisation by the Communist Parties, especially in Italy, of the post-war wave of popular left wing struggles meant that the widespread revolutionary mood which attended the end of the First World War was present only in a muted form after the Second World War. Furthermore, sustained arms spending at a level quantitatively higher than during the inter-war period led to a 30 year period of economic expansion unparalleled in capitalism's past. In this respect the period after the Second World War was quite unlike the crisis ridden 1920s and 1930s. The international scene was also transformed during the long boom. The old European colonial powers, whether victors or vanquished, ended the war economically exhausted. Faced with twin pressures to open their markets to competition from newly dominant US corporations and from growing anti-colonial resistance, they were unable to sustain their empires. The second half of the 20th century became the great era of decolonisation, although economic power wielded by the imperial states proved to be as disabling for the mass of the population in the former colonies as the old set-up of direct rule had been. ·

These great anti-colonial transformations combined with the previous defeats suffered by the international working class movement and the economic growth which attended the long boom to throw the dynamics of the revolutionary process into a unique new pattern. The assumptions which lay behind Trotsky's theory of permanent revolution were called into question by these new developments. Trotsky's theory had been constructed between two poles. One was the fact that the bourgeoisie was incapable of recreating its revolutionary past under modern conditions, and therefore of carrying through the construction of a unified, independent capitalist state in the face of concerted opposition from pre-capitalist or colonial ruling classes. The second was that the working class would fill the political vacuum thus created, simultaneously solving the problems of the democratic and the socialist revolution. But what would happen if the first of these conditions, the objective weakness of the bourgeoisie, remained true while the second, the subjective potential of the working class, remained unrealised?

Trotsky could not have foreseen the unprecedented conditions which conspired to bring about just this situation after the Second World War. Nevertheless, such conditions required a fresh analysis. This was provided in Tony Cliff's pioneering essay 'Deflected Permanent Revolution'.[41] In analysing the Chinese Revolution of 1949 and the Cuban Revolution of 1959, Cliff demonstrated that in periods where the working class was unable to mount a challenge to the old order, and yet the old order was decomposing as a result of a wider social crisis, other social forces were able to play a significant political role. The peasantry often provided the forces for popular mobilisation in these circumstances but, since modern revolutions are overwhelmingly urban events, they could not provide indigenous or effective political leadership. This leadership could be provided, however, by sections of the middle class intelligentsia—lawyers, state bureaucrats, teachers, literary figures, owners of small businesses, academics, and so on.

This layer had, in an earlier incarnation, often been a crucial element of the practical leadership of the classical bourgeois revolutions. The bourgeoisie proper does not often directly provide its own political representatives. The middle classes are often professionally engaged in forming general ideological conceptions of society, and live closer to the mass of the population whom they are trying to lead. They are, therefore, better political representatives of bourgeois political programmes than the oligarchs of the bourgeoisie themselves. This is a relationship which holds to this day: better for the ruling class that they be represented by a university educated grocer's daughter like Margaret Thatcher (and the lawyers who dominate the House of Commons) than that Rupert Murdoch and his fellow plutocrats attempt to directly represent themselves.

One of the great strengths of the analysis which Cliff provided was a political profile of this layer of people as they appear in modern 'developing' societies. The intelligentsia in these societies is peculiarly open to playing a leadership role in popular movements when the working class is quiescent. But the revolution made under these circumstances is a modernising, nationalist, anti-colonial revolution, not a socialist revolution.

The intelligentsia is...sensitive to their countries' technical lag. Participating as it does in the scientific and technical world of the 20th century, it is stifled by the backwardness of its own nation.[42]

Thus the intelligentsia turns its face against the ruling class, whose 'mismanagement', 'corruption' and 'cowardice' in the face of imperialism has brought the nation to this pass. Such individuals are in search of a new god, which they find in the abstract notion of 'the people', especially those sections of the people who have the greatest difficulty in organising for themselves, the peasantry.

The spiritual life of the intellectuals is also in crisis. In a crumbling order where the traditional pattern is disintegrating, they feel insecure, rootless, lacking in firm values. Dissolving cultures give rise to a powerful urge for a new integration that must be total and dynamic if it is to fill the social and political vacuum, that must combine religious fervour with militant nationalism.[43]

But this desire to be part of 'the people' and to end the subordination of the nation is always combined with a sense of superiority, the elite feeling that the masses are too backward or apathetic to accomplish a revolution for themselves:

They are great believers in efficiency, including efficiency in social engineering. They hope for reform from above and would dearly love to hand a new world over to a grateful people, rather than see the liberating struggle of a self conscious and freely associated people result in a new world for themselves. They care a lot for measures to drag their nation out of stagnation, but very little for democracy. They embody the drive for industrialisation, for capital accumulation, for national resurgence. Their power is in direct relation to the feebleness of other classes, and their political nullity.[44]

This political profile made the whole strategy of autocratic, state led capital accumulation very attractive for this social class throughout the 30 years of the long boom. China and Cuba were only the purest expressions of this trend. But, as Cliff noted, 'other colonial revolutions—Ghana, India, Egypt, Indonesia, Algeria, etc—more or less deviate from the norm. But...they can best be understood when approached from the standpoint of, and compared with, the norm'.[45]

As the post-war colonial revolutions ran their course, the long boom came to an end and the terminal crisis of the East European regimes set in, this model lost its attractiveness. But the class who saw modernisation as the key objective of popular movements did not disappear. And although its members no longer held to Stalinist derived economic models, they continued to see the state as the crucial vehicle for their political strategy. In some cases, for instance in South Africa, they remained caught within the old Stalinist ideology until the very collapse of Stalinism itself. As the leadership of the liberation movement, and the working class struggle as it revived, they influenced it accordingly. In Eastern Europe, where opposition necessarily defined itself against Stalinism, other ideologies were pressed into service and often had to contend with socialist and revolutionary alternatives for hegemony. In the Indonesian Revolution, very little of the old nationalist and Stalinist ideology survived the 1965 coup which brought Suharto to power, simultaneously overthrowing the nationalist founder of Indonesia, Sukarno, and crushing the Indonesian Communist Party. Some 32 years of dictatorship have united aspirant members of the excluded middle class around pro-democratic sentiments. They now seek to benefit from the overthrow of Suharto by pacifying the movement which achieved it. So wherever other social forces, principally the working class movement, were weak or lacking in coherent, socialist political leadership, this crucial layer of the middle classes has continued to play a role long after its state capitalist ideological incarnation has passed away.

The revolutions of 1989

The causes of the East European revolutions of 1989 exist in three registers: firstly, the international register, which is the arena of economic and military competition with the West; secondly, the imperial register, which is the internal economic and political decay of the national economies and the Russian empire; and lastly, the class register, which is the way in which these forces expressed themselves as class struggles and political strategies.

The deepest and most lengthy processes which resulted in the East European revolutions are primarily to be found in the first register. In these regimes, the 'normal' political function of the state, the exclusive use of force in a given territory, was combined with the 'normal' function of a capitalist class, the exclusive right to hire and fire wage labour. They were therefore best defined as 'state capitalist'. In Eastern Europe such regimes resulted from the Russian occupation at the end of the Second World War. But although the Russian model and its East European copies saw the state capitalist method of industrial development at its most extreme, elements of this approach were clearly visible in many economies of the 1930s and 1940s. The international experience of the economic crisis of the 1930s, followed by the centralising imperative of total war, meant that state capitalist elements were strongly

present in Hitler's Germany as well as in Stalin's Russia, in the New
Deal United States as well as in wartime and welfare state Britain. This
is why state led economic development became such an attractive model
for post-colonial regimes as well.

The attraction was not wholly based on illusion. In the immediate
post-war period the state capitalist regimes' economic expansion was
faster than that of the Western powers. Indeed, the correlation appeared to
be that the more state capitalist the regime, the faster the economic expansion. The index of industrial production in West Germany rose by seven
times between 1950 and 1969—but Poland's rose by almost the same
amount. Britain's rose less than twofold, while Hungary's rose nearly
fivefold. France's increased by just over two times, yet in the same period
Romania's index rose over 10 times.[46] Of course these figures only
measure the rise in industrial production, not the absolute size of the
various economies. Nevertheless, they show that the picture of the state
capitalist economies as stagnant by their very nature is a myth.

In the same period, however, the world economy as a whole expanded
massively, making it the most sustained period of growth in the history of
capitalism. And the character of the world economy was transformed as it
grew. Private monopoly and multinational firms came to dominate the
Western economies as never before. International trade expanded as never
before. These developments began to undermine the progress that was
possible using state capitalist methods of accumulation. This was especially true for the autarkic state capitalisms of Eastern Europe, those
states which had attempted the most complete isolation from the rest of
the world market. Isolationist state capitalist methods had been very good
at developing an industrial base from weak beginnings in a post-war
world where the international economy was itself weak. But when the
Western economies recovered and grew, and when international trade
expanded, the isolated Eastern economies were at a disadvantage.
Western corporations, whether private or state owned, were free to
organise and trade on a global scale, searching for the cheapest raw materials, plant and labour, and for new and lucrative markets. The Eastern
state corporations traded in a bloc which had always been weaker than its
Western rivals, even in the pre-war years. Now non-convertible curren-
cies, restricted resources and the imperial demands of the Russian state
undermined their competitiveness on a world scale.

The very isolation of the Eastern state capitalist economies protected
them from this fact for a time, but ultimately it was brought home to
them in two crucial ways. Domestically, it was obvious that the industrial progress of the post-war period was not being converted into a
'second revolution' in consumer durables. Internationally, and this is
where the second, imperial, register is important, the inability to keep

up economically eventually meant an inability to keep up militarily. The state capitalist ruling class was losing the Cold War. Détente was the result: an attempt to transfer resources from the military to the civilian economy, the better to be able to develop military capacity in the future. The stakes in this game had become very high by the 1980s when Ronald Reagan proposed the Star Wars defence system and Mikhail Gorbachev, fearful of another huge hike in defence spending, countered with a series of disarmament proposals which he hoped the US could not refuse. He was right, but it was too late.

Gorbachev was too late because developments in the class struggle, the third register, were already closing the road to the kind of reform for which he hoped. To understand this process we have to look at how the economic crises of state capitalism and the attempts by the ruling class, including the Russian ruling class, to deal with these crises were expressed in the class struggle. Poland is the key to this process—indeed, the key to understanding the whole dynamic of the revolutions of 1989.

This revolutionary narrative, however, begins much earlier. In the 1970s the then Stalinist leader of Poland, Edward Gierek, attempted a new strategy to deal with mounting unrest, notably the massive wave of strikes and factory occupations which had toppled his predecessor in December 1970. He tried to undertake a 'second industrial revolution' by borrowing from the West. New plant would be built with Western loans and repaid by exporting Western quality goods back to the West. The plan was a catastrophic failure, in part because the world economy was no longer expanding as it had done in the post-war period but actually entering the current prolonged era of slump and slow growth. In 1976 Poland's hard currency debt stood at $10 billion. Three years later it had reached $17 billion.[47]

Other East European leaders had tried the same 'consumer socialism' experiment—Janos Kadar in Hungary, Erich Honecker in East Germany—and by the late 1970s per capita debt in these countries had reached the same level as in Poland. Economic failure led to political change: Honecker tried cautious rapprochement with the Protestant Church, Kadar implemented a slight easing of restrictions on intellectual freedom.

But Poland had sustained the longest and deepest tradition of mass working class resistance to the state, and it was this which was to be the decisive factor in the overthrow of Stalinism. In 1976 workers were once again involved in a huge wave of strikes against price increases. Several thousand workers of the Ursus tractor factory in Warsaw marched to the rail lines, ripped them up and stopped the Paris-Moscow express. In Radom, south west of Warsaw, workers burnt down the Communist Party headquarters. The price rises were withdrawn, but the workers paid for their victory in other ways: thousands were sacked, many jailed and, in Radom and Ursus, those who kept their jobs were beaten back to work between lines of truncheon wielding police.

To defend the workers in the aftermath of the 1976 strikes, activists and intellectuals formed the Workers' Defence Committee (KOR, by its Polish initials). In September 1977, a year after KOR was founded, it began to produce its own newspaper, *Robotnik* (*The Worker*). On May Day 1978 the Founding Committee of Trade Unions on the Coast was announced in Gdansk, and it soon began producing its own paper, *Robotnik Wybrzeza* (*The Worker on the Coast*): 'KOR worked very much as Lenin recommended (in *What is to be Done?*) the conspiratorial communist party should work, raising the political consciousness of the proletariat in key industrial centres'.[48] The activists drawn together in these and other similar initiatives were to become the leadership of Solidarity in the wake of the greatest of all Polish strike waves in 1980. Their political development was crucial to the whole process of revolution in Eastern Europe.

The workers' movement which gave birth to Solidarity was insurrectionary in its scope. In July 1980 the government announced another round of price rises, and again these were met with a series of rolling strikes. Despite the regime's attempt to pacify the workers with a wage increase, the strikes spread. By August they had reached Gdansk, and the Lenin shipyard was occupied in response to the sacking of *The Worker on the Coast* activist Anna Walentynowicz. The yard management conceded the occupiers' demands, but the occupation continued in solidarity with the local strikes which the action at the Lenin yard had sparked. An Inter-Factory Committee (MKZ) was established for the whole of Gdansk. The strikes and occupations spread, involving mines and steelworks in southern Poland for the first time. So too did the MKZs, springing up one after another across the whole country. In September they united in one national organisation, Solidarity. The government was forced to negotiate an unprecedented agreement, the '21 points', granting a host of reforms, most importantly the right to 'independent, self governing trade unions'.[49]

This unprecedented rupture in the authority of a Stalinist state effectively created a situation of dual power. The state tried, but failed, to undermine Solidarity in the months after the initial strike wave. And Solidarity for its part came to take on more and more of the actual running of society. One KOR activist paid eloquent testimony to this fact, though he saw it as more of a problem than an opportunity:

At this moment people expect more of us than we can possibly do. Normally, society focuses on the party. In Poland nowadays, however, society gathers

*around the free trade unions. That's a bad thing. Thus there is an increasing
necessity for us to formulate a political programme. It would be a good thing
if the party took the lead and removed the people's expectations from our
shoulders. But will it do so now? In the eyes of the people the new trade
unions should do everything: they should fill the role of trade unions, participate in the administration of the country, be a political party and act as a
militia.*[50]

Unless Solidarity was willing to meet these expectations by overthrowing the government it was bound to gradually disappoint its own
supporters. Worse, it began to limit the actions of its rank and file in the
name of not provoking the government. Worse still, such a policy
divided and exhausted the movement, giving the ruling class its chance
to regain the initiative and organise the military coup headed by General
Jaruzelski in December 1981.

What brought the Solidarity leadership to act in this way? Why did
they not support the demands of the rank and file, and of the radicals
within the Solidarity leadership, and use the power which they acknowledged the union to have to overthrow the government? Crucial to this
decision was the political strategy developed by the KOR leadership in
the period before Solidarity was created. Jacek Kuron is perhaps the
pivotal, certainly the emblematic, figure in this story.

Kuron was a longstanding militant with an impressive record of
opposition to the Polish regime. As early as 1965 he had written, with
Karol Modzelewski, the pathbreaking *Open Letter to the Party*. This
document, which still has an impressive power when read today, was a
Marxist critique of the Polish state. Similar in its social analysis to the
theory of state capitalism, it insisted on revolutionary conclusions: it
called for a return to genuine workers' councils, the arming of the
workers, and an 'anti-bureaucratic revolution'. Indeed, it went on to call
for 'the organisation of workers' circles, nuclei of the future party'.[51] But
by the time he played a leadership role in KOR and then Solidarity
Kuron had abandoned this revolutionary perspective. Why?

Paradoxically, the economic and social fate of the state capitalist
regimes played an important part. The economic success of Stalinism in
the 1950s and 1960s allowed the opposition in Poland and throughout
Eastern Europe to think that what was necessary was a renewal of
socialism, a return to the genuine Marxist tradition and to the democracy
of the early Russian Revolution. Even those who broke completely with
the notion of 'reform Communism', as Kuron did, could not help but be
influenced by the evidence that state ownership was a viable economic
model. Furthermore, Kuron developed his position and maintained it
during a period of international working class advance, but abandoned it
when the great wave of international struggles had been defeated, after

the Prague Spring and the Polish struggles of the early 1970s as well as the May events in France.

The *Open Letter* had argued that the threat of armed Russian intervention would be met by the spread of the revolution to the rest of the Eastern bloc. It could therefore paralyse the Russian ruling class's ability to intervene. By 1980, however, Kuron was defending the reformist perspective precisely by reference to the Russian military threat. Just as the Western left was abandoning the revolutionary perspectives of 1968 in favour of the reformist perspective of the 'long march through the institutions', so Kuron was coming to believe in a 'self limiting revolution', in which the institutions of civil society would be built up within the old order, gradually forcing it to accommodate to liberal democratic norms.

Kuron's change of heart was equally marked on the question of party organisation. The *Open Letter* had been unambiguous on this issue:

> In order that the working class can have the chance to play the leading role, it must be conscious of its distinct, particular interests. It must express them in the form of a political programme and organise itself—as a class fighting for power—into its own political party or parties.[52]

But by the time KOR was founded Kuron and fellow activist Adam Michnik were writing a series of essays calling for a 'New Evolutionism'. KOR itself was renamed the Committee for Social Self Defence, and although the central role of the working class was never abandoned, as it would have been difficult to do given the combativity of Polish workers, this force was now to be harnessed to a gradualist political strategy. New political allies were to be sought, especially among the intellectuals gathered around the Catholic Church. This new 'popular front' reformism had little need for the revolutionary organisation outlined in the *Open Letter*. When, in the midst of the crisis which engulfed Solidarity in 1981, radicals began to call for the formation of such a party Kuron spoke against them.[53] As we shall see, such ideas were not peculiar to Kuron but became the common coin of oppositions throughout Eastern Europe in the 1980s.

The military coup of 1981 was a brutal refutation of this perspective— or at least it should have been. Yet the reformist vision continued to be held by the leaders of Solidarity even as they were imprisoned and chased into the underground by Jaruzelski's troops. But if the 1981 coup was a defeat for Solidarity, it was not a victory for the regime. The Polish ruling class was so burnt by the cost of imposing martial law that it seems to have concluded that it could not repeat the experience. Marian Orzechowski joined the Central Committee of the Polish CP in 1981, its politbureau in 1983, and was effectively the party's last foreign minister. He says:

I personally feel that 13 December 1981 had been a hugely negative experience for the army and the police. I had discussions with General Kiszczak and General Siwicki that martial law could only work once. The army and the riot police could not be mobilised against society. Most of the party leadership realised this... You couldn't rerun martial law.[54]

The Russian ruling class had, ironically given Kuron's fears, been unwilling to act and seemed to have drawn the conclusion that it would henceforward not be possible to intervene against civil unrest in its empire. The 'Sinatra doctrine', 'I Did it My Way', as Gorbachev's spokesman Gennady Gerasimov would later call it, was sung to a Polish tune. General Jaruzelski himself recalls:

Gorbachev on many occasions said that Polish changes were an impulse to perestroika... He often requested materials about what we had tried and tested... I was closely linked to Gorbachev. We spoke to one another without reserve, saying that old men like Zhivkov [of Bulgaria] *and Honecker* [of East Germany] *did not understand a thing.*[55]

And as the crisis sharpened again with the 1988 strikes, Gorbachev had an immediate political motivation for continuing to support the Polish government's decision to attempt to hang on to power by compromising with, rather than cracking down on, Solidarity. Polish foreign minister Orzechowski again:

When in February 1988 I told him [Gorbachev] *that the position of Jaruzelski was under attack, he was very worried...Gorbachev realised that if economic reforms in Poland were to collapse, his hardliners could argue that deviation from the principles of socialism must lead to catastrophe. He came to Poland in June 1988 to provide moral support. At every meeting with Jaruzelski, Gorbachev approved of what was happening in Poland.*[56]

This underlines the degree to which the ultimate cause for the change of political heart towards Solidarity was rooted in economics: Poland and other East European states were now connected to Western regimes by trade and debt. Poland's external debt totalled over $38 billion in 1988, the highest in the Eastern bloc. Armed intervention would endanger both trade and loans. It would therefore worsen an already dire economic crisis, thus precipitating civil unrest, the very thing intervention was meant to suppress. Beyond these internal consequences the whole project of détente would have been destroyed by Russian police action in Eastern Europe.

Solidarity itself maintained an underground structure. Renewed strike action in 1988 left the Polish regime with no other option but to try and negotiate its way out of the impasse. Despite continuing strikes—which Lech Walesa tried to demobilise—student protests, and protests from the radical wing of Solidarity, 'round table' negotiations with the government began in January 1989. Kuron's response to the radical critics of the 'round table' strategy reveals the degree to which he had now adopted a fully articulated reformist strategy:

> Many of our friends, members of the opposition in Poland, asked us, 'Why did you go to the roundtable discussions? Wouldn't it have been better to continue organising people and to increase the potential for social explosion—a social explosion which would wipe out the totalitarian system?' Our answer was 'no'. We don't want to destroy the system by force...the road to democracy has to be a process of gradual evolution, of gradual building of democratic institutions.[57]

The round table went ahead and resulted, in June 1989, in elections which the regime thought it might win, especially as they were rigged in its favour. In the event Solidarity swept the board with an electoral victory far greater than many in Solidarity had imagined possible. The path to the 'velvet revolutions' in Eastern Europe now lay open. But Jacek Kuron was right when, looking back from 1990, he wrote:

> The real breakthrough took place in 1980, when a massive wave of strikes led to the founding of Solidarity, an independent union that the government was forced to recognise. This was truly the moment when the totalitarian system in Poland was broken.[58]

At the same time as these events were unfolding in Poland, the Hungarian ruling class was feeling its way towards a similar reconstruction of the political regime. Indeed, six days after Solidarity swept the board in the Polish elections, the Hungarian Stalinists opened their own round table discussions about reform. A week later over 100,000 people gathered at the reburial of Imre Nagy, the murdered leader of the 1956 Hungarian Revolution. But there was comparatively little popular mobilisation in Hungary in 1989, and certainly no recreation of the workers' councils of 1956. Yet if the Hungarian events do not tell us very much about the role of the working class in the revolution, the very quietude of the transition in Hungary allows us to see the reconstruction of the ruling class in its purest form.

In the 1970s Hungary followed many of the same policies and confronted many of the same problems as Gierek's Poland. Opening the economy to the West meant accepting Western loans and increased indebtedness. Hungary's external debt rose from $0.9 billion in 1973 to

$5.8 billion in 1978.[59] But the Hungarian ruling class pushed on down this road, combining economic liberalisation with a degree of intellectual liberalism. Elemer Hankiss, a Hungarian academic and, after 1989, head of Hungarian television, writes:

> In the 1970s in certain places a kind of social democratisation began. Already during the late 1960s in Hungary the Kadar regime introduced a more tolerant policy to the opposition and society in general. It allowed a 'second economy' to evolve; it allowed a process of cultural pluralisation to emerge, though of course it did not allow political pluralisation.[60]

The formal economy continued to slide into deeper crisis during the 1970s and 1980s, but the 'second economy' grew. The number of independent craftsmen in Hungary was 50,000 in 1953. By 1989 it had risen to 160,000. In the 1970s there were reckoned to be 2 million Hungarian families involved in the 'second economy'. The numbers of entrepreneurs, shopkeepers and their employees rose from 67,000 in 1982 to almost 600,000 in 1989. Of course, these figures are tiny compared to the formal economy, and the economic activity these forces generated could not reverse economic decline. Their importance is sociological and ideological, not economic. They were one indicator showing the Hungarian ruling class a way out of the crisis.[61] By the mid-1980s this growth was combined with limited but real political change. A popular groundswell, unsuccessfully resisted by the state, got genuinely independent candidates elected in the 1985 general election. Independents won 10 percent of parliamentary seats. This was unheard of in any Stalinist state and was another straw in the wind for a ruling class which at that very point must have been absorbing the lessons of the Solidarity era in Poland.

The question of whether or not the whole Hungarian ruling class would attempt a transition to a more market oriented form of capitalism would be decided by the behaviour of the upper echelons of the state bureaucracy and the managers of the major industrial enterprises. In this respect Hankiss notes, 'Since the writing appeared on the wall in 1987, the Party and state bureaucracy have been trying to convert their bureaucratic power into a new type of power which will be an asset that can be preserved within a new system, namely in a market economy or even a democracy.' The result 'may be called the rise of a kind of 19th century grande bourgeoisie'.[62] This class is an amalgam of different elements of the old ruling class. Firstly, the state bureaucracy of the old order used its family ties to diversify its power:

> There are various ways of converting to new power if you are a Kadarist

oligarch... The characteristic oligarchic family in the mid-1980s was the
*father or grandfather, a party **apparatchik**, a high level party or state offi-*
cial; his son a manager of a British/Hungarian joint venture; his son in law
with a boutique in Vaci Street; his daughter an editor for Hungarian televi-
sion; his nephew studying at Cambridge or Oxford; his mother in law
having a small hotel or boarding house on Lake Balaton, etc... These family
businesses are absolutely top secret. However, we did discover more than
250 businesses belonging to this kind of diversified oligarchic family, and
there must be several hundred more.[63]

Secondly, as soon as the dam broke in 1989, party bureaucrats found
they 'could convert power on an institutional level', and so they began to
transform high value properties and real estate, including party buildings, training centres and holiday complexes, into semi-private or joint
stock companies. And besides the party bureaucrats proper there were
also the managerial bureaucrats, the 'Red Barons', who were busy relo-
cating themselves as private capitalists.

This process naturally led to a generalised consciousness on the part
of the ruling class: 'A third way for the regime to convert power was,
ironically, to transform the Hungarian economy into a market economy.
This...has been carried out in such a way that this new *grande bour-*
geoisie profits most from the new laws'.[64] Indeed, this consciousness
predated the upheaval of 1989 and provides a crucial part of the explanation of the peaceful nature of the transition in Eastern Europe. The
political institutions of Eastern Europe were transformed in 1989, but the
ruling class was not overthrown and no new mode of production was
advanced by the revolutions. Rather, the ruling class transformed one
method of capitalist accumulation, the autarkic state capitalist method,
for another method of capitalist accumulation which involves a combi-
nation of private monopoly, orientation on the world market and a
continuing element of state ownership and regulation. That is, a repro-
duction of the really existing capitalism of the West, but not the fantasy
'free market' model of ideological fame.

The relationship between this new model of capital accumulation
which arose within the womb of the old state capitalist model and the
quietude of the political changes of 1989 is well expressed by Hankiss:

I have tried...to answer the question, 'Why did they not shoot?'... Let me
focus on one single factor which played an especially important part in the
Hungarian (and to a lesser extent in the Polish) process of transition: loss of
interest in preserving the party. In the late 1980s a substantial part of the
Hungarian party and state bureaucracy discovered ways of converting their
bureaucratic power into lucrative economic positions and assets (and also
indirectly into a new type of political power) in the new system based on

market economics and political democracy... When in the late 1980s they discovered the possibility of...becoming part of an emerging new and legitimate ruling class or **grande bourgeoisie**, *they lost interest in keeping the Communist Party as their instrument of power and protection. And, as a consequence, on the night of 7 October 1989 they watched indifferently, or assisted actively in, the self liquidation of the party.*[65]

This process of self transformation by the ruling class is probably more extreme in Hungary than elsewhere in Eastern Europe and none of it is conceivable without the actions of the Polish working class in 1980-1981 and again in 1988. It was the Polish workers' struggle which both demonstrated to the ruling classes of Eastern Europe the impossibility of continuing to rule in the old way and the penalty that might be paid if they persisted in trying to do so. Furthermore, it was the experience of Solidarity combined with Russia's own economic problems and the consequent need to break into the world economy which created the Sinatra doctrine of non-intervention. And this in turn created the space in which the Hungarian and other ruling classes could recompose themselves.

The Hungarian events did, however, contribute one vital link to the chain of the East European revolutions. Early in 1989 the still ruling Hungarian Communist Party decided to open its border with Austria. It was a dramatic move which broke apart the then intact Eastern bloc. The then Minister of Justice, Kalaman Kulcsar, explained why his government acted:

We wanted to show that we meant what we were doing and saying. Poland and Hungary were then the only two countries on the road to reform and it was by no means excluded that others in the Warsaw Pact would try something against us. We were pretty sure that if hundreds of thousands of East Germans went to the West, the East German regime would fall, and in that case Czechoslovakia was also out. We were not too concerned about Romania, the only danger to us came from the DDR [East Germany]. *We took the step for our own sakes.*[66]

But even though the Hungarian government correctly foresaw the international implications of opening the border, they did not see the domestic consequences. Kulcsar again: 'Our internal situation changed completely. Suddenly conscious of the strength of its position, the opposition was able to advance the date of the elections, and that was the end of the party'.[67] Even so, it was still not clear in all cases that a peaceful transition was inevitable, as the case of East Germany shows.

The East German ruling class instantly understood the meaning of the Hungarian decision to open the borders. When a Hungarian government delegation met its East German counterparts and told them of the decision,

Erich Mielke, the head of the Stasi secret police, 'called it treason'.[68] The East German leader Erich Honecker described it as 'nothing short of treachery'.[69] Some 24,000 East Germans left the country by this route between 10 September and the end of that month.

East Germany was the western watchtower of the Russian Empire. Its fate was always closely tied to the fate of the empire which created it from a Cold War partition. Two thirds of East Germany's trade was with Russia. Honecker himself remembers being told by Russian leader Brezhnev in 1970, 'Never forget that the DDR cannot exist without us; without the Soviet Union, its power and strength, without us there is no DDR'.[70] East Germany could not simply be 'hollowed out' by its own ruling class in the way that the Hungarian regime had been. Neither had there been the long tradition of combativity by which the Polish working class had worn down the resistance of its ruling class.

Consequently the East German regime fell as a result of the decay of the empire which sustained it and the simultaneous pressure, both through mass demonstrations and mass emigration, of its ordinary people. The fact that the regime did not attempt a violent counter-revolution was not a result of lack of will on the part of its leaders. It was the result of the fact that imperial decay ran just ahead of popular mobilisation, eroding the regime's capacity for repression.

The East German state marked its 40th anniversary on 6 October 1989. Gorbachev arrived to attend the celebrations. *Neues Forum*, the dissident civil rights organisation, had already been banned shortly after its formation the previous month. Some 1,000 people were arrested the day Gorbachev arrived, and another 3,456 during the few days of his visit. To mark the anniversary a triumphal torchlight procession marched past a saluting stand in Berlin on the night of 6 October. But, though they marched to order, the crowds could not be made to chant to order. Instead they chanted 'Gorbi, Gorbi'. The following morning Gorbachev and Honecker held their final private meeting. In the corridor afterwards Gorbachev deliberately let slip a phrase which, although it was not his intention, damned the East German state: 'Whoever acts too late is punished by life'. He then delivered a speech to the SED (Communist Party) central committee which was a oblique attack on the speed of reform in East Germany, beginning the process of upheaval in the SED leadership which would see Honecker replaced by Egon Krenz on 18 October.

But as the succession was being decided in the old way, very different things were happening in the streets. On 7 October violent arrests accompanied a 6,000 strong march in East Berlin; the next day 30,000 marched in Dresden. On the same day, 8 October, special security forces were put on alert. For the following day's demonstration in Leipzig huge numbers of police, plus ambulance and hospital services, were

mobilised. Honecker is reported to have ordered the use of live ammunition. On 9 October 50,000 marched in Leipzig. There was no shooting.
Honecker's order to shoot had been lost by one vote at the central committee.[71] Local district party bosses also refused to carry out Honecker's
orders any longer.[72]

It is not clear who led the opposition to Honecker's plan at the highest
levels—Krenz, the Russian leaders, or both—but it is obvious why the
governing class as a whole were no longer willing to follow Honecker.
He had been publicly deserted by Gorbachev, and his rivals were already
beginning to campaign for his removal. No one thought that the end of
the regime was at hand, merely that the new line from Moscow must be
respected. Honecker had lost the trust of Moscow and with it the confidence of his fellow rulers. Consequently, the East German government
stayed its hand.

The effect of such governmental paralysis was dramatic. A week
later, on 16 October, 100,000 marched in Leipzig. By 23 October the
marchers were 150,000 strong; by 30 October 300,000 marched. On 4
November 500,000 attended a rally in East Berlin as tens of thousands
left the country through the now open border. In an attempt to stem the
tide the regime announced, on 9 November, that border crossings to
West Germany were open. The unexpected consequence was that crowds
gathered on both sides of the Berlin Wall and began to dismantle it with
picks, hammers and chisels. A round table on the Polish model followed,
but its only real achievement was to set the date for elections: 18 March
1990. Helmut Kohl and the Christian Democrat machine filled the void
left by the collapse of Stalinism, winning the election and setting their
own stamp on the process of German unification.

For events to have taken a left wing direction during the East German
revolution would have required a left wing organisation and ideology of
rare consistency. In the polarised ideological atmosphere of a partitioned
country, only an alternative as clear and consistent as either the old
Stalinist certainties of Honecker or the Western imperial *realpolitik* of
Helmut Kohl, and equally opposed to both, could have sustained
support. The East German opposition had few of these qualities. One of
the founders of *Neues Forum*, Jens Reich, recalls the atmosphere of the
opposition in the early 1980s:

> *The new opposition was individualistic and bohemian, and composed of a*
> *kaleidoscope of 'counter-culture' social groups: hippies, Maoists, anarchists,*
> *human rights groups, greens, gays, lesbians, the protesting 'church from*
> *below'—a very colourful mixture...in fact, to professional people, frankly*
> *somewhat alien! My wife Eva and I felt like fish out of water.*[73]

Of course, it is perfectly possible that out of such a milieu a core of people could emerge who clarify their ideas, formulate a revolutionary strategy and start to build links with workers. This, for all their ultimate weaknesses, was the path taken by KOR in Poland. But this was not the path taken by the people who founded *Neues Forum*. Jens Reich argued that those who represented an 'extreme rejection of the status quo...really could not become a mainstream political force.' They were 'too isolated from the culture of the bulk of the population'. Instead:

> *We had to reach out to a more 'respectable' middle aged generation, to give them the courage to come out of their snail shells...We wished to ensure that we were properly representative; to ensure that* **Neues Forum** *incorporated not only clergymen, not only Berliners, not only intellectuals, not only young dropouts from the social ghetto. This criterion brought us together...a cross-section of normal people with normal professions and different political leanings.[74]*

Such a strategy was initially successful, but as the revolution radicalised, and as global political issues quickly came into play with the fall of the Berlin Wall, *Neues Forum* was thrust aside by more robust political forces. From the one side it was undermined by Helmut Kohl's pro-market capitalist ideology and the huge CDU and state machine that he could mobilise. But, even though many East Germans rejected this model, and many more came to reject it as they experienced life under 'really existing capitalism', *Neues Forum* could not even present itself as an adequate vehicle for discontent. And so, from the other side, it was undermined by the reconstituted social democratic SED, now called the Party of Democratic Socialism.

This is not the inevitable fate of the kind of petty bourgeois groups who formed the core of *Neues Forum*. They can often play a very effective political role, as we saw from the theory of deflected permanent revolution, by benefiting from the impotence of the two major classes. Or, as in the case of the KOR activists in Poland, they can ally themselves to the working class. Or, as in the Hungarian case, they can align themselves with a section of the ruling class, although this option allows them very little distinctive political profile. The East German opposition could not align themselves with the ruling class, did not align themselves with the working class and were a dispensable commodity as far as the West German ruling class was concerned. They bloomed briefly in the revolution of the flowers, but wilted quickly in the heat generated when real class forces came to dominate the scene.

The fall of the Berlin Wall signalled that the end of the state capitalist system in Eastern Europe was only a matter of time. Jan Urban, a leading figure in Czechoslovakia's Civic Forum, recalls:

> *Poland, Hungary and now East Germany were moving. What about us? On 9*
> *November 1989 the Berlin Wall was breached. Now it was completely clear*
> *that Czechoslovakia would be next on the list.*[75]

The difference between the Prague Spring of 1968 and the revolution
of 1989, as far as Urban is concerned, is that '20 years ago it was predominantly a matter of a crisis of legitimacy within the governing
Communist elite in one country of the Communist bloc. In 1989...it was
the Czechoslovak variant of the crisis of legitimacy of whole Communist
system'. Although the Czechoslovak regime did not accumulate debt on
the Polish scale it did, consequently, create a 'painful internal debt...so
the structure and equipment of industry became unmaintainable. The
transportation system was old, services undeveloped and natural envi-
ronment devastated'.[76] In common with other ruling classes in Eastern
Europe, the Czechoslovak ruling class was losing faith in the state capitalist method of accumulation. The onset of perestroika in Russia from
the mid-1980s deepened this mood.

There had long been dissident groups in Czechoslovakia. The most
famous of them was Charter 77, patterned on KOR in Poland but more
oriented on achieving 'civic rights' and less on working class activity.
But the real mobilisation of the mass of the population only really took
hold after the fall of the Berlin Wall. Throughout 1988 and 1989 many
thousands signed petitions of protest against the Czechoslovak regime,
the largest of which were organised by the church. Demonstrations did
not attract more than 10,000. Indeed, as late as 28 October 1989 this was
the number in Prague's Wenceslas Square when at the same time Leipzig
was seeing demonstrations of 150,000 to 300,000. These demonstrations, and the ones that followed, were met with beatings and mass
arrests by the police.

Sections of the regime clearly hoped they could stage manage a transition which would maintain nearly all their power. They needed to
reform the political system by separating party, state and economic structure and, at the same time, win Gorbachev's approval. But events ran
beyond their control, although not so far beyond as to endanger the
whole process of transition to capitalist parliamentary democracy. On 17
November riot police made a violent attack on a Prague demonstration,
and a carefully planned security operation was mounted to make it seem
as if a student, Martin Smid, had been killed. The incident was meant to
be reported by the dissident press. The security forces then planned to
produce the unhurt student, discredit the opposition and pave the way for
'reform Communist' Zdenek Mlynar to replace Husak as president. At

the same time a StB security service briefing was arguing:

> *Use influential agents to intensively infiltrate opposition parties. Aim to disinform the opponent. Compromise the most radical members of the opposition and exacerbate divisions within the opposition. At the same time, create conditions for StB officers to obtain civil service promotions and posts at selected companies.*

The narrower part of this plan, to replace Husak, failed for two reasons. Firstly, Mlynar refused to play his allotted part, even though Gorbachev sought to persuade him. Secondly, and more importantly, after the fall of the Berlin Wall the mass movement took on a momentum which swept aside such plans for an orderly succession.[77]

A week after the Berlin Wall came down the numbers protesting in Prague rose to 50,000. Two days later, on 19 November, they doubled to 100,000. The next day the numbers doubled again to 200,000. Four days later, 24 November, 500,000 demonstrated in Wenceslas Square and listened to Alexander Dubcek, the disgraced leader of the Prague Spring in 1968. The same day the entire politbureau of the CP resigned.

On 25 November, another crowd of 500,000 gathered to hear Civic Forum leader Vaclav Havel and Dubcek speak. On 27 November three million workers took part in a two hour general strike, and 200,000 demonstrated in Wenceslas Square. The result of this massive spasm of popular activity was that Civic Forum announced the suspension of the demonstrations and the government conceded free elections. Within a week a majority reformist government took over.

The Civic Forum leaders were thrown to the head of the movement, but they did not create it. Indeed, it was not until 19 November 1989 that 400 activists founded Civic Forum. But the long history of dissent by the leaders of Civic Forum, many of whom were Charter 77 activists, made them natural figureheads, symbols of the revolt. But it could not be said that they *actively and organisationally prepared* the revolt in the way that the KOR activists prepared for, and then built and led, Solidarity. The deficiencies of organisation and ideology were made good by the cumulative weight of the revolutions in Eastern Europe, which led directly to massive mobilisations and the internal decay of the regime. Jan Urban's recollections make explicit both the rapidity of the regime's collapse and the limited aims of the opposition:

> *The entire political power structure collapsed in front of our eyes. We didn't want to allow the state to collapse with it, so we had to act. There was no one else to do so. There were even moments when we had to support some Communist Party officials against whom we had just fought.*[78]

Martin Palous, a philosopher at the university in Prague and one of the founders of Civic Forum, describes a similar experience:

Civic Forum leaders were constantly shocked that their proposals, dreamlike, turned into reality. It gave everyone a false impression that they were really marvellous politicians... The party structure of communications and power disintegrated.[79]

The crucial weakness lay in the 'popular front' style political strategy which the Civic Forum leadership had long espoused. Urban again:

In a few hours we had created, from the far left to the far right, a coalition with only one goal: to get rid of Husak... We did it ourselves, and having done so, we found out it was not enough. Now we had to change the whole system! We decided that the best way to achieve this was through free elections.[80]

Here the forces which determined the fate of the Czechoslovak Revolution stand out in high relief. An exhausted empire was collapsing. The national regime fell apart under the impact of popular mass mobilisations. The working class was willing to take part in general strike action under the leadership thrown to the fore by the revolution itself. But these leaders previously committed themselves to a perspective which limited the revolution to achieving the kind of political structure which dominates the Western powers. They chose to pursue this aim by a cross-class alliance stretching from the political left to the far right. At the crucial juncture they found that this ideology, and the consequent lack of real roots among the mass of the working class, led them to suspend further mass mobilisations and strikes. What followed was an accommodation between the Civic Forum leaders and members of the ruling class which allowed that class as a whole, barring only a few symbolic political figures, to maintain its power by utilising the new political and economic methods of exploiting the working class.

The Christmas revolution in Romania was significantly different from the revolutions in the rest of Eastern Europe. The violent overthrow of the Ceausescu regime requires careful analysis. Certainly, the Romanian regime was engulfed by the rising tide which had already swept away nearly all the East European dictators by the time it overcame Ceausescu. Demonstrators in Romania chanted, 'We are the people', copying those in East Germany. But if the mass movement was inspired by and had much in common with the other revolutions of 1989, the state against which it was pitted was significantly different.

Romanian state capitalism was an unreconstructed and unreformed model. External debt had peaked in the early 1980s and been reduced by means of impoverishing the working class. By 1988 food and fuel rationing was in operation. In Bucharest electricity was reduced to one kilowatt per day per household. The Romanian regime had been less undermined by growing economic links with the West. There was some of the gradual demoralisation obvious elsewhere in Eastern Europe, but it found an impenetrable barrier at the core of the state machine in the tightly knit clique of the Ceausescu family circle. Ceausescu had a long history of distancing himself from Russian foreign policy and defence strategy, and had no sympathy with 'reform Communism' of any description. This independence from Moscow earned Ceausescu the admiration of Western rulers and resulted in the granting to Romania of 'most favoured nation' trade agreements with the US. Consequently, when faced with unrest the Romanian regime was far more inclined to take the traditional stance of East European rulers—military repression, the response of Jaruzelski in 1981 rather than the response of Jaruzelski in 1989.

The revolt came late in the East European revolutionary calendar when, on 15 December 1989, pastor Laszlo Tokes of the town of Timisoara was served with a deportation order. Tokes was an ethnic Hungarian, a fact that was significant for two reasons. Firstly, Ceausescu had announced the previous year a 'systemisation' plan for agriculture which involved the demolition of 7,000 of Romania's 12,000 villages, many of them in areas heavily populated with ethnic Hungarians. Secondly, a diplomatic war between Hungary and Romania had been raging ever since Hungary began its reform programme, and Ceausescu responded with a series of hardline public criticisms. A few months before the deportation order was served on Tokes, Hungarian television had broadcast an interview with the pastor.

The day after the deportation order was served, 16 December, several hundred blockaded Tokes' house to stop it being enforced. The following day Ceausescu ranted to his Political Executive Committee about the necessity of opening fire with live ammunition: 'I did not think you would use blanks; that is like a rain shower... They have got to kill hooligans, not just beat them'.[81] The same day the Securitate police opened fire, killing 71 protesters. In the following days the protests grew in Timisoara and around the country. Troops withdrew from Timisoara on 20 December after workers threatened to blow up the petrochemical plant, and 50,000 demonstrated and sacked the CP headquarters. The next day Ceausescu's power collapsed after a staged rally turned into a protest demonstration. The scale of resistance required more than the Securitate to repress it, but the conscript army refused to intervene. The Securitate did fight back, firing on demonstrators. Fighting spread, and during the course of the revolution 700 lost their lives. Ceausescu tried, on 22 December, to address a crowd outside the CP central committee building. The crowd broke into the building and Ceausescu had to flee by helicopter from the roof. The army joined the battle against the Securitate as crowds captured the TV and radio stations. Ceausescu and his wife were captured and shot three days later, on Christmas Day 1989.

The newly formed National Salvation Front dominated the provisional government, which also included some 'dissidents' and religious leaders. Romania was one of the most repressive states in Eastern Europe. Its dissidents were hardly numerous or well organised enough to be called a movement. There existed no widely recognised programme of reform even among the intelligentsia. There was no KOR, no Charter 77, no *Neues Forum*. The National Salvation Front was therefore not a dissident organisation, but one of the groups competing for power which emerged from the old governing class. Given the vacuum of political leadership, such a group was always most likely to be composed of former Stalinists who knew the system and were able to take it over more or less intact. The National Salvation Front's president, Ion Iliescu, was a former leader of Ceausescu's youth organisation from the 1960s; the NSF's second in command was a former Securitate officer and diplomat; another senior NSF figure, Silviu Brucan, was a former editor of the party daily paper and an ambassador. Their 'opposition' to the regime was limited to the fact that they had all quarrelled with Ceausescu in the past.

The background of some of the leading figures of the revolution, and their relationship to the *apparatchiks* of the NSF, is revealing. Ion Caramitru took part in the invasion of the TV studios. He was a well known actor and head of Romania's National Theatre. Octavian Andronic was a cartoonist and news editor of the party paper *Informatia* before he launched the free paper *Libertatea* during the revolution. Nicolae Dide made film sets before he helped storm the central committee building. Later he became a parliamentary deputy. Petre Roman was a professor at the polytechnic when he pushed into the central committee building with the first wave, making his way to the balcony to famously declare that the people had taken power.

The relationship between these middle class activists and the core of the old regime that survived in the NSF is described by geologist Gelu Voican-Voiculescu. He was involved in fighting around the Intercontinental Hotel. He remembers coming to the TV centre the following day: 'I entered the television centre, just like that, someone off the street. By five o'clock I was one of Iliescu's team, and five days later I was deputy prime minister. It's almost unimaginable!'[82] Petre Roman found that his brief moment of revolutionary heroism gained him a similarly swift induction to the elite. At a meeting in the central committee building he remembers, 'The former top bureaucrats of the Communist system were gathered and I remember

The mark of restoration is sterility. Sterility of government, lack of ideas, lack of courage, intellectual ossification, cynicism, and opportunism. Revolution had grandeur, hope and danger. It was an epoch of liberation, risk, great dreams and lowly passions. The restoration is the calm of a dead pond, a marketplace of petty intrigues and the ugliness of the bribe.[85]

And it is the conduct of Solidarity itself which Michnik holds mainly responsible for this state of affairs:

One does not have to like the Solidarity revolution anymore... With that revolution the time of Solidarity and Walesa had passed. The great myth turned into caricature. The movement towards freedom degenerated into noisy arrogance and greed. Soon after its victory it lost its instinct for self preservation. That is why the post-Solidarity formations lost the last elections... Let us emphasise this: it is not so much that the post-Communist parties won as the post-Solidarity parties lost.[86]

But Solidarity lost its imagination and its ability to preserve itself because the aims to which it was limited by its leaders had been achieved—a capitalist economy and a fragile and corrupt parliamentary system. Only a deeper revolutionary policy could have maintained Solidarity's engagement with its base, but this was precisely the policy that Michnik was instrumental in jettisoning from Solidarity in the 1980s.

Michnik is not alone in his disillusionment. Jens Reich of *Neues Forum* says:

Strange to say, I am not happy and neither are others around me. Now that the state is decaying, people begin to yearn for some of its more sympathetic traits. In a peculiar way, many of us feel homesick for that inefficient and lazy society which is so remote from the tough and competitive society into which we have been thrust.[87]

Reich laments that 'one cannot deny it makes a difference whether a young mother, made late for work by her child's sudden illness, can stay at home and afterwards excuse herself without fuss, or whether such a commonplace family event puts her under considerable stress because there is no spare labour capacity at work...and she knows that she will find little sympathy or understanding of her plight'. Others, like Jan Urban of Czechoslovakia, see 'real problems before us', and that 'economic difficulties await us'. These include 'nationalist frictions' and 'clashes with dissatisfied workers'. But for Urban this is simply the price which has to be endured in order to secure the 'beginnings of parliamentary democracy'.[88]

If all that were being recorded here were the disappointments of a few

how everyone was of the opinion that Iliescu should assume respor
bility... Among the old guard, Brucan, General Militaru and so on, I v
the only one to come from the street'.[83] Nicolae Dide also remembers
scene inside the central committee building:

> In the afternoon Iliescu arrived, and that was the point where we lost the r
> olution. We gave it to him not because we wanted to but because we were
> good at revolution. For about two hours we had been an alternative gove
> ment, the first government of the revolution. When Iliescu and comp
> entered the building they spread out... General Gheorge Voinea appeared
> said, 'I want to talk to the revolutionary political structure.' All of
> remained rooted on the spot. None of us had any conception of political str
> ture. At that moment Petre Roman stepped up from behind us, to say, 'We
> here.' And he took General Voinea off to meet up with Iliescu and his frie
> to form the National Salvation Front and then they went off to televisi
> General Voinea was part of it. And that's the way they did it.[84]

Thus a paradox was created: the most complete revolutionary expe
ence of 1989 resulted in the least fundamental social change of 1989.

The velvet restoration

The experience of revolution in Eastern Europe in 1989 was a mixture
achievement and disappointment. The real achievement of the 1989 r
olutions is that they overthrew a dictatorial political system and repla
it with a form of government in which working people have the rig
join trade unions which are not state controlled, to express thems
and to organise politically with a freedom they did not have unde
Stalinist regimes. The disappointment is that such a powerful int
tional revolutionary movement ended with the installation of a
economic and political order which preserved the wider power
ruling class, enabling it to renew the process of capital accumulat
further exploiting the working population. This disappointment
seen in two spheres; firstly, in the disillusionment of many of the l
figures of the 1989 revolutions, and secondly, in the economic ex
tion and political exclusion of the mass of workers throughout
Europe.

Many of the leading opposition figures now look on the resul
1989 revolutions with a profound sense of disillusionment. N
regard the limits which they imposed on the revolutionary deve
as necessary, but they regret the effects of what Adam Michnik
velvet restoration'. Comparing the mood in Poland in the 19
previous periods of restoration, Michnik writes:

revolutionary dreamers then their sentiments might only be of limited interest. But that is not the case. These are some of the leaders of the 1989 revolutions, and the programme with which they entered those events was anything but extreme. They held a view of the West which incorporated an idealised view of parliamentary democracy and a misapprehension that the kind of economic performance demonstrated by the US in the 1950s was the norm for any capitalist economy. What they got was the crisis ridden, monopoly dominated, anti-welfare capitalism of the 1990s wedded to barely reformed state machines, glossed by a thin varnish of parliamentary representation within which corruption has become rife.

The extent of the failure of capitalist democracy in Eastern Europe is captured in the economic statistics. In all the major economies of the area, except Poland, real GDP was lower in 1997 than in 1989. In Hungary it is 10 percent lower; in the Czech Republic 11.4 percent; in Romania 17.8 percent; and in Russia there has been a drop of over 40 percent. Real wages in the same economies dropped by between 8 and 54 percent between 1989 and 1995. Full employment gave way to unemployment of over 10 percent in most of the economies, excepting Russia (3.4 percent), Romania (6.3 percent) and the Czech Republic (3.1 percent). The numbers suffering low incomes have risen to between 20 and 60 percent of the population across the region.[89] Looking out over this vista the *Financial Times'* Philip Stephens was forced to concede:

> *The common assumption was, and still is, that the defeat of communism marked the triumph of democracy. In fact, the victor was capitalism...the EU's contribution to the creation of a democratic Russia has amounted to a few billion euros and the despatch of a handful of economists from the Chicago School. And to Moscow's former satellite states, the union has offered plentiful promises and precious little else.*[90]

This is what lies beneath the disappointment of the revolutionaries. The mass unemployment, the destruction of welfare rights, the speed up and intensification of the work process have created this mood. Two major social forces have emerged to fill the vacuum where the revolutionaries had no further programme to deal with these issues. The first is reformism, often embodied by the reconstituted Communist parties of the old order. The second is nationalism and national rivalry, which has made two countries of Czechoslovakia and ignited internal conflict across the former Eastern bloc. But by far the most catastrophic effect of the 1989 nationalist revival has been the break up of Yugoslavia.

The destruction of Yugoslavia is, as much as any of the more trumpeted gains of 1989, a child of the revolutions of that year. Firstly, like Romania, there was an enormous upsurge of class struggle inspired by the other East European revolutions. And the former Communist ruling class met this challenge by playing the nationalist card, notably in Serbia, Croatia and Kosovo. But this process was enormously accelerated by the acts of the Western powers who were keen to dismember the country. Germany led the way, flushed by its unexpectedly easy victory in shaping the unification of the country, by encouraging the independence of wealthy Slovenia. But at every step of the way in the last decade all the major powers have concentrated their efforts in the continued dismemberment of the area, finally provoking in 1999 the first war involving the main imperial powers on European soil since 1945.

Thus the disillusionment of the revolutionaries of 1989 was qualitatively different from that which afflicted their forebears. The Levellers, the Sons of Liberty and Babeuf were disappointed because their programmes could not be realised. The Bolsheviks' programme was simply defeated by counter-revolution. But the democratic revolutionaries of 1989 were disappointed because their programmes were realised. The fault lay in the programme, not in the limits of the objective situation or the power of the forces opposing them.

South Africa and the ANC: the bitter fruit of freedom

It might seem that there were few similarities between the Stalinist states of Eastern Europe and the apartheid state in South Africa. Yet there were strong likenesses in certain crucial areas—both societies were industrialised by a process of strong state direction and in relative isolation from the world economy. South African apartheid, like Stalinism, faced its terminal crisis because it was unable to transform this method of capital accumulation when new realities faced it in the 1970s and 1980s. And the South African ruling class, like its East European counterparts, tried to meet the opposition of a revolutionary mass movement with a strategy of partial reform and negotiation.

Deep racial segregation marked the South African state all this century, but it became codified and further institutionalised in 1948 with the ascendancy of the Afrikaner National Party in the elections of that year. This system endured the major challenge which resulted in the 1960 Sharpeville massacre. But in the 1970s the Soweto uprising and the rise of the black consciousness movement, followed in the 1980s by the growth of independent black trade unions, marked successive phases in the crisis of apartheid.

During this 30 year period the structure of South African capitalism was transformed in some vital respects. In the pre-war period South African capitalism had been dominated by its agricultural and mining sectors. In 1936 these contributed a total of 34 percent of GDP, compared with manufacturing and construction's 13 percent. But industrial development during and after the war, sponsored by state direction of industry and import controls, transformed the economy so that the manufacturing and service sectors became predominant. By 1970 agriculture and mining had dropped to a total of 18 percent and manufacturing and construction had risen to 27 percent of GDP.[91]

Protectionism had been a feature of the inter-war South African economy, as of many others. The Second World War saw tremendous growth of manufacturing industry behind the natural protective wall of the war economy. By 1957 local capital formation accounted for 97 percent of total investment and represented a reinvestment of 30 percent of national income.[92] But after the war South African industry faced increased international competition both within its borders and from other African states. Protectionism was increased in 1959, and after Sharpeville import controls were introduced: 'Policies of domestic procurement, especially in strategic products such as armaments, energy and transport, also contributed to local expansion'.[93] This method of state led, protectionist development did result in high growth rates for a whole era. But there was a price to be paid, and the price grew greater the more the economy developed. As Merle Lipton notes:

> *Hothouse development behind protective barriers was for some years effective in maintaining profitability, new investment and growth in manufacturing. But it* **raised the cost structure of the whole economy,** *as expensive SA goods had to be used in preference to cheaper imports. As the economy developed and diversified, the costs of protection became clearer, not just to consumers, but also to businessmen, because their inputs were also protected and therefore costly.*[94]

State control of the economy was closely linked to apartheid. The maintenance of segregation in the labour market, on which white petty bourgeois and working class support for the state depended, could only be maintained through state direction of industry and isolation from the international economy. Opening the economy to international competition would have meant that South African firms would have had to compete more directly with foreign companies which did not have the burden of apartheid to carry, either in terms of higher wages for whites or the low skills and training of blacks.

But the longer the South African variant of state capitalism remained unchanged, the more it exhibited some of the same signs of crisis as the economies of Eastern Europe. Growth rates declined, as they did throughout the world when the long post-war boom ended. But the resulting problems were made worse by the nature of apartheid. From 1946 to 1970 average annual growth in manufacturing was 7 percent;

from 1969 it declined to 2.6 percent; by 1977 it was negative. The restriction of the internal market, an unavoidable consequence of apartheid's impoverishment of the black population, further limited growth. A restricted internal market encouraged manufacturers to look abroad for sales—yet the protected nature of the South African economy meant that their goods were not competitively priced in international markets. Thus the contradictions of apartheid resulted in a massive expansion of borrowing from the international banking system.

Some sections of the South African ruling class had long believed that partial reform of apartheid was necessary. The words of Anton Rupert, chairman of the Anglo-American conglomerate, were representative of this view: 'We cannot survive unless we have a free market economy [and] a stable black middle class.' Eventually a majority were driven to this conclusion by a mixture of economic imperatives and the threat of revolution from below. Yet even while they reached this conclusion, and even while arguments about the speed and direction of reform continued amongst them, a majority of the ruling class also remained convinced that their economic security, and therefore the role of the state as the guarantor of safe conditions for capital accumulation, could not be endangered by the reform process. To the extent that either reform or pressure from below threatened the fundamental existence of private property, the ruling class turned its face against compromise.

This explains the chequered history of attempts at 'top down' reform of apartheid. Prime minister Vorster's attempts at reform and at détente with the frontline African states in the 1970s collapsed in the face of the Angolan war and the Soweto riots. A new clampdown followed. The Riekert and Wiehahn reports, both issued in 1979, renewed reform by trying to develop a black business class and a stable working class which could act as a consumer base for a modern capitalist economy. The most important aspect of these proposals was the Wiehahn report's provision for the legalisation of independent black unions, which expanded enormously through the early 1980s.

The expansion and militancy of the black independent unions was decisive in convincing the ruling class that unreconstructed apartheid was resulting in the build-up of revolutionary pressure within the system. But only when it seemed possible to separate the reform of apartheid from any threat to capitalist property did the majority of the ruling class accede to the reform project. Crucial in confirming to the ruling class that reform of apartheid and a challenge to capitalist relations of production were not the same thing was the attitude of the leaders of the African National Congress (ANC) and the South African Communist Party (SACP).

The ANC was born in 1912 as a predominantly middle class led organisation focused on constitutional change: 'The ANC...drew its leadership largely from the small urban elite—teachers, priests, lawyers and doctors. Its policy was termed "moderate"—removal of discrimination, constitutional means of change, the gradual extension of a qualified franchise'.[95] The relationship with the Communist Party and the ascension to the ANC leadership of former Youth League members Nelson Mandela, Oliver Tambo and Walter Sisulu radicalised the organisation in the late 1940s. In 1955 the ANC adopted the Freedom Charter, the document demanding a number of democratic and civil rights reforms which remained the foundation of ANC politics until the final victory over apartheid in the early 1990s.

The guiding principle of the Freedom Charter, the ANC's general strategy, and the politics of the Communist Party which informed both, was the stages theory of revolution. The principal argument of this approach is that South African society was in all essentials a colonial society, 'colonialism of a special type' as the SACP described it, in which the colonial ruling class resided within the borders of the colony. The first stage of the revolution would be a democratic anti-colonial struggle, and only after this struggle was complete would it be possible to fight for socialism. In the course of defending the Freedom Charter in 1956 Nelson Mandela put it like this:

> *The Charter does not contemplate economic and political changes. Its declaration,'The people shall govern', visualises the transfer of power not to any single social class but to all the people of the country, be they workers, peasants, professionals, or petty bourgeoisie.*[96]

As Mandela makes clear, the adoption of the stages theory not only precluded a struggle for socialism, but also effectively submerged specifically working class activity in an all-class 'popular front'. Furthermore, the aim of such an 'anti-colonial' movement was to rid the country of apartheid, but not to smash the capitalist state. As Ronnie Kasrils, leader of the ANC's armed wing, explained in 1990:

> *There are revolutionary movements which, at their foundation, addressed the question of seizing state power. These immediately recognised and analysed the use of state power and the need to develop a force to seize state power. With us that was not the ethos.*[97]

This broad commitment to a national democratic revolution was combined with a wide range of rhetoric—running from appeals for insurrection to demands for compliance—and an equally variable series of tactics, spanning guerrilla struggle and peaceful negotiation. Which of these strategies were prominent in ANC propaganda was determined by the nature of the struggle between the mass movement and the regime. When guerrilla struggle became fashionable on the left in the aftermath of the Cuban Revolution it also became much more central to the ANC's approach. When the massive growth of the trade union struggle became the dominant feature of the South African mass movement in the 1980s, the ANC necessarily had to adapt its approach accordingly. But throughout the various phases of the ANC's political development the overarching theoretical framework remained constant: a stages theory of the revolution in which socialist demands had little immediate relevance. Indeed, it was this conception of the democratic revolution which made such catholic attitudes toward the agency and strategy of the revolution possible. After all, if an alteration of the political regime was the limit of the revolution, then it was possible to imagine that a variety of social forces and strategies might achieve such a goal. If, however, the aim had been socialist revolution, then working class self activity would have determined both agents and strategies with much greater precision.

The ANC's approach did not go uncontested. Perhaps the greatest challenge to the authority of the ANC and the SACP came with the growth of the independent unions in the early 1980s. These unions, first gathered in the Federation of South African Trades Unions (FOSATU), were originally highly democratic in structure, workplace based and militant. The activists who led them at first developed an approach to the struggle which laid far greater stress on working class self activity, and on socialist ideas in general, than had previously been common in the ANC.

The SACP and its trade union organisation, the South African Congress of Trade Unions (SACTU), were at least as surprised by this development as was the regime. The SACTU had held that the South African state was virtually 'fascist', and that no genuine trade unions could grow in this atmosphere. As late as June 1982 a SACTU position paper was arguing:

SACTU was forced underground. And there is nothing to suggest that the apartheid regime will ever tolerate a strong, progressive and open trade union movement for very long. It would be a mistake to act on this basis.[98]

The new unions created an alternative pole of attraction inside the working class movement and provoked an enormous and critical debate about the future of the revolution. FOSATU general secretary Joe Foster and president Chris Dlamini forcefully argued that the experience of anti-colonial revolutions proved that the regimes they created did not give workers power or even guarantee the most basic demands of the working class. 'Worker liberation can only be achieved by a strong, well organised worker movement,' Dlamini stated. Following a visit to

Zimbabwe, he observed that the people were liberated but the workers were not.[99] The ANC and the SACP reacted sharply to this challenge insisting that the CP was *the* party of the working class:

> *Dare FOSATU ignore this? And dare it ignore the confusion and division it will sow in the ranks of the working class if it sets up a new 'workers' movement' in competition with or alongside the still living Communist Party?*[100]

The debate between the 'workerists' from the new unions and the 'populists' of the ANC continued up and through the expansion of the independent union movement to include the huge National Union of Mineworkers, among others. The enlarged federation was called the Congress of South African Trade Unions (COSATU). Even at this point:

> *There was still a great deal of antipathy towards the SACP and their two stage national democratic revolution strategy. Some saw the SACP...formulations as diluting specific working class concerns in its alliance with the ANC and of placing the struggle for socialism on the back burner. The SACP itself continued to argue that 'workerism' was necessarily 'reformist' and lashed out at the 'workerists' who mooted the idea of forming a specifically workers' party as not dedicated to the 'overthrow of capitalism'.*[101]

Ultimately the SACP and the ANC were able to win both this argument and the allegiance of the best 'workerists', like Moses Mayekiso, the general secretary of the National Union of Metalworkers of South Africa, because they could provide a wider political perspective than their opponents. The 'workerists' were right in their criticisms of the SACP/ANC strategy, but they had no theory about how the struggle for socialism and the struggle against apartheid could be combined in a way which did not subordinate one to the other. This allowed the SACP leaders to portray themselves as more 'revolutionary' and more 'political' than their workerist rivals. SACP central committee member Jeremy Cronin recalls this debate:

> *The party intervened around...the so called populist-workerist debate by saying: The way forward lies neither through workerism in the narrow sense of economism or syndicalism nor through populism... We need a class perspective, we need to defend socialism, but also the national liberation struggle was the immediate struggle to be fought.*[102]

The syndicalist approach of the workerists played into the SACP's hands. The workerists' inability to show how the working class struggle was central to a broader assault on apartheid and capitalism, that is to

develop a strategy drawing on the insights of Trotsky's theory of permanent revolution, was a decisive weakness. Instead, they saw the unions as
defending workers' interests 'within the wider popular struggle', as Joe
Foster put it during a crucial policy debate.[103] Neither could they show that
they had an alternative and superior model not only of working class self
activity but also of revolutionary organisation. Thus they were always at
an ideological and organisational disadvantage when dealing with the
SACP. The experience of the socialists in the South African unions, like
that of KOR activists in Poland, is testimony to the fact that faith in rank
and file militancy is only the beginning of a revolutionary perspective. To
bring such a project to a successful conclusion in the face of rival political
projects, a broader revolutionary theory, and a party which attempts to win
a minority within the class to that theory, is necessary.

In the absence of such a commitment on the part of the workerists, the
ANC was able to incorporate the massive social force represented by the
new unions into its democratic revolution strategy. The ANC gained a
huge and decisive addition to its arsenal by this adoption:

> *The intensity of grassroots struggle continued well into 1986. The ANC and
> its internal UDF* [United Democratic Front] *allies were riding high...With the
> added strength of COSATU an attitude of supreme confidence reigned that
> liberation, or as the nationwide slogan proclaimed, 'People's Power', was
> just around the corner.*[104]

The ANC never abandoned the rhetoric of revolutionary struggle.
Indeed, the decline in the international significance of guerrilla struggles
(and its obvious ineffectiveness in the South African case) combined
with the rise in organised working class resistance, both in the unions
and the townships, to propel the ANC into adopting an insurrectionary
language more akin to the classical Marxist tradition. There was talk of
'dual power' as the basis of a revolutionary challenge to the regime. But
such an approach could never become the settled strategy of the SACP
or the ANC without the wholesale rejection of the stages theory of revolution. Only when smashing the capitalist state becomes the objective
can the question of dual power be raised seriously. If removing apartheid
and establishing a non-racial parliamentary capitalist regime is the objective then the mass movement is only necessary to compel change in the
political superstructure. Thus the mass movement of the 1980s became
the adjunct of a strategy aimed at a negotiated settlement, just as the
ANC's previous adherence to the armed struggle had been. In 1985
Oliver Tambo told a radio audience:

> *They* [domestic capital]...*want to reform the apartheid system in such a way*

that the result is a system that secures their business but is minus racial dis-
crimination. And that is...a system that falls short of the stipulation of the
Freedom Charter... Well, we do not think that such a system is different.[105]

But a year later Tambo was arguing that the ANC's aim was not 'military victory but to force Pretoria to the negotiating table'.[106]

Despite the state of emergency declared by P W Botha in June 1986,
the union-dominated struggles of the 1980s were the final, crucial conflict which propelled the regime down the path of reform. The victory of
the SACP in the ideological battles inside the union movement during
the 1980s meant that COSATU now shadowed the national negotiations
in the industrial sphere. COSATU signed accords with the state and
began participation in the National Manpower Commission, devoting
increasing energies to institutionalising bargaining arrangements with
the state and the employers. But there were also other factors at work.

As part of the Reagan-Gorbachev summit in Iceland in 1986 it had
been unofficially agreed that aid to Third World clients would be scaled
down. The cessation of Russian and East German aid in everything from
weapons to the printing of journals was a blow to the ANC and a further
pressure in the direction of a negotiated settlement. The 1988 New York
agreement involving Russia, Cuba, the US and South Africa ended the
war in Angola. It was a defeat for South Africa and so helped to create a
willingness to reform. But the New York agreement also underlined the
fact that Russia was no longer willing to support the ANC's armed
struggle. And in the wake of these developments the US sponsored a
massive propaganda offensive through a variety of non-governmental
organisations. Financial assistance was channelled through a 'Human
Rights Fund' and a 'Labour Union Training' operation. This last organisation was controlled by the African-American Labour Institute of the US
union federation AFL-CIO, previously denounced by the SACP as a CIA
front. More aid poured in through the 'Special Self-Help Fund' for 'community development', projects for students to be educated in the US, and
the National Endowment for Democracy's fund for 'strengthening democratic institutions', another project thought to have close CIA links.[107]

The crucial element, however, was the growing sense among South
Africa's rulers that the ANC would negotiate a settlement which would
leave their fundamental economic power untouched. As Zach de Beer,
executive of the giant Anglo-American corporation, had put it in 1986:

We all understand how the years of apartheid have caused many blacks to
reject the economic as well as the political system. But we dare not allow the
baby of free enterprise to be thrown out with the bathwater of apartheid.[108]

It was on precisely this crucial point that the ANC's stages theory of revolution allowed it to compromise with the desires of capital. In 1987 the ANC's national executive unequivocally stated:

> *Once more we would like to affirm that the ANC and the masses of our people as a whole are ready and willing to enter into genuine negotiations provided they are aimed at the transformation of our country into a united and non-racial democracy.* ***This, and only this, should be the objective of any negotiating process.***[109]

The path to the eventual majority rule settlement was still the subject of great conflict between the mass movement and the regime. But this conflict was no longer over whether or not there would be a social revolution in which capitalist relations would be challenged. Now the conflict was reduced to one in which the contending parties fought to decide who would have how much power inside a new parliamentary capitalist system. The de Klerk regime was quite willing to use the violence of the security forces, and to stir up reactionary forces like Inkatha, to force the ANC into accepting a more disadvantageous settlement than it wanted. The ANC for its part realised that it could not operate effectively without mass mobilisation as a counterweight to the violence of the state. This was its sole bargaining counter of any real value. But on both sides it was understood that these forces were now adjuncts to the negotiations. Just 12 weeks after the fall of the Berlin Wall, de Klerk used the state opening of parliament to announce the unbanning of the ANC and the SACP. This, and the freeing of Nelson Mandela nine weeks later, was a watershed. The regime could not go back to full blooded apartheid and the ANC would not go forward to a struggle against capitalism. Even those who were critical of the slow pace and inadequate gains made in the negotiations, like Ronnie Kasrils, saw the mass movement as a tool which could create a 'Leipzig option' in which 'de Klerk is propelled out the exit gate'. That is, the democratic revolution would be attained by faster, 'bottom up' methods.

Even this was not to be, but not because the popular movement lacked the desire to take this path. There was constant dissent and outbreaks of struggle which threatened to break the limits of the ANC/SACP's strategy. Even SACP central committee member Jeremy Cronin later admitted that 'there was a tendency to underemphasise socialism... I think the party underrated the mass support, particularly working class support, for socialism'.[110] And this estimate is supported by survey evidence stretching back through the 1980s and 1970s showing sustained support for revolutionary ideas among a substantial section of black militants and workers:

*The Buthelezi Commission found 'a growing climate of revolutionary ide-
ology', with violence becoming a 'respectable option', particularly among
the educated. However, militancy was not necessarily correlated with racist
or undemocratic views... Hanf concluded that 'the more democratic a black
South African is, the stronger his demands for political rights, and the readier
he is to adopt non-peaceful means to attain them'... Marxism has become
influential among younger blacks, and surveys showed a growing hostility to
capitalism, though this may have been mainly to white capitalism.*[111]

Yet the ANC's hegemony, and its two stage theory, survived. Indeed,
it survives to this day with opinion poll support well above 50 percent in
the population as a whole and 70 percent among blacks. But nearly a
decade after the ANC entered negotiations the bitter fruits of compromise are easy to see. The central promise to build a million homes has
still not been delivered, in part because of corruption and mismanagement by the new black elite, but mainly because resources have not been
made available. It is the same story with the provision of education.
Unemployment, at more than 40 percent, is higher than it has ever
been.[112] And in 1997 state expenditure on health was a smaller per-
centage of the total budget than it was in 1991.[113]

This is the tragedy of a working class movement which both objectively had the power and subjectively had the willingness to overturn
the capitalist system. Yet it is still suffering the same injustices and
deprivations under the black bosses it elected as it did under the white
bosses it did not elect. But such is the reality of power in capitalist societies, as workers in the parliamentary capitalist regimes of the West
have long experienced. Whatever power parliament possesses is easily
negated by the economic power of the capitalist class. Changing the
skin colour of government ministers may signify a defeat for racism, but
it does not alter the fundamental fact of class exploitation and oppression for the vast majority of black South Africans.

The left and the Indonesian Revolution

Indonesian society in the 1950s and 1960s, the two decades after independence from the Netherlands, was dominated by a state bureaucracy
which became the leading force in investment and corporate ownership.
No great landed families existed as they had done in Europe and Latin
America. Consequently, the state bureaucracy which led the industrialisation process was not subordinated to the same degree to a pre-existing
conservative oligarchy. The middle classes, the other crucial contending
class force in earlier transitions to capitalism, were also weak. The middle
classes were composed of a small layer of professionals and intellectuals
allied to a wider group which depended almost entirely on the state

bureaucracy for their employment. This state machine and its huge military industrial complex increasingly dominated Indonesian society, from independence under Sukarno, through Suharto's bloody coup in 1965, until the 1980s.

Over this period the international economic climate changed dramatically, and so did the economic role of the state. As the world economy grew in the post-war period the Indonesian state adopted the autarkic, isolationist model of development common to the Stalinist states and many post-colonial Third World regimes in the 1950s and 1960s. As late as the early 1980s the economy was more highly regulated and controlled than at any time since the 1930s. But in the late 1980s and into the mid-1990s, just at the end of the 15 year period in which the South East Asian boom doubled Indonesian GDP, the state moved towards a strategy of promoting international investment and attracting foreign investment. This process was accelerated in 1982 and 1986 by the decline in state controlled oil revenues, which had helped boost annual growth to 7 percent between 1973 and 1981.[114] The result was greater reliance on private investment. The finance sector was deregulated and state monopolies in banking, television, airlines and public utilities were brought to an end. The result was a massive surge in private corporate capital during the 1980s.[115]

The resulting overproduction produced an economic crash which was, in turn, a major cause of the May 1998 revolution. The fate of the revolution is caught up with the transformation of the class structure which accompanied the earlier economic growth. The rise of a newly confident middle class is obvious from the sight of the canyons of corporate skyscrapers which line the main highways of Jakarta, interspersed with luxurious, air conditioned shopping malls whose patrons go home to the new security guarded and enclosed housing developments. The number of new apartments aimed at the middle class and corporate elite, and worth between US$100,000 and US$500,000, rose from 753 in 1985 to 8,427 in 1992.

This new middle class remains tied to the state in many ways and certainly looks to the state to protect it from 'the mob'. But in recent years it has also chafed against the limits of the old Suharto power structure. Such divisions have limited the political effect of this class:

It is little wonder that middle class reformers have made such limited political progress in the last 40 years. Internally divided, dependent upon the state and fearful of social and economic chaos, they have largely been immobilised.[116]

But the economic transformation of the last two decades has built up pressure on the regime from the middle class. Some of this pressure is not directly political: demands for efficient public services, medical facilities, rational building codes and so on. One account, written before the overthrow of Suharto, noted:

> ...*stronger demands from the 'new capitalists' who are not part of the large conglomerates for a level playing field, a more transparent regulatory regime, and stricter control over the business activities of the families of high government officials. Such demands...have been increasingly heard during the 1990s, reflecting the growing strength and confidence of the indigenous middle class, working in the private sector as white collar employees, as employers or as independent, own account workers.*[117]

These demands meshed with the kind of pressures from the major powers that we have seen also existed in South Africa:

> *By attempting to ignore...politically unpalatable but nevertheless important new issues within its supposedly all encompassing corporatist structures the state has allowed room for institutions and expertise outside its apparatus to take the lead. This has resulted in rapid expansion of non-governmental organisations (NGOs) in areas such as legal aid and human rights, environmental matters, community development and social research. Often receiving foreign funding, especially from Western European foundations, NGOs now employ many highly qualified younger generation lawyers, economists, managers, researchers and organisers.*[118]

This layer of the middle class and their allies in the ruling class were certainly not the moving force behind the overthrow of Suharto. But once that had been achieved by other forces, their political representatives, whether in the elite already or figures who had been excluded from it during previous dynastic quarrels, moved to ensure that their own agenda dominated the movement. They, like a previous generation of middle class activists in the deflected permanent revolutions discussed earlier, could only act because of the space created by other classes. And, unlike their forebears, the Communist Party had not been their political organisation nor revolutionary nationalism their ideology. For this generation the NGOs and academic forums provided much of the organisation, and the 'Western values' of democratic civil, society and free market economics provided the ideology.

So who did create the revolutionary situation which allowed the middle class politicians to act? In May 1998 the Suharto dictatorship was broken by a mass student movement which coincided with, and gave political direction to, an uprising of the urban poor. There has been some discussion on the Indonesian left about whether the fall of Suharto can be called a revolution at all. The evidence usually adduced to support the claim that nothing approaching a revolution took place in May 1998 is that Suharto was deposed by a kind of 'internal coup' within the governmental machine, and that the figures who replaced him at the apex of government, President B J Habibie and armed forces chief General Wiranto, were both members of the Suharto elite.

It is certainly true that there was no *social* revolution in May 1998. No class was overthrown, no mode of production transformed. But was there a political revolution in which the nature of the governmental system was changed? The fact that the immediate cause of Suharto's resignation was that all his 14 senior economic ministers refused to serve in his cabinet and his senior army officer told him the security situation was bleak does not prove the case one way or another.[119] The key question is why these long serving elite figures acted in this deeply uncharacteristic way. After all, the regime was a personal dictatorship and nothing of this kind had ever happened before. The governmental elite acted in this way because the student demonstrations, the occupation of the parliament building and the urban riots made it plain that if Suharto did not go then the entire economic system, as well as the existing political system, stood under threat. The elite reacted to the economic crisis and under pressure from below— and so began a process of transformation which has not yet run its course.

The Habibie regime is a classic example, on the political level at least, of a provisional government. The parallels with the provisional government in Russia after the February 1917 revolution are especially striking. The February revolution resulted in a regime that preserved much of the tsarist state while forcing the abdication of the tsar himself, just as the May revolution in Indonesia resulted in a regime which preserved much of the Suharto state while forcing the abdication of Suharto himself. The provisional government of 1917 was led by Prince L'vov, a member of the tsarist aristocracy, and in 1998 the Indonesian government formed in May 1998 was led by a 'prince' of the Suharto 'aristocracy', B J Habibie. The Russian capitalist class, with the conditional support of the officer class of the army which was central to the tsarist state, hoped that the new regime would stabilise the situation and preserve their power:

> *The February revolution of 1917 which overthrew the Romanov dynasty was...welcomed and utilised by a broad stratum of the bourgeoisie and of the official class, which had lost confidence in the autocratic system of government and especially the persons of the tsar and his advisers; it was from this section of the population that the first provisional government was drawn.*[120]

The Habibie government represented very similar forces with very similar intentions. The first provisional government in Russia was almost exclusively composed of ruling class figures. Indeed, the Bolsheviks' paper *Pravda* denounced the provisional government as 'a government of capitalists and landowners',[121] just as socialists and others in Indonesia today denounce the Habibie government as a continuation of Suhartoism without Suharto.

That the provisional government came during successive crises throughout 1917 to include socialist ministers was a product of the force exerted on it from the outside by the revolutionary movement. Such 'socialist' evolution had nothing to do with the intrinsic nature of the provisional government itself. Indeed, if we look at the policy of the provisional government, rather than at its personnel, it becomes obvious that the fundamental nature of the government was not changed at all by the inclusion of socialist ministers. The government continued to prosecute the imperialist war, continued to oppose the seizure of the factories by the workers and the land by the peasants, and continued to resist the pressure of the workers' councils. It continued on this path after the socialists joined it, just as it had done before they arrived.

Nevertheless, for all these striking similarities between the provisional government of 1917 and the Habibie government, there are also some equally striking differences. Most importantly the provisional government of 1917 represented a break between an old semi-feudal governmental layer around the tsar and a more modern pro-capitalist layer represented by the provisional government. This break was a product of the highly uneven and rapid social development in Russia before the revolution.

In Indonesia the situation is different because capitalist development before the revolution lasted much longer and is more deeply entrenched than in Russia in 1917. The most important index of this fact is the development of the working class: in Russia in 1917 it numbered 12 million out of a total population of 160 million; in Indonesia today it numbers some 86 million out of a total population of 200 million. In short, the Russian working class in 1917 was 10 percent of the population, whereas in Indonesia it represents 43 percent of the population. If we look at the proportion of GDP contributed by the agricultural sector of the economy we see the same extensive growth of industry from another angle. According to the World Bank, agriculture accounted for 53.9 percent of Indonesian GDP in 1960. This fell to a mere 19.5 percent by 1991. In the period 1975-1993 alone the contribution of agriculture to total GDP fell by 50 percent. In 1993, according to the Asia Development Bank, it stood at only 18.4 percent. Russian agriculture was still standing at 19 percent of national product in 1960, a full 53 years after the revolution.[122]

Even before the Indonesian revolution, one commentator noted that 'growing numbers of unskilled and semi-skilled wage workers in the non-

agricultural sectors of the economy were demanding more autonomous
worker organisations which could press for better wages and working conditions'.[123] This reflects the changing profile of the Indonesian working
class where there has been a 'particularly striking...increase in the proportion of the labour force comprising employees in both industry and
services.' Indonesia, like many developing countries, still possesses a huge
pool of surplus and semi-employed labour—the urban poor. But the economic growth of recent decades has had an effect even here: 'Accelerated
economic growth...from the late 1960s has pulled labour from...the traditional economy into wage employment in modern enterprises run along
capitalist lines'.[124] This is important because the popular base of middle
class politicians like Megawati is often composed of the urban poor and
the smallest of the petty bourgeoisie who live among them. But the
growing weight of the working class enables socialist arguments to carry
greater weight among these sections of the population than they would
have done before, provided such arguments are clearly articulated by
socialist organisations who do not allow the liberal bourgeoisie an open
field.

The increasingly capitalist nature of Indonesian society can also be
seen if we look at the ruling class. The Suharto regime was dictatorial
and militaristic as far as its political form was concerned, but it was not a
semi-feudal regime in its economic content. Nor did it rest on semi-
feudal landowning classes. It was a fully capitalist regime intent on using
the state machine to develop the economy and break into the world
market. This difference becomes politically important when we consider
the nature of the Habibie regime. The Russian bourgeoisie wanted to
clear away the tsarist excrescences and remodel the state machine,
although in the event they were too cowardly to do so. The Indonesian
bourgeoisie has even less reason to want to interfere with the state which
Suharto built. This is obviously true of Habibie, Wiranto and their like
because they have been loyal servants of this state from the beginning.
But it is also true of the liberal opposition of Megawati and Amien Rais.
They represent would-be alternative governmental parties. They certainly do not represent an alternative class to the present government.
The *Financial Times* had this to say at the time of Megawati's party con-
gress in Bali last October:

> The upside of this for foreign investors is that Mrs Megawati...rejected
> appeals to restrict access to foreign investors, hamper the free market or
> break up the conglomerates which dominate the Indonesian economy but are
> also, in times of crisis like this, the main source of cash.[125]

Amien Rais's economic programme is not qualitatively different to that of Megawati, who he joined in an electoral alliance in May 1999. The desire of Megawati and Amien Rais to run the Indonesian state with as little alteration as possible does not mean, however, that they will not give voice to demands for reform if they believe that raising such issues are necessary to unseat Habibie. But they will prefer to do this with as little threat to 'order' as possible, they will pray that they can do so constitutionally, that the popular movement will not force them to make uncomfortable choices. They hope that demonstrations, riots and strikes will give way to peaceful, 'democratic' development. One Western diplomat accurately captured Megawati's dilemma:

> *The elite feel they can trust her. But her base is clearly with the poor people. People who have been disempowered, who want wealth and power sharing. She can't be both a leader of the elite and the poor.*[126]

If, however, the mass movement does not agree to fulfil its allotted role as stage army and voting fodder for the liberal opposition there is little doubt that the fundamental loyalties of both Megawati and Amien Rais will be to the Indonesian ruling class and its state.

Certainty in this question rests in part on the analysis of the similarities and differences between Russia in 1917 and Indonesia today. In Russia the bourgeoisie really did need to clear away elements of a pre-capitalist state machine. Even so, they were still too cowardly to do so. The Indonesian bourgeoisie already has a capitalist state machine. Some sections of the bourgeoisie may now wish for a governmental reform which will re-establish the credibility of their state in the eyes of the mass of the population and at the same time hoist their party into power. But the Indonesian liberal bourgeoisie are even more afraid of the popular movement than the Russian bourgeoisie were, because they in no sense represent a fundamentally different class and have no desire for a fundamentally different state.

The only forces that can maintain the forward momentum of the revolution are the workers, students and urban poor who have been the sole source of all its progress to date. And, of these forces, the workers are by far the most important. But this raises the question of what attitude socialists should take to the democratic demands which dominate the revolution at the moment. This question became centrally important when the movement, which subsided after the overthrow of Suharto, revived on an even grander scale in demonstrations at the November 1998 meeting of the People's Consultative Assembly (MPR).

The sessions of the MPR focused discontent with the Habibie government's lack of commitment to real change. The mass of workers and students clearly saw how tied to the old Suharto state the new regime remains. This transformed the call for the overthrow of the Habibie government from being the property of relatively small and fragmented demonstrations in September to being the popular aim of mass demonstrations in November 1998. In wide layers of the movement the demand for 'reformasi' gave way to the call for 'revolusi'. These demonstrations, the largest of which involved hundreds of thousands, culminated in the killing of 18 protesters by the Indonesian army and marked a new stage in the Indonesian Revolution.

The November demonstrations failed to unseat the government and replace it with a 'proper' provisional government as many of the organisers hoped it would. But the Habibie regime's attempt to break the opposition movement in a 'Tiananmen style' crackdown also failed. The killings outraged many students, workers and urban poor but did not break the movement. The armed forces were weakened by internal divisions as some army units either sided with the demonstrators or remained neutral, including elements of the elite marine units. All these factors meant that the Habibie government, already unstable, was propelled down the road of reform.

The elections, which there had been plans to delay, were called for June 1999. Early in 1999 a pledge was given that a referendum would be granted on autonomy for East Timor. East Timorese and other political dissidents began to be released from jail. The People's Democratic Party (PRD), the party furthest left on the Indonesian political spectrum, was legalised and allowed to stand in elections, although some of its leading figures remain behind bars. All these reforms were urged on by the US, backed up by Australia. As in South Africa, a variety of NGOs, often with links to the opposition, have been urging on the rapid transition to capitalist democracy.

But the regime did not just trust the outcome of the elections to pro-democratic sentiment. It has reshaped the armed forces, giving the police a separate structure it did not have before. It recruited hundreds of thousands of 'civilian militia', armed with shields and bamboo canes, and under military command. And it continued to spread religious and ethnic conflict through *agents provocateurs*. The aim is not to totally suppress the movement in the Suharto manner, but to keep it within the bounds of the election process and so destroy the possibility of a revolutionary alternative arising among the mass of the population, a fear common in ruling circles at the start of 1999.

The Indonesian bourgeoisie, including its liberal wing, is in an analogous position to the bourgeoisie that Marx described in 1848. It is even now 'grumbling at those above, trembling at those below'. Megawati and Amien Rais are, like their German precursors, 'revolutionary in relation to the conservatives and conservative in relation to the revolutionaries, mistrustful of their own slogans, which were phrases instead of ideas, intimidated by the...revolution yet exploiting it; with no energy in any respect, plagiaristic in every respect'.[127] But the Indonesian liberal bourgeoisie is not in this condition because it is tied to an old feudal order by its late development, but because it is tied to an already developed capitalist state, which they want to reform but not to overthrow. They are also confronted by a working class of far greater size than that which so terrified the German bourgeoisie in 1848.

The Indonesian student movement and the left have been caught off guard by these developments. They did not see the Habibie government as a provisional government, but as a continuation of the Suharto state, and so did not expect this 'democratic' development. On the contrary, they expected the state to resist any such change and assumed that it would have to be fought for in a 'proper' democratic revolution. Early in 1999 it became apparent that the student movement was divided on this issue. Some wanted to continue fighting under the previous year's slogans, 'Down with Habibie' and 'End the political role of the armed forces', in order to push for a real provisional government. Some wanted to settle for making sure that the elections were 'free and fair', and so volunteered as election monitors. The PRD seemed split between standing in the elections because the masses were clearly looking to them and boycotting the elections because they were not called by a democratic provisional government.

The solution to this quandary is to be found in the history of previous revolutions. Every revolution, including every socialist revolution, begins with the battle for democratic demands. Socialists should be in the forefront of the fight for all kinds of democratic reforms. The characterisation of the Indonesian state as capitalist and of the Indonesian bourgeoisie as wedded to the state is simply meant to show the limits of democratic politics, the speed with which socialist politics can emerge in the course of the further development of the revolution, and the importance of raising socialist politics. More important still is that socialists raise democratic demands in a different way to those who are simply adherents of the 'democratic revolution' and use very different methods and techniques in organising to achieve these demands.

In 1848 Marx insisted that workers stay one step ahead of the liberal opposition and that their demands, while 'democratic', should have a specific class content which sets the workers at odds with the liberal democrats. This is why in Indonesia today socialists should not just echo the slogans of the popular movement, slogans which are quite acceptable to Megawati and Amien Rais. For instance, 'End the dual function of ABRI [the armed forces]' should always be combined with the slogan, 'Cut the arms budget, feed the starving.' The second slogan is still a 'democratic demand' in a certain sense, but it raises issues specific to the working class and combines them with an attack on the state which Megawati and Amien Rais will be reluctant to endorse.

And for Marx this approach to the tactics and slogans of the day was part of a wider strategic understanding that a socialist revolution was the goal to which the movement was headed. He did not talk of the workers forming a provisional government, nor did he speculate on what shape a provisional government formed by the bourgeois democrats would take. Marx and Engels understood that class polarisation was dividing the democratic camp. Engels noted that all revolutions begin with a cross-class 'democratic unity' against the old order. But, as the revolution develops, the initial phase, the 'revolution of the flowers', gives way to political divisions within the revolutionary camp based on underlying class differences. This has been the case in all previous revolutions, including the very first bourgeois revolutions.

But in all the revolutions after 1848 there was the potential for this class differentiation to develop to the point where workers created their own distinctive organs of power: workers' councils. Of course there are no workers' councils in Indonesia, and therefore no organised form of dual power. Yet it is not true to say that the Habibie government, or the government formed after the elections, could rule without having to take account of the power of the mass movement. The demonstrations which coincided with the meeting of the MPR clearly forced the government onto the defensive, at least in the short term. The crucial question is how this power can be consolidated into an institutional form which commands the allegiance of wide layers of the working class, and which can become an organising centre of opposition to the government.

One thing seems clear: a 'real' or 'democratic' provisional government cannot simply be declared. The students' attempt to create an alternative 'parliament' during the November demonstrations was a valuable propaganda weapon, but a real alternative to the Habibie government will have to built from the bottom up, not just proclaimed. Local meetings of activists including students and workers could have begun such a process. Even if these beginnings of workers' power cannot yet be built, socialists can argue that they *should* be built and gather around them the best militants in the movement, even if they are a small minority of the working class, on the basis of this programme of action.

For an illustration of this process at work we can turn to the experience of French workers during the strikes of 1995. These strikes involved an all out strike by rail workers combined with a series of one day public sector general strikes. The strikes were called in opposition to the austerity plans of then prime minister Alain Juppé which increased workers' retirement age, raised the taxes paid by the poor, increased health charges and cut welfare benefits. The strikes were massive by comparison with any struggles in France since 1968, but still far from a revolutionary situation. And while the reformist left in France was represented by two large organisations, the Socialist Party and the Communist Party, the forces of the revolutionary left were small. Nevertheless, French workers began to form rank and file forums in a way which is instructive.

As different sections of public sector workers came out on strike they began to pull out other sections, fuse their separate strike committees and call local assemblies of workers. What follows is the story of one teacher in one local area of Paris. His school had just voted to go on strike:

> We went down to the local postal depot which was out on strike. There were about 100 of them having a meeting in the canteen. It was amazing, everyone was applauding us, just a little school! They proposed a local demonstration on Thursday morning, before the national march, to go around the local workplaces. Everyone thought that was a great idea and it was decided straight away to contact other local strikers. Armed with leaflets we set off on a tour of local workplaces—the office of the Paris water company, where a delegation walked straight in while the rest chanted outside, a large residential nursing home, where a group of the home's workers comes to the door, nearly all low paid, women and black, the big Monoprix supermarket, into which about 20 striking teachers, postal workers, bus workers and school students marched.[128]

Such work made it possible to organise a meeting of 500 workers from workplaces across the locality a few days later. This meeting set up a regular coordinating committee. Similar initiatives were taken in other areas of Paris and in other cities. In Rouen, western France, the rail workers held daily 'general assemblies' at the goods yard, where other workers were invited to participate and argue out plans to fight the government. Something similar happened in Dreux, a town of 35,000 people 60 miles from Paris:

> The rail workers pushed for a new, open form of struggle against the Juppé plan... Discussions took place in front of comrades from other parts of the private and public sector.
> The small premises by the railway line became a humming beehive of activity where everything was debated—how to carry the movement forward, the preparation of demonstrations, providing daily meals, the organisation of the creche for strikers' children...and the making of links with other sectors. The railway workers went to meet the postal workers, the hospital workers, the gas workers, the teachers, the council workers. And then everyone found themselves together

in front of private factories with loudhailers, songs, red flags, leaflets with the
call for the general strike in the public and private sectors.[129]

Such councils of action have arisen, frequently spontaneously, in
every revolutionary upheaval: in Germany in 1918, in Hungary in 1919,
in Italy during the two red years, 1919 and 1920, in Spain in 1936, in
Hungary in 1956, in Czechoslovakia and France in 1968 and in Portugal
in 1974. They are non-party bodies representing as wide a cross-section
of the working class struggle as possible. There may be long periods
when they are dominated by moderate socialists who want to compromise with the provisional government, as the Russian soviets were
dominated for much of 1917 by the Mensheviks and SRs. The outcome
of the Russian Revolution was decided by whether or not the revolutionaries won a majority in the soviets during the course of the revolution.
When they did, it enabled them to lead the soviets in smashing the provisional government.

What is the People's Democratic Party strategy?

The People's Democratic Party (PRD) is the best known left wing organisation in Indonesia and its members have a brave record of opposition to
the Suharto regime. Its strategy has widespread support far beyond its
own membership. What is the PRD's assessment of the Indonesian
Revolution? The statements, manifestos and interviews with PRD
leaders available on the party's publications and website give a clear
account of the PRD's strategy.[130]

The overwhelming majority of PRD statements, including the
'Manifesto of the PRD' issued in July 1996, talk in terms of fighting for
'a government that is democratic and people-oriented' and of the need
'to unify and mobilise the existing democratic forces'.[131] In discussion of
the PRD's approach to the June 1999 elections, Muhammad Ma'ruf,
editor of the party's fortnightly magazine, *Liberation*, says, 'We would
like the elections to be organised democratically by a provisional government'.[132] In a recent interview Ma'ruf explains, 'The PRD, Student
and People's Committee Against the Dual Function of the Armed
Forces, KOBAR, and KPM (Megawati Supporters Committee) are cam-
paigning for a democratic coalition government comprising forces that
have struggled consistently for democracy'.[133] The attainment of a
'democratic provisional government' is undoubtedly the PRD's immediate aim, and so discussion of specifically anti-capitalist struggles and
of working class self activity is a secondary factor in these statements.
There is no discussion of fighting to set up councils of action as sources
of independent working class power in opposition either to the provisional government of Habibie or to any future, more democratic

provisional government.

US based PRD supporter Malik Miah believes that the Indonesian Revolution is a 'democratic revolution' which aims at the establishment of 'a more democratic capitalist regime'. He argues, as do many in Indonesia, that there is no possibility, given the current consciousness of the Indonesian working class, for socialist arguments to gain an audience: 'There is no discussion about overthrowing the market or establishing a government based on a planned economy. That consciousness does not exist there any more than it exists...in the United States'.[134]

It follows that all socialists can do in this situation is 'build a stronger democratic movement' by raising 'demands to further isolate Habibie and the military from the masses'. This sentiment is echoed by the PRD central committee document entitled 'Let's Create Democracy Without ABRI's Dual Function', in which it is argued that there are positive benefits for the armed forces if they stay out of politics, such as 'ABRI will no longer be confronting their own people because they are devoting themselves to the interests of certain social groups'.[135] Malik Miah believes that this strategy is founded on the experience of the Bolsheviks during the Russian Revolution:

The real lesson of the Russian Revolution was the programme followed by the Bolsheviks before 1917... The pre-1917 programme was to end tsarist rule and establish a bourgeois democratic republic.

*It was that correct programme (see Lenin's **Two Tactics of Social Democracy in the Democratic Revolution**, discussing the 1905 revolution) that laid the basis for the toilers to have a chance to achieve their own rule. Lenin always defended that strategy. In fact, it was the socialists who disagreed with the Bolshevik strategy and took a more leftist position who were not able to build a party before 1917.*[136]

Let us take these points one by one. As we have already seen, it is only partially true to describe the Indonesian Revolution as a 'democratic revolution'. Indonesia's revolution is democratic in the sense that it has overthrown a dictatorship and that the Habibie government was forced into making democratic reforms. Actually it would be more accurate to say that the mass movement has *de facto* created a degree of political freedom which the Habibie regime has been forced to endorse. Indonesia's revolution is also democratic in the sense that all the major political currents, from Habibie through Megawati to the PRD, now express themselves in favour of democratic government of some kind.

But the Indonesian Revolution is not a simply a democratic revolution in the sense that this term has been used in the Marxist tradition. For Marxists, the democratic revolution refers to conditions in which it is *objectively impossible* to go beyond the limits of a capitalist economic system and a parliamentary republic. These conditions prevail where a feudal or semi-feudal class still controls and shapes the state, where the working class is too weak to take power, and where the bourgeoisie is the main opposition to the old order. These were the conditions under which the classical bourgeois revolutions, like those in 17th century England, and in America and France in the 18th century, took place. The democratic revolution in these cases was not merely a *political phase*, created by the subjective weakness of the working class and its political representatives, but a *social transformation*. It is therefore more properly called a *bourgeois revolution*, the culmination of the economic and social transition from feudalism to capitalism, not simply a democratic transformation of the political superstructure.

The 1848 revolutions occurred when the further development of capitalism had created a more powerful and numerous working class than had existed during the classical bourgeois revolutions. This development alarmed the bourgeoisie to such an extent that they became more afraid of the class rising beneath them than they were of the old order standing above them, as we saw that Marx and Engels discovered at the time. In 1917 Lenin once again discovered that even in backward Russia the working class would have to directly proceed to *simultaneously* solve the problems of the democratic revolution and the socialist revolution. The fact that there were 'phases' in the development of the consciousness of the working class in 1917 was not a result of objective economic barriers to the socialist revolution. Workers always begin a battle with faith in their traditional leaders, because these leaders tend to reflect the compromises with the system which are the inevitable experience of most workers most of the time under capitalism. But these factors and the consciousness that arises from them only mark the workers' point of departure; they do not place any limits on the distance they may travel under the impact of revolutionary struggles and the urgings of that organised minority of the class which is its revolutionary leadership.

The social structure of Indonesia is much more advanced than that of Russia in 1917. Indonesia is a capitalist country with a massive working class. More than 30 years ago this working class could support a Communist Party of three million members. Indonesia has no feudal landowning class. The army is controlled by capitalist bureaucrats. The Indonesian state is a capitalist state. Megawati and Amien Rais are bourgeois democrats but they do not face a feudal or semi-feudal state; they face a capitalist state run by the very same class from which they themselves come. What separates Megawati and Amien Rais from Habibie and Wiranto is a difference of political strategy, not a class divide of any kind. This is why the two forces so easily compromise with each other all the time.

Is it at least true, as many on the Indonesian left assert, that the Indonesian working class lacks the consciousness that will permit discussion of a socialist solution to the crisis? It seems obvious that this assertion cannot be true. It hardly seems likely that a class which is suffering from the ravages of a market produced crisis of the depth of that now afflicting Indonesia will be unwilling to listen to criticisms of pro-capitalist policies. Is it really being argued that when the IMF, one of the leading international capitalist agencies, enforced the removal of the rice subsidy there was no Indonesian worker willing to listen to anti-capitalist agitation? When the whole revolutionary movement considers ABRI to be its main enemy, and when this same military machine dominates the state and defends the capitalists' property from the starving, is it really impossible to combine democratic and anti-capitalist demands?

Moreover, in a country whose Communist Party was the largest outside the Stalinist states it seems clear that, despite the destruction of the left in 1965, a memory of what it stood for will persist among a sizeable minority of workers. Proof of this was inadvertently provided by ABRI's attempt to start 'red scare' in late 1998. The military claimed that the Indonesian Communist Party (PKI) was mounting a comeback and that it was infiltrating the PRD. In response *The Jakarta Post* ran an opinion poll asking respondents if they believed that the PRD was infiltrated by the PKI and if they equated 'radicalism' with 'communism'. The responses were as follows: 75 percent said they did not equate radicalism with communism and 73 percent said they did not think that the PRD had been infiltrated by the PKI.[137] The form in which these questions were posed does not allow us to draw many conclusions about whether or not people supported radicalism, communism or the PRD, although in one of the survey's most interesting findings, 22 percent said that they believe that 'communism is very much alive as an ideology'. But it does allow us to prove conclusively that a broad cross-section of Indonesians are aware of the issues and are quite willing and able to engage in debate about them. Among these there certainly exists a militant minority capable of forming a genuinely revolutionary organisation.

Indeed, opinion about the current consciousness of the Indonesian working class seems to be divided in the PRD itself. Although wishing to limit the current demands of the movement to the call for a democratic provisional government, Muhammad Ma'ruf argues that the current consciousness of the movement is running beyond this perspective: 'Workers' unrest in particular is increasing everywhere. These last weeks there have been four demonstrations each day in Indonesia. All of them were political and are directed against government leaders at regional

and local level'.[138] And when asked in an earlier interview about the
'thirst for Marxist ideas among campus students in Indonesia', Ma'ruf
replies:

> That is true. For 32 years, under the Suharto regime, people were not
> allowed to learn about Marxism. The government has always said that
> Marxism is bad, vile, atheist and so on, so many students are anxious to find
> out what was actually taught by Marx... Following the May uprising which
> overthrew Suharto, more and more students have begun to develop a high
> level of political consciousness. Even on the city buses there are people
> selling books and photocopied material—usually attacking Suharto.[139]

So even though Ma'ruf contradicts his own report by saying that 'the
workers' consciousness is still low', he does not share the pessimism
common on the Indonesian left about the consciousness of those in the
mass movement. Indeed, his more recent statement following the
November demonstrations raises issues which normally receive little
attention in PRD material. Ma'ruf argues that 'no face of capitalism can
bring a solution. The only government that can solve the economic catastrophe is a government that is 100 percent supported by the people and
that puts into practice an economic programme that is 100 percent controlled by the people.' He continues:

> We are in favour of an uninterrupted movement, an uninterrupted revolution.
> The struggle for democracy means a freeway for socialism. A strategic
> demand for the actual situation is the building of people's councils at every
> level... In our propaganda we can make no illusions in bourgeois democracy.
> We must propagate socialism widely. For instance with the nationalisation of
> crony capitalism the workers will gain experience about how to nationalise
> all capitalism. The people's councils will be the instrument to put the socialist
> programme into practice.[140]

There is much to welcome in this approach, even though it is not the
general approach of the PRD. But, even here, there are still some important issues which need to be clarified. Peoples' councils—it would be
better to call them councils of workers, students and the poor, or simply
councils of action—should not been seen as the base on which a new
'democratic' provisional government rests, as Ma'ruf has argued.[141] They
are *organisers of struggle* of the working class *against the provisional
government*, even if the political leadership of the provisional government is composed of democrats or socialists. The councils of action can
only become governmental bodies if they *smash* the capitalist state,
headed by the provisional government. Until that time, no matter how

many administrative functions they begin to take over from the government, they remain primarily organisers of the struggle against the
provisional government.

Any provisional government which comes to office before the
soviets take power, even if it were to be composed exclusively of
members of the PRD and possessed of the best intentions in the world,
would still be faced with a state machine which is capitalist and an
economy which is still run by the capitalists. Not until the workers'
councils are strong enough to overthrow both the provisional government and the bosses in the factories can revolutionaries think of being
part of the government. This is the whole lesson of Lenin's *State and
Revolution* and of the practice of the Bolshevik Party between February
and October 1917. Without this perspective Trotsky's epitaph for the
struggles in France in the 1930s might also come to apply to the
Indonesian Revolution:

> *Recent history has furnished a series of tragic confirmations of the fact that it
> is not from every revolutionary situation that a revolution arises, but that a
> revolutionary situation becomes counter-revolutionary if the subjective
> factor, that is, the revolutionary offensive of the revolutionary class, does not
> come in time to aid the objective factor.*[142]

And if this tragedy comes to pass, the ethnic and religious rivalries,
on which the army and the electoral parties are already playing, can take
centre stage. This has already begun to happen since the fragmentation
of the student movement earlier this year. It will not cease unless the
Indonesian ruling class can recreate the boom conditions which suppressed these divisions before the crash of 1997. And if this unlikely
eventuality does not come to pass then capitalist democracy will not
enjoy even the limited stability it has achieved, at enormous cost to the
working class, in South Africa and Eastern Europe. Neither could the
major powers stand aside and watch a renewed crisis unfold in
Indonesia without intervening. Richard Nixon famously described
Indonesia as 'the greatest prize in South East Asia'. Its importance to
the West has risen since then. That is why the US police commanders
are now training their Indonesian counterparts in riot control, why Japan
is considering sending police to Jakarta, and Australia has mobilised
troops to Darwin ready to intervene in East Timor. All of this is
regarded by China with the greatest suspicion. Liberation for workers
and the oppressed of Indonesia or descent into a crisis of the
Yugoslavian type are the alternatives which rest on the outcome of the
current struggles in Indonesia.

The prospects for revolution

Not every revolution involves the same range of political forces as the East European, South African and Indonesian cases. The Iranian Revolution of 1979, for instance, was ultimately dominated by a very different Islamic ideology to the parliamentary capitalist ideology that triumphed in Eastern Europe and South Africa, although this fact has served to disguise a more fundamental similarity in the class forces which made that outcome possible. Neither is it the case that the transition from authoritarian rule to capitalist democracy is in some way the inevitable outcome of modern economic trends. China, the most populous country on earth, is set on a course of 'totalitarian market capitalism'. The Tiananmen Square massacre reminds us that the price that opposition forces can pay for adopting a 'democratic revolution' strategy can be a great deal higher than a velvet restoration. Indeed, just such a counter-revolutionary solution still hangs over the Indonesian Revolution as one of its possible fates.

The pattern of revolution in the last ten years is also distinct from developments in the parliamentary democracies of the West. All the 20th century revolutions examined above took place in collapsing dictatorships. In these cases the reformist and centrist currents necessarily emerge as *interior* to the revolutionary camp. This was true of the Mensheviks, the ANC, KOR and the PRD. In the West reformism is already organisationally and politically distinct and feels no need to adopt revolutionary language or methods in the face of an intransigent authoritarian regime. Here, consequently, the undermining of reformism involves a longer process of work by existing revolutionary organisations which utilise united front tactics to win layers of workers away from established labour party type politics. Yet, even while such work is in progress, any revolutionary crisis in the West will throw up new left reformist and centrist currents with similar programmes to KOR, the ANC or the PRD. Learning from their mistakes today can save Western revolutionaries from defeat tomorrow.

But, after all the qualifications have been duly noted, the patterns described in this article are now common enough to justify close examination. Moreover, there have also been similar transformations from authoritarian rule to capitalist democracy in Brazil, Chile, South Korea the Philippines, Portugal and Spain, to mention only some of the most important examples in the last 30 years. The Portuguese Revolution was the equal of any the events of the last ten years in carrying the same explosive charge of popular mobilisation. Others did not. But much of what happened in these cases can best be understood using the framework described here. So what are the principal lessons of recent attempts to revive the idea of the democratic revolution as we face a new century?

In the English, American and French revolutions the level of industrial development and the restricted size, organisation and consciousness of the working class prevented any socialist solution to the conflicts which emerged within the revolutionary camp. But for the revolutions in Eastern Europe, South Africa and Indonesia this was not the case. Each of these countries is an industrialised society in which the ruling class is a capitalist class and the working class is not only a substantial proportion of the population but also has behind it a considerable history of self organisation and a developed class consciousness.

The revolutionary crises which have occurred in these societies in the past decade have been crises of capital accumulation. A particular form of state led capital accumulation which was laid down in the post-war period has proven an inadequate vessel for the renewed conditions of worldwide capital accumulation which have emerged in the period since the end of the long boom in the late 1970s. In each case, authoritarian regimes previously thought impervious to revolt from below were brought to the ground. In the decisive stages of the confrontation in Poland and South Africa the organised working class was a key element in that revolt.

Once the rebellion was under way a process of polarisation within the revolutionary camp took place, much as it had done in all the revolutionary situations analysed in this account—1649, 1776, 1789, 1848 and 1917. What determined the eventual outcome in all these cases was the way in which the revolutionary leadership which emerged in the course of these struggles interacted with the class battles of which they were a part. What separates the early bourgeois revolutions from the later revolutions is that the organisation of the revolutionaries in the first case mainly emerged only in the course of events and it mainly represented a programme of the bourgeoisie, not an alternative to it. With KOR in Poland, the SACP in South Africa and the PRD in Indonesia the fact that such organisations existed and influenced even quite small numbers before the outbreak of large scale struggles allowed them to become the political beneficiaries of those struggles—even when the objective logic of events pointed in quite another direction than these organisations' declared strategies.

The industrial struggles in Poland and South Africa in the 1980s might have raised the spectre of social revolution, and this may even have been the more or less conscious aim of the activist rank and file in these struggles (just as it is of the PRD today in Indonesia). These same activists were nevertheless drawn to organisations like KOR and the SACP. And to the extent that KOR and SACP strategies became hegemonic they actually demobilised the struggle by settling for achievements far short of those which the movement was actually capable of attaining. The same would have happened in Russia in 1917 had the Bolsheviks not replaced the Mensheviks as the dominant force in the workers' movement.

Even those organisations with an orientation on rank and file workers were unable to overcome the problems with which they were confronted by the development of the revolution. In these cases there was a political failure to correctly apprehend the implications of the debate over the socialist revolution and the democratic revolution. KOR had an orientation on the working class, and so did the activists who built the independent unions in South Africa in the early 1980s. And many of the best activists in the PRD and the student movement in Indonesia today also acknowledge the importance of organising workers. But the key activists in KOR came to see Solidarity as the engine of a democratic revolution, and did not maintain their earlier commitment either to the goal of a socialist revolution or to building a revolutionary party. In South Africa a syndicalist orientation on rank and file workers could provide no adequate alternative to the political strategy offered by the SACP—and so eventually became absorbed by it. Even though many of the activists in the new unions were socialists highly suspicious of the ANC's downgrading of working class struggles, they had neither the ideological reserves nor the party organisation to provide an alternative. Similarly, in Indonesia an orientation on workers is essential to any socialist project, but in itself building militant union organisation will not provide an alternative to the PRD's democratic revolution strategy.

This points to the high premium to be placed on theoretical clarity and organisation in the revolutionary movement. In all the cases examined here a small and determined minority have exerted massive influence during a revolutionary crisis. But they have only done so by expressing a political programme which reflects the class interests of one major force in the revolution, or by interposing themselves in the vacuum created by contending class forces which have neutralised each other. In many cases, though not all (the Bolsheviks being the most notable exception), these groups were predominantly middle class in origin. This need not be decisive for their political orientation if they choose ideologically and practically to build among the working class, as KOR chose to do. What is decisive is whether they then choose to build on a reformist or a revolutionary basis, and whether they correctly apprehend the class forces involved in their own revolution. This essay is an attempt to help socialists make those judgements correctly.

Notes

1   Quoted in G Rudé, *The French Revolution* (London, 1996), p14.
2   K Marx, 'Speech at the Trial of the Rhenish District Committee of Democrats', 8 February 1849, first published in *Neue Rheinische Zeitung* nos 231 and 232 (25 and 27 February 1849). A text of this is available in K Marx, *The Revolutions of 1848* (Penguin, 1973), p262, but I have used the translation available on the Marx-Engels Archive website: www.marx.org
3   The definitive account of this process is B Manning, *The English People and the English Revolution* (Bookmarks, 1991).
4   See Rudé's excellent synopsis of class consciousness in the bourgeois revolution in *Ideology and Popular Protest* (Chapel Hill, 1980), p75.
5   Quoted in L Trotsky, *Writings on Britain*, vol 2 (London, 1974), p90.
6   Quoted in P Gregg, *Oliver Cromwell* (London, 1988), pp88-89.
7   See S R Gardiner, *Oliver Cromwell* (E P Publishing, 1976), pp167-168.
8   B Leviné et al, *Who Built America?*, vol 1 (New York, 1989), p140, p148.
9   Ibid, p132.
10 Ibid, p163.
11 Quoted in H Zinn, *A People's History of the United States* (Longman, 1980), p94.
12 For an excellent short introduction to the French Revolution see P McGarr, 'The Great French Revolution', in P McGarr and A Callinicos, *Marxism and the Great French Revolution* (International Socialism, 1993).
13 A Soboul, *A Short History of the French Revolution 1789-1799* (University of California Press, 1977), p71.
14 B R Mitchell, *European Historical Statistics 1750-1970* (London, 1975), pp799-800. The figures for England and Wales are from 1788.
15 Quoted in A Soboul, *A Short History...*, op cit, p10.
16 Ibid, p23.
17 See G Rudé, *The French Revolution*, op cit, p38.
18 Quoted in A Soboul, *A Short History...*, op cit, p79.
19 Quoted ibid, pp86-87.
20 Document 22, an account of a Cordeliers Club session, in D Andress, *French Society in Revolution* (Manchester, 1999), p188.
21 G Rudé, *The French Revolution*, op cit, p103.
22 A Soboul, *Understanding the French Revolution* (London, 1988), p23.
23 Ibid.
24 A Soboul, *A Short History...*, op cit, p97.
25 Quoted in G Rudé, *The French Revolution*, op cit, p118.
26 See I Birchall, 'The Babeuf Bicentenary: Conspiracy or Revolutionary Party?', in *International Socialism* 72 (Autumn, 1996), pp77-93. Also I Birchall, *The Spectre of Babeuf* (London, 1997).
27 K Marx and F Engels, *The Manifesto of the Communist Party*, in K Marx, *The Revolutions of 1848* (Penguin, 1973), p98. The *Manifesto* was of course written before the outbreak of the revolution.
28 Ibid, p97.
29 D Fernbach, Introduction to K Marx, *Revolutions of 1848*, ibid, p38.
30 K Marx, *The Bourgeoisie and the Counter-Revolution*, ibid, pp193-194.
31 K Marx, *Address of the Central Committee*, ibid, pp329-330.
32 F Engels, quoted in H Draper, *Karl Marx's Theory of Revolution*, vol II (London, 1978), p257.
33 K Marx, *Address of the Central Committee*, op cit, p330.
34 A good account of the bourgeois revolutions from above can be found in A Callinicos, 'Bourgeois Revolutions and Historical Materialism', in P McGarr and A Callinicos, op cit.

35   V I Lenin, *Two Tactics of Social Democracy in the Democratic Revolution*, in *Selected Works* (Moscow, 1975), p60.
36   Trotsky's theory is given in full in the Pathfinder Press book *Permanent Revolution*. But perhaps the best account of the theory of combined and uneven development as it applies to Russia is given in the chapter on 'Peculiarities of Russia's Development' in Trotsky's *History of the Russian Revolution*.
37   L Trotsky, *The History of the Russian Revolution* (Pluto Press, 1977), pp180-181.
38   Quoted in E H Carr, *The Bolshevik Revolution 1917-1923*, vol III (London, 1966), p53.
39   See ibid, pp17-18.
40   Ibid, p59.
41   T Cliff, *Deflected Permanent Revolution* (London, 1986). Originally published in the first series of *International Socialism*, no 12 (Spring, 1963). Also see T Cliff, *Trotskyism After Trotsky* (London, 1999), ch 4.
42   Ibid, p20.
43   Ibid.
44   Ibid.
45   Ibid, p21.
46   Calculated from figures in B R Mitchell, op cit, p358.
47   T Garton Ash, *The Polish Revolution: Solidarity* (London, 1985), p17.
48   Ibid, p25.
49   See the excellent account in C Barker and K Weber, *Solidarnosc: from Gdansk to Military Repression* (International Socialism, 1982).
50   Quoted ibid, p29.
51   The latest English language editon is J Kuron and K Modzelewski, *Solidarnosc: the Missing Link? The Classic Open Letter to the Party* (Bookmarks, 1982), pp72-82, p86.
52   Ibid, p56.
53   See C Harman, *Class Struggles in Eastern Europe 1945-83* (London, 1983), pp279-280.
54   See interview with Orzechowski in D Pryce-Jones, *The War That Never Was: the Fall of the Soviet Empire 1985-1991* (London, 1995), p213. Pryce-Jones's book combines unreconstructed right wing Cold War commentary with genuinely valuable interviews with some of the leading figures in the East European revolutions.
55   See interview with Jaruzelski ibid, p215.
56   See interview with Orzechowski ibid, p212.
57   J Kuron, 'Overcoming Totalitarianism', reprinted in V Tismaneanu, *The Revolutions of 1989* (London, 1999), pp200-201.
58   Ibid, p199.
59   C Harman, op cit, p297.
60   E Hankiss, 'What the Hungarians Saw First', in G Prins (ed), *Spring in Winter: the 1989 Revolutions* (Manchester, 1990), p15.
61   Ibid, pp25-26.
62   Ibid, p26.
63   Ibid, p27.
64   Ibid.
65   Ibid, pp30-31.
66   See interview with Kulcsar in D Pryce-Jones, op cit, pp224-225.
67   Ibid, p225.
68   Interview with Istvan Horvath, then Hungarian minister of the interior, ibid, p232.
69   Honecker quoted ibid, p274, by the then Russian ambassador to East Germany.
70   Quoted ibid, p236.
71   See the account in J Riech, 'Reflections on Becoming an East German Dissident', in G Prins (ed), *Spring in Winter*, op cit, p81.

72 Ibid, p88.
73 Ibid, pp71-72.
74 Ibid, pp72-73.
75 J Urban, 'Czechoslovakia: the Power and Politics of Humiliation', in G Prins (ed), op cit, p116.
76 Ibid, p108.
77 The events surrounding the 17 November demonstration and the degree to which they were shaped by a plot to replace Husak have been the subject of two Czechoslovakian government commissions of inquiry. The account in this paragraph is based on evidence cited ibid, p116-117, and in D Pryce-Jones, op cit, p322.
78 Ibid, p121-122.
79 Quoted in D Pryce-Jones, op cit, p321.
80 Quoted in G Prins (ed), op cit, p124.
81 From the transcript of the Political Executive Committee meeting, quoted in D Pryce-Jones, op cit, p341.
82 See ibid, p358.
83 Ibid, p353.
84 Ibid, p350.
85 A Michnik, 'The Velvet Restoration', in V Tismaneanu, op cit, p248.
86 Ibid, p249.
87 J Reich, op cit, p97.
88 J Urban, op cit, p136.
89 M Haynes and R Husan, 'The State and Market in the Transition Economies: Critical Remarks in the Light of Past History and Current Experience', *The Journal of European Economic History*, vol 27, no 3 (Banca Di Roma, Winter 1998), pp367-368.
90 P Stephens, 'Dark Continent', *Financial Times*, 23 April 1999.
91 M Lipton, *Capitalism and Apartheid* (Gower Publishing, 1985), Table 4, p380.
92 Ibid, p286.
93 Ibid, p240.
94 Ibid.
95 Ibid, p263. See also D T McKinley, *The ANC and the Liberation Struggle* (London, 1997), p6.
96 Quoted in D T McKinley, op cit, p22.
97 Quoted ibid, p34.
98 D MacShane, M Plaut and D Ward, *Power! Black Workers, their Unions and the Struggle for Freedom in South Africa*, (Spokesman, 1984), p119.
99 Ibid, p125.
100 As the CP's journal *African Communist* put it in 1983. See ibid.
101 D T McKinley, op cit, p70.
102 Interview with J Cronin in A Callinicos (ed), *Between Apartheid and Capitalism: Conversations with South African Socialists* (London, 1992), p81.
103 J Foster, 'The Workers' Struggle—Where does FOSATU stand?', a keynote address given to the April 1982 FOSATU Congress. See Appendix 1 in D MacShane et al, op cit, p150.
104 D T McKinley, op cit, p71.
105 Quoted ibid, p85.
106 Quoted ibid, p78.
107 Ibid, p92.
108 *Financial Times*, 10 June 1986.
109 Quoted in D T McKinley, op cit, p89. Emphasis in the original.
110 J Cronin, in A Callinicos (ed), op cit, p85.
111 M Lipton, op cit, p359.

112   A Duval Smith, 'ANC Heading for Election Landslide', *The Independent*, 7 May 1999.
113   Statistics South Africa, Health and Welfare, 'Table 8.2: State Expenditure on Health Welfare'. This is the South African government's statistical service, available on the following website: www.statssa.gov.za/
114   A Booth, *The Indonesian Economy in the Nineteenth and Twentieth Centuries* (Macmillan Press, 1998), p87.
115   This account of the class structure in Indonesia draws on Richard Robison's excellent account, 'The Middle Class and the Bourgeoisie in Indonesia', in R Robison amd D S G Goodman (eds), *The New Rich in Asia* (Routledge, 1996), pp79-84.
116   Ibid, p87.
117   A Booth, op cit, p323.
118   R Robison, op cit, pp83-84.
119   See the account of Suharto's fall in M R J Vatikiotis, *Indonesian Politics Under Suharto: the Rise and Fall of the New Order* (Routledge, 3rd edn 1998), p231.
120   E H Carr, *The Bolshevik Revolution 1917-1923*, vol 1 (London, 1966), p81.
121   Ibid, p84. There was one socialist in the first provisional government, Alexander Kerensky, who broke the discipline of the Petrograd soviet in order to join the government.
122   B R Mitchell, *European Historical Statistics* (London, 1975), p813.
123   A Booth, op cit, p323.
124   Ibid, pp324-325.
125   *Financial Times*, 10 October 1998.
126   Ibid.
127   K Marx, *The Bourgeoisie and the Counter-Revolution*, op cit, p194.
128   Quoted in C Harman, 'France's Hot December', *International Socialism* 70 (Spring, 1996), p87.
129   Ibid, p69.
130   Malik Miah, 'The Dynamics of Revolution', in *Against the Current* 76 (Detroit, September/October 1998), pp43-44. The PRD's website can be accessed through www.peg.apc.org/~asiet/
131   'Manifesto of the PRD', 22 July 1996. Even since the fall of Suharto, leading PRD figures still call for the creation of a 'democratic coalition'. See the interview with jailed PRD leader Dita Sari, 'Dita Sari: "I am so Optimistic" ' by Jill Hickson on the PRD website, op cit.
132   'How We Fight Habibie', an interview with Muhammad Ma'ruf by James Balowski, PRD website, op cit.
133   'Indonesia: "The Radicalisation Will Spread"', interview with Max Lane for the Australian publication *Green Left Weekly*, PRD website, op cit.
134   Malik Miah, op cit.
135   Wilson bin Nurtias, 'Mari Ciptakan Demokrasi Tanpa Dwo Fungsi ABRI', Central Committee, PRD (Jakarta, 26 April 1999), p3. My thanks to Tom O'Lincoln for this reference and translation.
136   M Miah, op cit.
137   'Communist Threat is Scapegoat Politics: Survey', *The Jakarta Post*, 21 October 1998.
138   'Interview with PRD editor of *Pembebasan [Liberation]*', *Socialist Appeal*, July 1998.
139   'How We Fight Habibie', op cit.
140   'Interview with PRD editor of *Pembebasan*', op cit.
141   See ibid: 'We…struggle for the organisation of people's councils that will be the base for a transitional government of those who participated in the liberation of the people.'
142   L Trotsky, *Leon Trotsky on France*, quoted in T Cliff, *Trotsky: the Darker the Night the Brighter the Star, 1927-1940*, vol 4 (London, 1993), p204.

Theses on the Balkan War

MIKE HAYNES

1) Capitalism is inherently a competitively expansionist and therefore conflict ridden system

The 20th century began with war in the Balkans and it is finishing with war in the Balkans. In the years between the first Balkan War that broke out in 1912 and NATO's war with Serbia in 1999, more wars have occurred, resulting in more military and civilian deaths, than in any other period in history. At each point it has seemed as if the 20th century, which potentially offered so much, has trampled hope down in the most brutal and nightmarish way. Its record as the 'century of extremes' is being carried through to its last days and the dawn of a new century.

Conflict, warfare and conquest seem to have been an ever present part of human history. The rise of the first class societies took collective control of human affairs away from the many and gave it to the few, who looked with envy on what their neighbouring rulers had. At the same time, they strove to protect their own property both from the equal avarice of their neighbours and the threat from those below who might rise against them. But capitalism has given this struggle a new intensity. Firstly, it has built competition for profits, resources and markets into the heart of the productive system itself. Secondly, through its continual technological revolution, capitalism has imparted a dynamic of military change not present in earlier societies. Thirdly, through the way in which capitalism has contributed to the development of a world of nation states, it has helped to divide the world and to consolidate the institutions of the state, and allow its huge resources to be mobilised in the fight for world power.

The forms of capitalist expansion have evolved over time, intensifying as capitalism has developed, so that the destructiveness of conflict has been more terrible in the 20th century than any other. In this process the early developing capitalist powers were able to conquer large parts of the rest of the world. By 1800 some 35 percent of the world's land surface was, or had been, a colony of a European power. By 1878 this figure had risen to 67 percent and by 1914 to 84 percent.[1] This led many to reduce the expansive drive of capitalism to formal colonialism and to equate formal colonialism with imperialism. This was a mistake. The expansionism of capitalism preceded formal colonialism and has taken many other forms. Formal colonialism, on the other hand, proved more transient with the widespread decolonisation of empire after 1945. Imperialism was, and is, something more. Imperialism is a modern phenomenon and it expresses the way in which the central axis of international competition is subordinated to interstate competition, with military force an ever present factor. The struggle over formal colonies was a part of this, but by no means the whole.[2] Instead the central axis of international competition was now over the control of the heartlands of the world economy. It was this that led to the First World War, the Second World War and the Cold War. Today these factors remain present. Despite talk of a 'globalisation' which transcends the boundaries of nation states, state power and military power cannot be relinquished. They remain essential ingredients underpinning the pseudo-'global' forms, helping to direct the process of international competition.

The optimism that the end of the Cold War might lead to a new world order has been shown to be false. The hope that it would release a peace dividend that would enable a new generosity in international relations has been belied by experience, as some of us sadly predicted it would.[3] Though the arms burden has declined, there has been no outpouring of aid to Eastern Europe, no new 'Marshall Plan'. The result has been that the burden of change has fallen on the broad masses of the population, wrecking lives across the old Soviet bloc in general and in one of its poorest components in south eastern Europe in particular. According to the World Bank, the number of people living in poverty (defined as having less than $4 a day) in the former Soviet bloc has risen from 14 million in 1990 to 147 million in 1998.[4] Worse still, the advanced countries have continued to reduce further the miserly sums they devote to aid to the even poorer areas of the world. The OECD countries are rhetorically committed to an aid target of 0.7 percent of their output. In

1990 they gave 0.35 percent, and by 1997 the figure had fallen to 0.22 percent, with the United States under this heading giving 0.09 percent of its output, a figure in startling contrast to the expenditure devoted to destruction.[5]

2) In the period 1945-1989 this conflict appeared to take the form of a Cold War between the military alliances of NATO and the Warsaw Pact representing two qualitatively different sides. But this idea obscured the similar roots of conflict on both sides and it enabled the US and Russia to make wider interventions under the guise of the East-West conflict

Already at the beginning of the 20th century the US had emerged as the most powerful capitalist economy in the world, but at this point it did not have a world role commensurate with its growing power. The fundamental imperialist clashes therefore took place in Europe both in 1914 and 1939 in the form of conflict between a British led alliance and a German led alliance. In the first instance the US intervened in 1917 to tip the balance in favour of the British led alliance. In the second instance, when the US came into the war in 1941, its power quickly made it the dominant force in the alliance. The result was that in 1945 it was in absolute and relative terms the most powerful economy in the world with, on some calculations, 50 percent of world manufacturing output. It now had a role of global leadership to match. This produced a degree of friction with Britain and France—powers in relative decline which still hankered after their old role. But this was minimised as a result of a more fundamental clash that now emerged with another former wartime ally in the anti-Hitler alliance, Russia. The result was the Cold War that lasted until 1989.

On both sides the Cold War was claimed to be something different from earlier imperialist clashes. Russia claimed to be socialist, though Stalin's regime and its successors developed on the ashes of the aspirations to real socialism as dictatorships with great power designs of their own. For their part, propagandists in the US and Western Europe claimed that their side of the Cold War was motivated by an attempt to halt Soviet imperialism and totalitarianism where they stood. For them, the Cold War was 'the brave and essential response of free men to Communist aggression'.[6]

The arguments were smokescreens obscuring the rapacious way in which both sides acted in their own interests and against the populations they claimed to defend. Those who argued that the point was to support neither Washington nor Moscow, but to take an independent stand and challenge both, were right then as they are right now—no matter how difficult the stance is to take.

But this is not to say that the Cold War was a clash of equals. Throughout there remained a fundamental imbalance of power. If the US was a global power in fact and name, the USSR was only a global power in name. In reality it was a regional power with some global aspirations but no means to achieve them. The dismissive phrase that was later attached to it—'Upper Volta with rockets'—was a woeful mischaracterisation of its economic power, but it captured in an exaggerated form the imbalance with which Russian leaders had to deal.

But the fact that the clash of interests could be presented as a global ideological clash—especially by US apologists—meant that friends could be rewarded and enemies penalised on an international scale as part of the fight against Communism, even though the real motivation, sometimes only half consciously understood by US leaders, lay elsewhere. In most of Western Europe, however, the democracy that had been achieved through past popular struggles, though limited, looked—and was—far superior to the forms of dictatorial rule that existed in the Eastern bloc, and not surprisingly, when people there got a chance to vote with their feet, in 1989 and beyond, in so far as the choice was 'West' or 'East', they chose 'West'. But this did not stop the US and its 'democratic allies' in Europe supporting the existing fascist dictatorships in Spain and Portugal, a succession of unpleasant regimes in Turkey, and encouraging military rule in Greece between 1967 and 1974. Beyond the boundaries of Europe, support for brutal regimes and intervention under the guise of the Cold War produced an even more sorry record to shame those who believed that their 'pro-democratic stance' invested them with moral supremacy over the dictatorships of the East.

3) When the Cold War ended it produced a more unstable world, but one in which new justifications had to be found for selective intervention in terms of a moral crusade against demonised opponents

When the Cold War ended it briefly appeared as if the basis for a new world order had been laid. Formal colonialism was now largely in the receding past. The great ideological divide in Europe and the wider world had disappeared with the triumph of the market, and in Fukuyama's famous phrase 'history', in the sense of the great clash of principles, 'had ended'. Democracy would not fight democracy. States based on the market and private property—linked by global business—would not fight one another. To popularise the idea some even talked of the 'McDonald's effect'—no two countries with a McDonald's restaurant, it was claimed, had ever gone to war against one another. Henceforth there would only be residual conflicts with leftovers of the old order.[7]

But far from being more stable, the post Cold War world has turned out to be less stable. The Cold War had, to an extent, produced a degree of international discipline—supported by the leverage of the US-USSR in their respective spheres of influence. Now this disciplining factor disappeared. Worse still, the less stable conditions in the world economy, accompanied in places by the strains of transition crisis, acted to inflame local antagonisms. Beyond this the big powers in general, and the US in particular, still needed to act to allow competitive expansion to continue and to deal with truculent states and minorities who refused to conform to the terms on offer.

For this to carry support at home, new justifications or reworked old ones had to be developed to support the deployment of power. Contrary to what is often imagined, earlier examples of imperialist action were rarely justified in terms of naked self interest. The claim was always that they served a higher purpose. Kipling's famous poem *The White Man's Burden*, where he gives advice to a US awakening to the first realisation that it has a global role, recalls this in its famous opening verse:

Take up the White Man's burden–
Send forth the best ye breed–
Go bind your sons to exile
To serve your captives' need

The First World War was, of course, famously conducted for 'humanitarian' ends on *both* sides, as was the Second World War. It is often not appreciated that when fascist or quasi-fascist states acted they were no less anxious to cloak themselves in altruistic humanitarianism. When Japan invaded Manchuria in 1931 the formal justification was to save the Manchurians from 'Chinese banditry'. When Mussolini invaded Ethiopia it was to bring the benefits of Italian civilisation. Hitler was no less adept at the argument, marching into Sudetenland to save the Sudeten Germans from 'Czech nationalist bullying' but intending to 'safeguard the national individuality of the German and Czech peoples' and 'filled with earnest desire to serve the true interests of the peoples dwelling in the area'.[8]

But now, after a Cold War invested with an apparently even nobler purpose and with what are deemed to be fickle mass electorates—it has become even more important to present the deployment of power and influence, of intervention (however selective, one sided and brutal in practice) as motivated only by benign intentions, benevolence, democracy, humanitarian concerns. It also became important to demonise your enemies to justify your actions even though, perhaps only months before, they had acted as your 'client' leaders or men 'with whom you could do business'. Thus international terrorist conspiracies were invented; pariah state supporters of terrorism isolated; drug states vilified; fundamentalist states made the objects of new crusades and ethnic nationalists seen as the recalcitrant leftovers of a past era.

And as this happened, as in other propaganda wars, it became more and more difficult to distinguish between the real atrocities and the imagined ones, to distinguish between the atrocities to which 'we' turned a blind eye (East Timor in Indonesia—perhaps 250,000 dead—or the ethnic cleansing of Kurds in Turkey where in a 15 year period an estimated 4,000 villages were destroyed, 30,000 killed and as many as 3 million displaced), atrocities which we looked at full in the face but bemoaned 'our' impotence to intervene in (Rwanda), and those which came to embody grounds for intervention as a new 'moral imperialism' (Iraq, Serbia).

None of this is to deny that a real tension exists between the aspirations to guarantee all people basic human rights regardless of their state and the fact that the world is organised by states which claim sovereign immunity. The United Nations tried to act as an international forum for the resolution of this tension. It could not achieve this because it remained a prisoner of the interests of the big states. International law existed as something to regulate and protect the strong rather than the weak. For this reason socialists have always been suspicious of the claims made on behalf of the UN. But so long as states remained committed to the UN in however loose a way it at least existed as a formal restraint on any state or group of states arrogating to themselves in a completely anarchic way the right to develop their own self defining pretexts for intervention. Now the US-UK led NATO action has specifically removed such intervention from the formal sanction of the UN, allowing it to become a self defining pretext for any other state or group of states to use. To do this they will only have to quote the justification offered by George Robertson, the British defence secretary: 'There can be no doubt...that NATO is acting within international law. The legal justification for air strikes rests upon the accepted principle that force may be used in extreme circumstances without the [UN] Security Council's express authorisation in order to avert humanitarian catastrophe'.[9]

4) Whilst the US has been prepared to intervene on its own in many conflicts, in the central area of Euro-Atlantic relations there has been a growing tendency to redefine and widen the purpose of NATO to orchestrate intervention

NATO was created primarily by the US and the UK as part of the Cold

War in 1949. Its formal function, set out in Article 5 of the original Washington Treaty, focused on the Russian threat:

> *The Parties agree that an armed attack against one or more of them in Europe or North America shall be considered an attack against all of them and...that, if such an armed attack occur, each of them, in exercise of the right of collective self defence recognised by Article 51 of the Charter of the United Nations, will assist the Party or Parties so attacked by taking...such action as it deems necessary, including the use of armed force.*

Article 6 then defined the geographical area to which this applied:

> *For the purpose of Article 5, an armed attack on one or more of the Parties is deemed to include an armed attack: on the territories of any of the Parties in Europe or North America...on the territory of Turkey, or on the islands under the jurisdiction of any of the Parties in the North Atlantic area north of the Tropic of Cancer.*

The organisation's first secretary-general, Lord Ismay, more brutally defined NATO's real role as keeping the US in Europe, keeping Russia out and keeping Germany down.

Even as late as 1991 an attempt to consolidate what is called the Alliance Strategic Concept formally held to this narrow definition of NATO's role, saying that 'the Alliance is purely defensive in purpose: none of its weapons will ever be used except in self defence'.[10]

But at the end of the Cold War the question arose as to why NATO should continue to exist at all. This question was at the heart of the development of a new strategic concept for NATO: 'History shows that traditional military alliances disappear once victory has been won. But NATO did not disappear... During the 1990s NATO has evolved to the extent that crisis management and conflict prevention are now its primary missions'.[11]

To understand how this happened it is important to realise that in a competitive world powerful states with similar interests have always needed to ally with one another to manage their joint interests, create a united front against other big states and police minor challenges to their detailed interests. Formally the UN exists as an organisation of all states to achieve this. Idealists therefore see it as the supreme expression of the collective interests of the community of states. It cannot, however, operate in this way. In many respects the UN is even weaker than its much maligned predecessor, the League of Nations. Not only does it lack its own forces but it was designed to give expression to the interests of the most powerful states. It can only act if the permanent members of the

Security Council (the US, UK, France, Russia and China) are united, and since each member has veto powers it will never be able to act when their fundamental interests conflict. One logical way of resolving this problem would be to diminish the power of the Security Council in favour of a real decision making forum of all states, something which has sometimes been allowed to happen in minor matters. But this would mean that the big powers would then be constrained by the smaller powers including those that they might wish to act against. They have therefore no interest in allowing this to happen on a significant scale and, to the extent that the US has been a victim of such alliances on minor matters, it has punished the UN by withholding its contributions.[12] The UN can therefore only ever be impotent when the big powers clash; it can only act in a unified way when their interests coincide, which will more often than not involve action against smaller and more minor players in the world economy.

When the Cold War ended, therefore, these wider factors encouraged all members of NATO to look for a continued and redefined role for the organisation through which their military and other interests could be orchestrated. This led to new policies which had four dimensions to them: (i) widening the European membership of the organisation, initially from 16 to 19; (ii) out of area actions with the unresolved question of how far afield NATO can operate—North Africa, the Middle East, the Caucuses or even wider? (NATO troops have already carried out training exercises in Kazhakstan); (iii) new forms of intervention—a rapid reaction force, the development of peacekeeping and policing roles, 'humanitarian' intervention; (iv) within NATO some attempt to rebalance its internal relations through an attempt to create a European Security and Defence Identity.

The internal debate over a European Security and Defence Identity has had a number of elements. One is the attempt to restructure the balance of effort in NATO. It is accepted throughout NATO that the US will continue to play the major role but there is US pressure for Europe to take up more of the burden. While NATO's European armed forces number 2 million, those of the US number 1.2 million, but two thirds of NATO defence spending is undertaken by the US and the US has not only led but carried NATO's past involvements. In the war on Serbia between 70 and 80 percent of the resources deployed and missions undertaken have been American.

This encouragement of a more 'European defence identity' in NATO has been welcomed by European leaders but they have been divided over its interpretation. For the British government and Tony Blair there is no question of it leading to an independent 'European' role. His vision is of a self financing European defence role explicitly subordinate to the US, what its pro-'European' critics call the 'Indian army of the Raj' scenario by analogy with the way that Britain ran its empire in India using Indian troops financed out of taxes on the Indian population. The alternative view, more evident amongst the French and German leaderships, toys with a 'defence identity' in which 'Europe' would be more of an equal partner with the US.

Beyond this the idea of a 'European defence identity' has a broader ideological role. It is supposed to enable the creation of a 'European security architecture' which will include not only the old NATO core, but its new members and the currently excluded members who are part of the 'Partnership for Peace' of which the most important is Russia. This is supposed to lead to what Solano, the secretary-general of NATO, calls 'a region of stability from Vancouver to Valdivostok'.[13] In addition this talk of 'defence identities' and 'security architectures' also helps to broaden terms on which NATO can intervene both on a wider European scale and beyond. If we take Solano at his word then, breathtaking and nightmarish though the idea might be, it is not illogical to suggest that guaranteeing such a zone against external destabilisation might mean that NATO's southern flank could extend from Mexico to Beijing.

The debate on these broader issues was still going on as the Yugoslav crisis erupted. Even as NATO was mobilising, its propaganda magazine was being issued with an article by Helmut Schmidt which accepted a wider role but explicitly argued, 'From a democratic standpoint, we urgently need a profound debate—similar to the quality of the euro debate that has taken place throughout Europe in the last few years— before fundamentally broadening or reshaping the aims of the Alliance'.[14] It seems likely therefore that one dimension of the Yugoslav crisis was that it provided an opportunity for NATO to decisively mark out on the ground its developing new strategic concept. It also enabled the internal debate to be short-circuited, ending what some have dismissively referred to as a 'partnership for prevarication'.

5) Intervention in Yugoslavia came to be seen as a crucial test of credibility of the evolving NATO strategy and US capacity for 'crisis management'

When Iraq invaded Kuwait the West's formidable firepower was turned on Iraq and much of it still remains focused on that country today. By contrast far worse problems, including initially those in the former Yugoslavia, were ignored or even encouraged to fester. The very clear material interest that the West had in oil supplies provided an obvious explanation for these double standards. In the dismissive phrase of the 1991 Gulf War debates, to have 'carrots rather than oil' was to fall beneath of gaze of the West's concern. The subsequent intervention in Bosnia and the sustained assault on Serbia in 1999 have led some to speculate that behind the rhetoric there are rather more substantial material interests at stake in the former Yugoslavia than 'carrots'.

Given the fulsome declarations of humanitarian motivation that have underpinned the rhetoric of NATO, it is important to recognise that crude material self interest does exist in the form of the anxiety of arms manufacturers for sales, the needs of oil companies for secure pipelines across the Balkan region for oil from the Caspian Sea, the interests of Western business in the former Yugoslavia, the role of the IMF-World Bank, the pressure of expatriate groups in the US and so on. More broadly still, it appears that the US State Department has been under considerable pressure from US business and Wall Street to push increased access to global markets as part of its strategy for endorsing the benefits of 'globalisation' as an ever wider open door for US business. No less on the Serbian side the equally fulsome rhetoric which claims Kosovo as the historic birthright of the Serbs helps to obscure the material interests of the Serbian regime in the rich mines of Kosovo as well as the interests of local Kosovan Serbs in extending their control of land in the countryside.

But to conceive of NATO's role in the Balkan War in direct material terms is to miss the wider role that Yugoslavia has come to play in the establishment of a world order under Western supervision—quite simply the former Yugoslavia, beginning as an irritant, became the test of credibility of US-NATO strategy and its capacity for what its propagandists call 'crisis management'.

That the growing crisis in Yugoslavia in the 1980s might lead to explosive consequences was long feared if not fully foreseen by Western leaders. According to the former German leader Helmut Schmidt:

> As far back as 1980, several European leaders, assembled for the funeral of Marshal Tito, concluded that this composite state, cobbling together at least eight nations and ethnic minorities and previously held together by the talented dictator and his brutal methods, would collapse in five or ten years at the most. No one suggested the possibility of Western intervention to deal with this, though there were certainly fears of Soviet military action. As it turned out, the Soviet Union and Yugoslavia collapsed simultaneously.[15]

Yet despite this initial reluctance to get involved as the former Yugoslavia disintegrated, Western meddling not only failed to control this process but materially assisted it. At each stage of the process the West has been drawn in deeper. In the 1980s it had intervened primarily by economic methods. The World Bank-IMF complex encouraged austerity programmes which would guarantee the repayment of Yugoslavia's large debt, even if they intensified the internal economic difficulties. Then as pressures leading to the break up of Yugoslavia developed the issue arose as to which states should be recognised and so granted legitimacy. Then the eruption of the Bosnian crisis eventually created the 'need' for direct intervention and Kosovo has seen this occur on a much greater scale.

Kosovo posed Western policy its sharpest dilemma. On the one hand there was recognition of the enormous weight Serb nationalism placed on Kosovo. One expert and policy adviser expressed the problem this way in 1992:

A poor, wretched land, Kosovo is important because the Serbs have deemed it so. Indeed, it cannot be emphasised too strongly that the future of Kosovo is non-negotiable as far as Serbia is concerned. The importance which the Serbs attach to Kosovo as the historic, cultural and spiritual centre probably knows no parallel except that of Jerusalem for the Jews, although even that comparison is inadequate since Jerusalem is a holy place for three religions.[16]

On the other hand there was also a long standing recognition that the predominance of ethnic Albanians in Kosovo and past Serb oppression made the situation potentially as explosive as the Bosnian one internally and more explosive externally since it might spill over to help unravel the borders of the successor states to the old Yugoslavia and perhaps the Balkans more widely.

To stabilise this situation, therefore, Western leaders were happy to go to Belgrade to do deals with Milosevic and, as the tension mounted, to denounce Milosevic, the Serbian side *and* the Kosovo Liberation Army, which had been formed in 1993 to conduct a more radical and, if necessary, violent campaign to defend the oppressed Kosovan Albanian population. A succession of UN resolutions called on both sides to reduce the level of conflict. But such appeals had little effect on either side. As the crisis developed, Western leaders and NATO had to decide between doing deals with Milosevic and making an example of him.

The threat to make an example of the Serb leader had been made as early as 1992 when George Bush apparently warned Belgrade that 'in the event of conflict in Kosovo caused by Serbian action, the US will be prepared to employ military force against Serbs in Kosovo and Serbia proper'.[17] Since every deal that failed to stick was seen as a mark of failure the balance began to tip against Milosevic and Serbia. This was helped by Milosevic's own inadequacies as a nationalist leader. He was not the only Yugoslav leader to come to power trying to play both a reformist and a nationalist card. Tudjman in Croatia had done the same and in the process woken just as many local fears about Croatian aggrandisement as Milosevic raised locally about Serbian aggrandisement. But Tudjman better managed not to rock the boat with the West. Milosevic and his group played their cards with much less finesse and, however well this may have gone down with Serb nationalism, it served only to create more Western suspicion of him and his power base.

So far, therefore, from being able to offer a constructive way out of the crisis by helping rebuild a shattered region, Western leaders were trapped in a series of ever narrowing options. In the summer of 1998 awareness of the worsening situation in Kosovo led to NATO renewing the threat of air attacks on the Milosevic regime. This forced a retreat in the autumn of 1998, as it had done earlier in Bosnia. Milosevic agreed to allow international observers into Kosovo and agreed to pull out Serb troops. But Serbian repression continued and the KLA fought back. Then in early 1999 the discovery of a massacre by Serbian forces at Racjek either appears to have convinced key figures in the Clinton administration that the time had now come to move, or provided them with the excuse they were looking for. While internal debate continued, pressure was put on the KLA to accept the Rambouillet Accords which required Serbia to allow NATO to police a peace—a demand which was highly unlikely to be acceptable to the Serbian leadership and which led eventually to the Serbian rejection of the accords and war.

The National Security Council in the US and wider policy circles reviewed what Clinton called 'a bunch of bad options' and apparently believing that there might be a 'hot Spring' in Kosovo they decided, after some last minute prevarication, that they could wait no longer and that they had now to carry out their threat to make an example of Milosevic whatever the resulting costs.

Undoubtedly they were helped in this by their recognition of more particular interests. No doubt too key 'hawks' like Madeleine Albright might have played an important role in tipping the balance. But to explain what happened in these terms is to localise the problem and to miss its wider logic that derives from NATO's attempt to police a competitive world in its interests and on its terms.

6) NATO made a major miscalculation about the ease with which its objectives could be attained

It is a commonplace of military strategy in the 20th century that it is necessary to strike hard, fast and at full strength to achieve your objectives. If successful, such a *blitzkrieg* tactic can create chaos for the enemy, demoralisation and a speedy surrender with minimum casualties to your self. Locally air strikes and ground troops should be combined fully and in quick succession. There is every indication that in narrow military terms this was the NATO High Command's view of the ideal military scenario in Kosovo.

But at the same time there appears also to have been a widespread belief among both political and military leaders that a demonstrative military action might be enough to achieve a humiliating Serbian retreat and so establish NATO's authoritative capacity to deploy minimum military force to achieve the maximum political ends. NATO operated, in Madeleine Albright's words, with the view that its objectives would be 'achievable in a relatively short period of time'.[18] The faulty intelligence on which this disastrous miscalculation was based need not detain us. It led to an underestimation of the air power needed (it took ten days to reach the level of intensity of the first night of the Gulf War), and it woefully encouraged the Serb regime by portraying the campaign as 'self limiting' in the refusal to deploy ground troops.

The result was catastrophic. Whatever Milosevic's intentions before the withdrawal of OSCE monitors, this signalled the impending attack while the effective breathing space that was created allowed the mass of the Kosovan population to be driven out through the combined impact of fear of the bombs, fear of actions of organised Serb forces and fear of the actions of ad hoc Serb civilians and paramilitaries. The victims of Milosevic's brutal nationalism became the victims of the incompetence of NATO's brutal power politics. Secondly, the huge refugee movements created an enormous destabilisation in neighbouring Albania, Macedonia and Montenegro—precisely the effect on Serbia's neighbours NATO claimed its action would avoid. Thirdly, the bombing solidified support for Milosevic in Serbia itself (and even more amongst the remaining Serbs in Kosovo), partly through the natural effect of a regime under attack coming together on reactionary terms and partly through the possibilities it afforded him to continue his destruction of all forms of opposition as, in effect, NATO traitors and betrayers of the national interest.[19] Finally the failure of NATO to achieve its objectives quickly in such a visibly incompetent way threatened the credibility of NATO, Britain, the US and their supporters far more than the original crisis.

Ironically it was this very fact that drew the NATO alliance more closely together. The open admission of NATO defeat by an otherwise tinpot leader of a tinpot state in the backward Balkans would have devastating consequences for the US, NATO and the West:

> *Failure will not just ensure that despots everywhere take heart. NATO is not serious, they will say. It has no stomach for a fight. When the fate of innocent Kosovars is in the balance that is bad enough. When Western national interests are at stake it will be grave indeed.*[20]

More immediately failure would put at risk the sometimes precarious coalition governments in some NATO member countries (for example,

Germany). Failure would also threaten the governments of the NATO members closest to Serbia which were in an even more difficult situation (Italy and Greece), and also put a question mark over states like Romania, Bulgaria and Slovakia that have been denied NATO membership and the promise of first wave EU membership, but to whom the carrot of some eventual linkage has been held out if they support the action.[21] Doubts were therefore suppressed and even those realists inside and outside the policy making circles who were critical of the original errors nevertheless insisted that the war had to be prosecuted to a visible victory for NATO. As one put it, 'We are committed to a policy that is quite frankly idiotic but which in a way would have to be continued to save some credibility'.[22]

Yet it is equally clear that the contradictions of a NATO victory will be no less devastating for the region, as we shall note in more detail later. On a global scale the ever widening ramifications threaten to set in motion a new round of tensions with implications barely foreseen at the start of the conflict. From the point of view of those who believe in the rightness of might this, however, will be acceptable if it ensures that the US can operate on a wider world scale with the continued support of its European allies.

7) In resolving these difficulties the interests of the wider Balkan peoples, the mass of the Serbian population and the mass of the Kosovan population will take second place to doing a deal with the Serbian leadership

The West claims that this is a humanitarian action designed to stabilise Kosovo, Serbia and the wider Balkans in the interests of the people there by bringing a local rogue government into line. But this is belied by the process that led to war, the way the war is prosecuted and the way it will be ended.

So far as the cause of the war is concerned, the collapse of Yugoslavia was underpinned by growing economic crisis and international debt in which the response of the West was to pressure first the Yugoslav government, and then its successors, to impose policies of 'structural adjustment' or more accurately an impoverishing process of readjustment which increased want and resentment on a huge scale while enabling Western loans to be repaid.

More specifically, so far as the Kosovans themselves are concerned, the callousness of Western policy is reflected in the indifference to the refugee problem. While we might allow that the enormous scale of the problem could not have been foreseen, the fact remains that not only was there no real planning for *any* significant movement but prior to the start of the war the refugee problem that already existed had been neglected.

In September 1998—eight months before the start of the aerial war— Kofi Annan officially reported for the UN on the earlier conflicts saying:

> *The hostilities triggered a dramatic exodus of the civilian population from Kosovo. According to the statistics of the United Nations High Commissioner for Refugees (UNHCR), the number of refugees and displaced people in the province amounts to 230,000 people, 60,000 of whom have chosen to leave Kosovo. Under considerable pressure brought to bear by the international community, the Serb authorities have taken action to attract the refugees back to their permanent places of residence, offering them material aid. However, this has elicited a tepid response from the Albanian population, which is suspicious of Serb guarantees.* **Humanitarian aid deliveries to Kosovo have so far been unequal to the situation on the ground.**[23]

Once the war was under way the prime consideration was, contrary to NATO's protestations, neither the Kosovan population nor the Serb population but the destruction of the infrastructure of the Serbian state—if necessary at the expense of both the Kosovan and Serb populations. This did not simply flow from errors which were inevitable in any scenario. NATO may well have tried to err on the side of civilian safety within the terms of its rules of engagement but these were set in such a way as to make this concern for civilians a marginal issue—good for propaganda but little else. NATO's real military policy was well characterised by Carl Bildt (the ex Swedish prime minister who played a leading role in the Bosnian 'settlement') as being 'one of minimum risk to itself and maximum risk to those it was supposed to protect'.[24]

This has been reflected in the reluctance to commit ground troops for fear of casualties; the form of the air war which has involved high altitude bombing for fear of risking the air crews, guaranteeing 'mistakes' and high levels of 'collateral damage' (or the mass destruction of civilian buildings with attendant deaths); and finally the gradually widening of the definition of what is a military target.[25]

So far as the bombing is concerned it remains for us to restate that 'smart bombing' is a myth. Firstly, as in the Gulf War, the vast majority of bombs dropped are not merely old bombs but often more deadly versions such as bombs tipped with depleted uranium and cluster bombs which leave a legacy of what are land mines by another name.[26] Secondly 'smart bombs' are only as 'smart' as the intelligence information that goes into their targeting and this is often at fault.[27] But in addition the oft quoted Pentagon data from the Gulf War suggests a high failure rate for 'smart weapons' with only a 60 percent success rate for laser guided bombs and only a 53 percent success rate for cruise missiles.

NATO policy can also be judged in terms of the treatment of refugees once the war had begun. While Western politicians were happy to have a photogenic day out in the camps, the real levels of aid that have been given have been pathetically inadequate not only to the task but in comparison to the military costs. As the Macedonian interior minister Pavle Trajinov bitterly remarked, 'They declare that they want to help the refugees but is it enough just to come to the camps, take photos with the refugees, and then tell the whole world, "See. We've done so much for the refugees"?' No less can policy be judged in terms of the unseemly wrangling over the movement of refugees in which the most disgraceful role has been played by Britain. As Trajinov put it, 'We've seen it before in other places, and it's happening here. They pass judgement on how the refugees are being cared for. At the same time, they come up with 300 excuses why they themselves shouldn't [take any refugees]'.[28]

At the time of writing it is not clear whether ground troops will be used before a ceasefire but it is already clear that the bombing has been intensified, widened and stretched so as to set the economies of both Serbia and Kosovo back a generation. Two scenarios now exist. One is an early ceasefire with a peace treaty with the Serbian leadership based on an assurance that NATO will achieve its major military objectives. The second is a widening of the war to achieve this through the use of ground troops. The common premise of both scenarios is the same greater intensification of the aerial campaign to bring a repentant Serbian government to heel or to prepare the way for enforcing that on the ground.

There is no suggestion, however, that NATO is prepared to invade Serbia and impose a different government on the country. This means that any deal must be with Milosevic or, if he is killed or removed, with a leader whose power base derives much of its support from his acceptance of the Serbian nationalist agenda. Therefore, even if a more amenable leader appears or Milosevic backs down and agrees to the creation of a largely independent Kosovo (whether greater or smaller), the full claims of either side will not be achieved or explicitly defeated but only supported/suppressed by superior force. Despite the war induced talk of a 'generous peace', there is absolutely no indication that the NATO countries are prepared to commit the massive long term aid necessary both to restore and improve the situation as well as to commit the military resources to police the peace.

8) So far from it being the case that social democracy and liberalism has a record of opposing Western imperialism, they have played a key role both in legitimising it and in leading it in times of conflict

The enthusiasm with which the war has been taken up by most liberal, social democratic and Green leaders in the NATO countries has come as a surprise to many on the left, as a considerable number of these leaders had only a few years before been prominent in peace movements. It is important to understand therefore that this is no momentary aberration. When confronted with past crises and wars, liberal and social democratic leaders have not only supported their governments but played a leading role in them. The scale of the betrayal in the First World War is too well known to require rehearsing. But the signs of this betrayal were already in the air before 1914—social democracy's 'internationalism' only existed when it could be made to coincide with 'national interests'. 'Social democracy can never be anti-national,' the French socialist leader Jules Guesde told the Balkan socialist Christian Rakovsky on the eve of 1914.[29] That key European leaders of the newly developed Green parties should similarly fail the test of war at the end of the 20th century is no less surprising given the nature of Green politics and the more benign view of the role of the state and parliamentary government that it shares with liberalism and social democracy.

The idea that all of these groups would have a more resolute anti-imperialist position today than in the past rested on a misunderstanding of recent history. In particular the anti-war movements in the US and Europe that developed in the 1960s over Vietnam and against the Second Cold War were very much a product of the unravelling of the US assault on Vietnam. Creditable though the opposition to this war was, it cannot be allowed to obscure the fact that in origin the Vietnam War was similar to other wars this century in being a 'liberals' war'. This was so not only in the sense that the liberal hero Kennedy played a leading role in its escalation, defining it 'a righteous crusade', but also in the way in which the liberal establishment initially swung behind it in the US, supported by the social democratic establishment in the West. This position reflected their earlier role in not merely endorsing but propagandising the Cold War. It was only when the Vietnam War began to go dramatically wrong and a peace movement developed outside these circles put pressure on them that they began to vacillate.

The role that left of centre political forces have played and continue to play in capitalism's wars can be explained in two main ways. One is their belief in the need to work within the system to change it, a view which means that in the short run they must accommodate themselves to its logic and assume the trustworthy character of capitalism in general and its institutions and leaders in particular. Their criticisms, doubts and hesitations are therefore only ever partial and they remain trapped by the logic of power—a logic that is manifested in an acceptance of the limited choices that capitalism's conflicts appear to create as well as the institutions that condition these choices.

But there is a second strand to the relationship of the left to capitalism's wars. It is often mistakenly assumed that the best interests of capitalist states are represented by the forces of the right. This is sometimes the case, but it is far from always so. Although the exact link between foreign policy and domestic politics and economic forces needs to be analysed on a case by case basis, as a generalisation we can say that the narrowness of the vision of the right often creates a space in which the policies of liberalism, social democracy and even the Greens, better reflect capitalism's needs. Faced with foreign policy conflicts the right tends to fracture. One part—usually the most backward—is often isolationist. Another section, priding itself on its realism, does not oppose action in principle, but wishes to tie it narrowly to its perception of the 'national interest', which may often paralyse action.

But, as we have argued, although capitalism is built on a competitive world of states it cannot just exist as an anarchical society. It is here that liberal and social democratic forces with an ostensibly wider vision of the 'national interest' can play a crucial role in developing the global institutions of capitalism and enforcing their domination or at least the domination of those institutions like NATO that they can control.

9) The intensity of the national question in the Balkans is the product of the late development of capitalism and the interests of the Great Powers in having a fragmented and competitive state system there

Many outsiders who look at the Balkans see a seething cauldron of irrational ethnic hatreds, which they would do well to steer clear of in person and also to steer clear of intellectually. But the Balkan peoples are no different from those anywhere else in the world and the enormous instability of the region is simply explicable in terms of the interaction of three factors.

The first is that this whole area was for centuries part of the Ottoman Empire (the word 'Balkan' derives from the Turkish for high range—reflecting the way the area is made up of mountains interspersed with broad plateaux). As part of the Ottoman Empire the region escaped the process of nation building that took place in Europe from the 16th century onwards. From the 15th century to the 17th century the Ottoman Empire was the most powerful political force in the world, controlling lands the size of the old Roman Empire whose eastern capital, Constantinople, the Ottomans took over. From the 18th century onwards, however, the Ottoman system began to fall into decay and this accelerated in the 19th century so the empire became, in the Russian Tsar Nicholas I's famous words, 'the sick man of Europe'. All of the major states in the Balkans derived from fragments of the Ottoman Empire (supplemented by fragments of the Austro-Hungarian and Russian empires). As children were taught in late 19th century Britain, the Ottoman Empire 'has, from 1672, been gradually dwindling... Kingdom after kingdom, state after state, has been cut out of it by Russia and Austria, with the consent of the other Great Powers'.[30]

In the 19th century the internal and external enemies of the empire condemned its rule as the 'Ottoman' or 'Turkish' 'yoke', attacking it as an 'uncivilised' and 'barbarous' 'Asiatic' relic in Europe. As central control weakened and in some areas it became hard to distinguish local rulers within the empire from bandits, 'the yoke' did come to lie more heavily. But in general terms the key thing to understand is that in comparative terms, throughout its history, Ottoman rule was relatively loose. In the West, for example, when Spain was unified in 1492, within a century Jews had been expelled (with an important community fleeing to sanctuary in the Ottoman Empire, including its Balkan lands) and so had the Muslims, and the Inquisition had done its worst.

There was nothing to compare to such attempts at expulsion and forced homogenisation under Ottoman rule. Instead Ottoman rulers were happy to allow different religions to develop and local peculiarities to exist provided that they did so in an ordered way and the resulting communities paid their dues to the empire. They therefore created a structure of rule which involved relatively autonomous and religious led organisations. So successful was this that at the high point of Ottoman power, despite later claims of forced conversions, some groups voluntarily converted to Islam and willingly identified themselves with the empire's aspirations.[31] Overall though it was the compromise with localism that was important because this allowed local traditions and differentiation to develop and be maintained at a time in which in western Europe they were being much reduced by the operations of capitalist development and the state.[32] Some 19th century romantic nationalists would claim that these traditions extended back to the glories of an imagined medieval independence and, in some instances—Greece or Macedonia, for example—even farther back to the glories of the ancient world. But these genealogies of nation were as spurious as those invented in western Europe around Robin Hood, William Tell, Joan of Arc and so on.

The second element in the instability of the Balkans was the eruption of capitalism in the 19th century. This came first as a demonstration effect. The economic development of western Europe, and more particularly the romantic vision of the French Revolution as the 'self proclamation' of the nation and of the 'nation in arms', encouraged stirrings among intellectuals within the Ottoman Empire but also, more importantly at first, in the expatriate communities on the borders of the empire.[33] Where Britain and France had gone before, they argued, now an independent Serbia, Greece, Bulgaria, Romania and so on could go in the future. Amongst the mass of the population who were peasants and whose life was bounded by their locality, such visions of national freedom had little resonance.[34] For them to be generalised a second element was needed in the form of the arrival of capitalism on the ground and the manipulation of state power to encourage the process of national identification. In the second half of the 19th century capitalism began to more fundamentally transform eastern Europe in general and south eastern Europe in particular. But while it began to unravel the old relationships and to create new ones, it failed to produce the prosperity that the nationalists hoped independence would bring.[35] The economic gap (measured roughly in output per head) between western and eastern Europe grew from around 20 percent in 1800 to perhaps 60 percent in 1860 and 80 percent in 1900. The overall levels of 'national' integration were also lower than in the west. But there also developed a marked pattern of uneven development with some regions developing faster and becoming more closely linked in a positive way to the world economy.[36] This enabled local differences to be played on and interpreted as part of a pattern of superiority and inferiority, domination and oppression, a pattern that soon trapped the new states that emerged from the Ottoman Empire. 'Building the nation' inevitably therefore involved a twin process of inclusion and exclusion.

To this was then added the third element—the interests of the Great Powers—Britain, France, Russia, Austria-Hungary and then from the 1870s Germany and Italy. As the 'sick man of Europe' the Ottoman Empire was ripe for picking off.[37] Russia (driving to the south and trying to accumulate more land, looking for an outlet to the Mediterranean and therefore eyeing control of Constantinople and the Straits, and playing on mythologies of Slav solidarity) had a major interest in its destruction. Numerous wars therefore took place between Russia and the Ottoman Empire.[38] But the last thing the other Great Powers wanted was that Russia should either seize or control land. These powers (Austria-Hungary, Italy) aspired to a strategic position that would allow them to dominate the others (Britain, France, Germany). Britain in particular was concerned with the threat both to its interests in south eastern Europe and more importantly to its strategic interests in the route to India through the Mediterranean and the Suez Canal. It was this that created the famous 'Eastern Question' that figured so prominently in the history of Europe between 1850 and 1945, but which for a period the Cold War division of Europe would turn into a half forgotten historical curiosity for most of the world. As one British expert told the Royal Institute of International Affairs in London in 1924, 'The Balkan problem, we must not forget, is not which town shall be Serb and which Greek...but which European race shall eventually hold the gate of Europe and Asia and control Europe's destiny'.[39]

The resulting power plays were sometimes breathtaking. At one point Russia would move against the Ottoman Empire, 'supporting the Slav peoples'. Then it would decide whether its interests lay in the empire's weakened survival rather than its complete destruction. Then it would turn against it again fearing that the newly independent Balkan states might themselves become too independent and challenge its interests in the region.[40] No less Britain and France viewed the Ottoman Empire with suspicion as the oppressor of Christians but then backed it as a better guarantee of their interests in the Balkans and the wider Mediterranean than a region controlled by Russia. Then, as demands for independence grew from different groups in the Ottoman Empire, this involved encouraging the fracturing of the Balkans into competing states (Balkanisation) which were often mutually hostile to one another and which could be played upon to secure the rival interests of the powers. As the competition increased, each of the powers, supplemented from the 1870s by the newly formed Italy and Germany, tried to maintain a grip on some part or other of the Balkans. German imperialism in particular began to look in a south eastern direction as its power grew before 1914 and then again in the 1930s under Hitler as it vied for the position of dominant power in the region. In the 1920s Mussolini paved the way for him and then acted as a truculent junior partner.

10) Local nationalist movements have always tried to work with particular great powers to gain leverage against enemies backed by other great powers

The paradox at the heart of the nationalist argument in the 19th century and beyond has been that, although nationalist movements have spoken in the name of 'peoples yearning to be free', nowhere have they gained enough support from these people to achieve their objectives. Their best hope therefore lay in movements from above which have often met with at best incomprehension and at worst opposition from the local populations but which have been able to lean on the support of the Great Powers which could then tip the balance in favour of national independence.

Since, however, the Great Powers had (and have) interests of their own and have rarely failed to be conscious of the disastrous results that might occur (as they did in 1914) if they fell out amongst one another, they rarely allowed those demanding national independence to get all that they wanted. This left these competing nationalisms with an unfinished agenda for a Greater Greece, a Greater Serbia, a Greater Romania, a Greater Bulgaria and, later, a Greater Albania. These agendas involved seizing territory and people from both the Ottoman Empire and sometimes the Austro-Hungarian Empire, as well as from one another. But to win these aims favour had to be continually curried with the Great Powers in the hope that one or other of them would force the others to accept the realignment of territory.[41]

Greece, on the fringes of the Ottoman Empire and seen by the Western powers as both a stabilising force as well as the mythical inheritor of the glories of the ancient world, was able, with one major exception in the early 1920s, to play this game spectacularly well.[42] Romania too managed to expand its lands by using the crisis of the Balkan Wars, joining the right side in 1916 in the First World War, joining the wrong side in the Second World War but then switching sides before it was too late. Bulgaria by contrast lost out. Having been a victor in the first Balkan War it became the country that the others ganged up against in the Second Balkan War. It joined the losing side in the First World War and then made the same mistake in the Second World War and then, unlike Romania, changed sides too late for it to make a difference.

But if state formation under Great Power supervision created a pattern of conflict over claims to external lands, the same process created the basis for internal destabilisation as nationalist movements developed (and were often tacitly encouraged externally) which claimed the right to secede and join the 'mother' country. Inevitably this accentuated the internal 'minority' conflicts within new states where concepts of identity were insecure. One consequence of this in the inter-war years was that as nationalist movements were driven to the right the attraction of Italian fascism and then German Nazism as both model and ally came for some groups to be overwhelming. This happened in Albania with Italy and Croatia with German fascism. Appendix 1 sets out in detail the growth of the Balkan states, their wars and claims and counter-claims that led to the bloody history of the region as it was buffeted by these forces.

But another consequence was that as common lands were fought over by different groups startling shifts in the position of nationalist movements could occur. Here the Macedonian case is perhaps the sharpest. No land or identity has even more disputed.[44] The complexity is reflected in the way in which the term *macédoine* came to be taken up in 18th century France to mean a mixture, being applied then to *macédoine de fruits* (fruit salad) and *macédoine de légumes* (hotchpotch). It is also reflected in the competing conceptions of the Macedonian lands and their rightful location. In each case the search for some authentic Macedonia, deriving from some ancient lineage, makes no sense at all but is best understood in terms of the interaction of Great Powers and local states with dissident nationalist groups struggling to carve out a niche for themselves.

Greek nationalism has always claimed the title of Macedonia as part of the ancient heritage of the Greek state going back to Alexander the Great, and speculated on the lands that might define this heritage. An area of land and a people with leaders claiming to be Macedonian were incorporated into Yugoslavia in 1918 emerging with the breakup of the country as the Former Yugoslav Republic of Macedonia. This phrase is bizarrely the correct title of the new state because Greek protests prevented it simply being called Macedonia lest this tarnish Greek claims to hold that land.[44] From the late 19th century, however, an even stronger case was developed that Macedonia was part of the Bulgarian inheritance and the lands that were supposed to be associated with should therefore be part of Bulgaria.

From the 1890s, however, a nationalist movement developed, based in Bulgaria, that looked to an independent Macedonia within a Balkan federation that would unite all the supposed Macedonian peoples. Known as the Internal Macedonian Revolutionary Organisation, it had a long history of wrecking itself in internecine warfare and Bulgarian politics more widely as it allowed itself to be a pawn of wider interests inside and outside the region. Its history has some striking echoes in the early life of the Kosovo Liberation Army and offers a telling vision of what its future might be. As one critical account from a previous generation expressed it:

> *The Internal Macedonian Revolutionary Organisation was a perfect example of a degeneration of a peasant movement which began as a real revolutionary movement but whose leaders, instead of accepting help for their pursuit of their own policies, became willing to take such help and to pursue the policies of the giver of aid. The Comintern tried originally to steer the IMRO movement away from individual terror and into alliance with the mass movement of the workers. The terrorists fell out among themselves over this policy and murdered each other. Then the movement degenerated completely and became a bandit racket.*[45]

These amalgams of Great Power rivalries, interstate conflicts and conflicts within states meant that while the best Balkan socialists supported the idea of national self determination as a general principle they could never simply and uncritically ally with national demands and nationalist movements. The result was that the most determined socialists were often abused and attacked by all sides as they stood out for a socialist solution that went beyond competing local interests and Great Power rivalry. And however real failings become visible with hindsight, there existed an admirable history of socialist argument and courage that is largely unknown in the West and which the socialist movement here, that often failed lesser tests, would do well to consider more seriously. In the Balkan Wars, for example, although some socialists supported their governments, many did not. Even more spectacularly in 1914, when the First World War broke ostensibly to protect Serbia from bullying by the Austro-Hungarian Empire, Serbian socialists courageously denounced the war as an imperialist one and suffered terribly for this. What inspired them was not simply the general vision of international socialism but a recognition that there was no solution to the problem of the Balkans so long as it remained a prisoner of the Great Powers and competing local leaders willing to beat the nationalist drum for their own ends. Against the prospect of permanent tension, national conflict and warfare they offered a prospect in the form of a socialist federation of the Balkan peoples which they hoped would allow the creation of a society that could eliminate the destructive roots of national conflict by attacking its roots in both local and international capitalism. But, like so much else in 20th century socialism, this alternative hope for a union of free peoples was first to be distorted and then destroyed by Stalin and his supporters in Russia and the system that they eventually helped to impose in Eastern Europe after 1945.

11) Stalinism in Eastern Europe in general and the Balkans in particular suppressed interstate and intrastate conflict, but attempted to co-opt the nationalist agenda for its own purposes

The Russian Revolution acted as a beacon for discontent throughout Europe, and in the Balkans a significant part of the left saw in the internationalism of the Bolsheviks and in their revolutionary policies the beginnings of a politics that could break with the disasters of the past.[46] But tragic errors were made, most notably in Bulgaria in 1923 when the Communist Party stood aside as sections of the ruling class turned on each other before the victorious group then turned on the left. Similarly the international Communist movement gave support to dubious peasant based parties such as that in Yugoslavia which turned against the Communists when a better ally appeared in the form of the Yugoslav king.

The detail of these mistakes can be found elsewhere.[47] The point is that they were never corrected. As the revolution degenerated in Russia under Stalin's leadership, mistakes were consolidated. The Communist parties in the Balkans, as elsewhere, became instruments of Russian foreign policy. In the Russia itself 'socialism in one country' became part of an ideology of national development in which, in foreign policy terms, the Russian leadership incorporated many of the earlier imperialist aims of Tsarist Russia. At the end of the First World War the various peace settlements had encouraged the consolidation of the Eastern

European states as buffer states against Bolshevism. Now the Communist parties, under Russian guidance, were pushed to the left or to the right as it suited Russian interests. But essentially they tried increasingly to incorporate a nationalist policy arguing for an independence from the West that would take the Eastern European and Balkan states into what was portrayed as the 'anti-imperialist' camp. Instead of these states being the West's buffer against Russia they would therefore act as Russia's buffer against the West.

In 1944-1945 the Russian army was able to push Hitler's armies back to Berlin. At first it appeared as if it might be possible to agree a new carve up of the Balkans between East and West. In the infamous informal percentages agreement Stalin and Churchill in October 1944 (half drunkenly) divided the Balkans between themselves. According to Churchill's own account:

> I wrote out on half a sheet of paper:
> Romania: Russia 90 percent, the others 10 percent.
> Greece: Great Britain (in accord with USA) 90 percent, Russia 10 percent.
> Yugoslavia: 50 percent, 50 percent.
> Hungary: 50 percent, 50 percent.
> Bulgaria: Russia 75 percent, the others 25 percent.
> I pushed this across to Stalin, who had by then heard the translation. There was a slight pause. Then he took his blue pencil and made a large tick upon it, and passed it back to us. It was all done in no more time than it takes to set down.[48]

But as the Cold War developed, Greece and Turkey were pulled into the Western bloc and Romania, Bulgaria and Yugoslavia and Albania into the Eastern bloc. But in consolidating its grip on the region the Russian leadership had to look two ways—against the West and for signs of disloyalty in its new bloc. This latter problem became serious in 1948 as a dispute with Yugoslavia developed. Yugoslavia was the only country in the region where the liberation had occurred without major direct intervention by the Russian army and where the local Communist leadership therefore did not need to kowtow to Stalin. This led Russia to establish an early pattern of rule which was likened to a wheel. On the rim of the wheel were the satellite states—able on minor matters to communicate with one another but controlled by spokes from the hub and having in major matters to relate to one another through Moscow. In particular early discussions of the most limited kind of Balkan federal unity were crushed as they appeared to be dangerous to Moscow rule.[49] Instead the countries were divided from one another by Soviet rule and encouraged to adopt their own ideologies of socialism in one country which had the additional advantage that it provided, in the short run, a way for the new ruling class and the ruling parties to sink some roots into the local populations. In the longer run it produced ideologies which reproduced nationalist agendas. Officially they were 'national in form, socialist in content'; in reality the socialist element was little more than 'form', if that, and it was the content that was nationalist. Ultimately though this was also to prove part of the downfall of the regimes, for their nationalism was compromised by their contamination with Russian interests.

12) The fracturing of Yugoslavia in particular was a product of the manipulation of a growing social crisis by competing sections of the ruling class to divert conflict and to secure their control over the remnants of the old society

The pattern of uneven development characteristic of capitalism took on an especially sharp form in Yugoslavia. As early as 1910 it is estimated that the per capita income of Slovenia was three times higher than that of the area that is today Kosovo.[50] After 1945, although Yugoslav governments made gestures to deal with this uneven development that helped to underpin national antagonisms, the Yugoslav system in the long run ended up reproducing these inequalities. For those who believed that there was some kind of socialism in Yugoslavia the explanation for this was often attributed to the imbalance of plan and market elements. But more centrally planned economies in the rest of Eastern Europe failed to solve these difficulties and more market economies in the West also failed to fundamentally restructure national economies so as to eliminate the problem of uneven development within countries, let alone between them.[51] The real explanation for the perpetuation of these inequalities lay in the effect of three main factors—class, international military-economic competition and the nationalist character of the Yugoslav (and other) regimes.

Despite its pretence of socialism the Yugoslav regime after 1945 remained one built on the alienation and exploitation of the mass of the population. Those in control directed the system in their own interests. This involved not only pressure on those below, but conflict for control over resources at the top. Different internal wings of the Yugoslav ruling class competed with one another, taking advantage of the language of nationalism when necessary both to consolidate support and paper over social divisions within the constituent republics and as part of a bargaining process between them.

The impact of military and economic competition increased this problem. No country's development takes place in a vacuum. After the split from Russia, Yugoslavia was caught between East and West, more nervous of Russia for much of the time and therefore accepting Western support but never really confident of European and US motives. To maintain Yugoslavia's independence, therefore, the government had first to pursue a policy of rapid growth which meant that, whether in terms of 'plan' or 'market', most resources had to be devoted to the areas of greatest return. This limited its ability to redirect resources on a large enough scale to make a serious impression on the problem of inequality. This was compounded by the strategic problem. Yugoslavia needed a strong military based on a strong military-industrial complex. But there was no point in locating this in areas that were vulnerable to outside attack. Ironically this meant that neither the more advanced nor the more backward areas benefited most from military expenditure, but an area in the middle. As Misha Glenny put it in 1992, believing that Yugoslavia was threatened by possible invasion from both East and West, 'Tito transformed Bosnia-Hercegovina into a huge fortress capable of resisting foreign aggression long after Zagreb, Belgrade, or Skopje had fallen. Although Bosnia-Hercegovina makes up only one fifth of the territory of Yugoslavia, 60 percent of the country's military industries and installations [were] there'.[52]

The third element was that Yugoslav governments, although they opposed local nationalisms, developed their own form of socialism in one country and therefore instead of challenging nationalism by real internationalism they challenged one form of nationalism with another form. The result was to legitimate the language and ideas of nationalism whatever the arguments about particular forms of it.

For a long period economic development allowed these tensions in the Yugoslav project (as elsewhere in Europe) to be submerged. But from the 1970s the impact of the decline in growth in the world economy began to affect the internal economy of Yugoslavia and to reinforce the latent tensions. Investment rates fell, unemployment and inflation rose and foreign debt accumulated to considerable levels. Austerity programmes became the order of the day as the government was encouraged to answer the demands of its financial creditors in the West.

By the 1980s these pressures were creating elements of radicalisation in the Yugoslav system. Milosevic understood better and earlier than most the triple value of nationalism as a means of diverting this discontent, as a means of consolidating his grip in his 'own' area, and as a means of strengthening his position in the infighting for the control of Yugoslavia's wealth. But other leaders in other republics also soon realised that if they were to ride out what at first appeared as centripetal tendencies and then a forthcoming implosion they too had to build support in the same way.

13) There is no way in which state structures can be made 'ethnically pure' without ethnic cleansing. This is why all Balkan wars have been dirty wars on all sides

The images of the television news reports bring home the brutalities of 'ethnic cleansing' and etch its horror for us in the tear stained faces or in the silent incomprehension of the victims at the scale of the brutality that has been inflicted upon them. Yet as the black and white images of refugees and mutilated bodies in the newsreels of past conflicts this century also show, this is not a new phenomenon. War has always brought with it refugee trains—people are forced out or flee and fall by the wayside and die as support is insufficient and takes second place to military priorities or creates complications in which the belligerents or neutrals prefer not to involve themselves. War too brings rape and sexual degradation. Whether it has been used systematically in the Balkans remains unclear—that it is everywhere present is clear for it has been in existence on a massive scale in every war, known to specialists but tucked far away from the concerns of those who glory in the heroic side of military history. And so too is the history of ethnic cleansing. The term is new—the phenomenon is not. Stinking, disease ridden refugee camps of 'cleansed' peoples litter the history of the 19th and 20th centuries, as do the graves of those who never made it to their relative safety. The scale of this forced movement and its extent throughout Europe and not just the Balkans is often not appreciated but, as one recent survey puts it:

> *In the 19th century, involuntary migrations were counted in thousands and tens of thousands; the Balkan conflicts* [of 1912-1913] *increased their numbers to hundreds of thousands, and World War One generated millions of them... The apogee of forced migrations came during World War Two and its aftermath when the uprooted were counted in tens of millions.*

One estimate is that 60 million were displaced in the Second World War itself and another 20 million after it. This forced movement resulted in the ostensible partial 'purification' of the ethnic base of European states by reducing 'national minorities'. These were reduced from 25 percent of the population of central Europe as a whole in the 1930s to 7.2 percent of the population in the 1970s.[53]

Not only have peace settlements rewarded such ethnic cleansing but they have often brought with them new rounds as people continue to be forced out or flee to escape location in a state that remains hostile to them and of which they might be rightly suspicious. Appendix 2 sets out some of the elements of the horrific process that this has created in the Balkans in this past century. It is solely concerned with the most identifiable movements of people, of 'ethnic cleansing' approved and unapproved. It says nothing of the deaths of those who died in the wars in the area or on the marches between countries.

What lies behind the sorry tale set out in Appendix 2 is the fact that state boundaries can never be drawn in such a way as to exclude all who are not of the right 'national' group and to include all who 'are'. The attempt to try to homogenise states must involve complicity in ethnic cleansing.

But the contradiction is that to defend state boundaries also involves in nationalist terms defending the subjugation of people who may wish to assert their difference. It is here that the simple, naive endorsement of an unqualified abstract right to self determination for everyone also founders, for if every self defined national group has the right to demand self determination we are looking potentially at a process without end. If socialists must never support the subjugation of peoples, their support for self determination cannot equally be a support for endless 'national' conflicts.

State boundaries of whatever kind are all artificial creations that divide people—Serbs as much as Croats, Slovenians as much as Bosnians. But this applies too with just as much force to the state boundaries of the US, Britain and France or wherever. Indeed the talk of the myth of nation and common nature of humanity is not worth a penny or a cent or a centime if it does not start with the attack on such myths in the West and the unqualified support of the right of peoples everywhere to free movement including to the West—the litmus test on which so much spurious internationalism comes to grief. The internationalism that bespeaks the need to make interventions in the name of humanity becomes the nationalism that denies humans the right to move freely, that passes immigration laws, denies asylum, builds walls around Europe and finances the erection of barbed war fences and the deployment of gunboats to ensure that people cannot even come ashore. The argument about the artificiality of boundaries then becomes no more than a cover to advance the interests of the most powerful at the expense of those who are weaker.

In the case of the former Yugoslavia there is no logical path that can be picked through the claims and counterclaims that does not endorse some at the expense of the others. The brutality of the Milosevic regime cannot in any way devalue the truth of its argument that the borders of the old Yugoslavia were simple administrative boundaries that in key areas bore no necessary relation to what people perceived to be realities on the ground. It cannot obscure the fact that the entirely justifiable demand of the Kosovans to be free of the brutality of Belgrade is also the same right that the Serbs in the Krajina were denied, their right to be free of the Croats. The internationalism that is prepared to support the former and not recognise the latter (or to accept it but cast it aside in the interest of realpolitik) demonstrates its spurious character by this very act of denial. In so doing, it tolerates one kind of deportation rather than another and so builds up problems for future generations.

Arguments about self determination only make sense if they are part of a wider challenge to the policies that divide and rule people whether they come from local leaders or the big powers. That challenge should have come from a strong socialist movement in the former Yugoslavia, built around internationalism—attacking the politics of the leaderships in Belgrade or Zagreb and defending the rights of the oppressed everywhere. But the destructive power of the myth of 'Soviet socialism' in general and 'Yugoslav socialism' in particular has meant that no such socialist force existed when Yugoslavia collapsed. In its absence the peoples of the former Yugoslavia have again become the playthings of local nationalist leaders and behind them the interests, direct and indirect, of the bigger powers.

14) The impact of the war will further destabilise the Balkans for at least a generation

Every day the war has gone on, its ramifications have widened even without the disasters of NATO's bombing failures. The immediate death toll in Kosovo, Montenegro and Serbia from the actions of both sides will only be more accurately known when post-war investigations strip away the propaganda, but it seems likely to be substantial.

What is already clear is that in terms of physical destruction the war has been more damaging than the combined impact of Nazi and Allied bombing in the Second World War in the area and has wrecked much of the economic infrastructure in both Serbia and Kosovo. 'Like Iraq, like Yugoslavia. Every day the definition of "military" subtly expands to embrace something we hadn't thought of', wrote one Western reporter who was observing the destruction.[54]

The evidence of past wars is that communications and transport can be relatively quickly restored and Western construction companies are already salivating at the prospect of the contracts that will come their way as 'aid' is sent to the Balkans—and then back out again to them. The reconstruction of the battered oil refineries, car plants, petrochemical works, engineering factories, even of the cigarette factory that has been destroyed, is another matter. So too is the reconstruction of the public facilities, the schools, the hospitals and the damaged housing stock.

Then there is the refugee problem. There is no prospect that the mass of refugees will return to the homes that they have left. This has not happened in Bosnia and it will not happen in Kosovo even if NATO achieves its widest objectives. In the Bosnian case, since the December

1995 Dayton Accords which effectively divided Bosnia and made it a UN/NATO protectorate, 75 percent of the 2 million displaced persons have not returned. Within Bosnia four main factors militate against return: fear of persecution in disputed areas; the destruction of housing stock, estimated at 60 percent; the legacy of land mines with some estimates as high as 2 to 3 million; and the dire economic and employment situation, with per capita income at two thirds of its 1990 level, but achieving that in part because of aid, as industrial production is 20 percent of its 1990 level. In Kosovo similar factors will be at work. Some will go back to their homes. Others will return but to other homes, possibly in the cities, near the NATO bases, to new camps and overcrowded slums. Still others, perhaps tens of thousands, will stay in camps either side of the Kosovo border in Europe's new 'Gaza strip'.[55]

The protectorate that NATO will create will itself become a new source of instability. Internally there will still be an aggrieved Kosovan population living in part on Western largesse, such as it will be, parasitic on serving the needs of Western forces stationed there but also disdainful of NATO's failure to deliver their real liberation. Perhaps too there will be a small population of Kosovan Serbs no less embittered against both the Kosovan Albanians and NATO. Across the border in Serbia, forced to retreat or be defeated, will be a population facing a bleak future with intensified grievances about NATO's actions and what will be portrayed as 'favouritism'. And, as in Iraq, the legacy of the war will be there not only in the memories, not only in the everyday view of the destruction that has not been remedied but in the aftermath of continuing deaths from environmental pollution, depleted uranium, unexploded cluster bombs and so on.

Beyond the immediate area of Kosovo and Serbia the ramifications will remain too. There is the uncertain position of Albania—already wrecked by a brutal ruling class that the West backed after 1989 because they embraced the free market with such alacrity. These selfsame heroic Albanian apostles of the free market established pyramid schemes that fleeced the whole population. When the bubble burst Albania was quickly dumped by its Western enthusiasts, save for a cynical aid effort whose sole motivation was to keep poor Albanians in Albania rather than allow them access to Europe. Then there are Macedonia, Montenegro and Bosnia—what of them? Or even Croatia caught between a triumphalism that the Serbs are 'getting it' and fear that it is suffering too as vital tourist revenues plummet, with prospects for the future dim. And what of Bulgaria and the other Danubian states? They neighbour the areas of conflict and have had their trade and economies disrupted by the blocking of the Danube and by the sanctions that they are expected to impose on Serbia.

No doubt some aid will be swung to all these, but it will not be enough. Nor will the foreign investment that was supposed to be private enterprise's contribution to the area be any more likely to come than it has in the past. Moreover in aid terms the key word is 'swung', for though there might be some increase in the aid budget simply to help resist chaos, part of it, on past performance, is bound to be redirected from other areas. The plans for EU expansion are now in chaos, as what appeared to be a central European and Baltic thrust which could ignore the south now at least has to consider south eastern Europe, not as part of a serious programme for EU entry, but as a competing and constraining area of interest.

Then there is Russia. Its economy has been firstly wrecked by the transition and then overwhelmed by the financial aspects of the economic crisis that developed in 1998. Even before the crisis in the Balkans developed, its leaders feared that NATO expansion was directed against them—an opportunity to take advantage of Russia while it was down to ensure that it would never be able to get up. The effect of the war has been to consolidate a huge opposition bloc and to give new authority and legitimacy to the right, offering confirmation of some of their wildest fantasies.

And the consequences have rolled on. Even before the start of the war informed observers were worrying that the crisis and NATO's determination to impose a more aggressive 'out of area' policy might have even wider implications beyond Europe. One aspect of this has been the pressure to increase the level of arms spending to 3 percent for all NATO members which if carried through would begin to ratchet up global military spending and do nothing to assist the arguments for disarmament elsewhere.[56] But perhaps more important than this is the indirect impact NATO's action might have on the arms race in Asia. Who can now trust the US and NATO to act, or not act, for it is the US-NATO bloc that now appears more than ever as the destabilising element in the international system. Consider, for example, the arms race between India and Pakistan. This has in part been provoked by India's uncertainty about the extent of Western support for them as the 'world's largest democracy'.

Instead Western policy has seemed to offer as much support or more to Pakistan and China—two countries with which India has had tense relations. All the more need, it is suggested, for India to have its own 'deterrent'. In its heart of hearts, is the leadership of India any more confident of Western support today? On the contrary, the West's willingness to intervene on such a massive scale on terms that it defines without the formal sanction of the UN seems likely to encourage doubt and suspicion.

But this policy has done nothing for relations with China either. Even before the bombing of the Chinese embassy, Chinese fears about the character of US-NATO policy had been growing. The bombing of the embassy has confirmed these. Thus the US and NATO have alienated a supposed 'friend' in the form of India to placate a supposed 'enemy' in the form of China, only to destroy whatever credibility they had gained there. The issue here is less the short term impact than the potential long term one. Diplomats are skilled at papering over cracks and massaging the public image. They are less skilled at repairing the deeper damage that breeds distrust and conflict and sets in motion processes that build more tension into inter-state relations.

15) No politics which does not challenge both the local ruling classes and the international ruling classes offers any way forward

There is a tendency to believe that when policies go badly wrong they do so because of mistakes or poor leadership and can be rectified by better policies and better leadership. The pressure to believe in the ultimate goodness of the system in which we live is considerable. If it is not a question of good versus bad, then it is the 'not so bad' versus the 'much worse'.

This illusion affects not only people in the West, but those who look to the West for support like the KLA. If only they cloak themselves in the Stars and Stripes or Union Jack then they will get the aid that they need to realise their dream. What NATO's Balkan War shows is that none of our rulers can be trusted because what drives them to act are motives that are in fundamental contradiction with the real needs and interests of humanity. What hope does NATO offer after its role in Kosovo-Serbia? What hope does Milosevic offer, or the rest of the Serbian leadership? What hope does Rugova or the moderate Kosovan Albanian leadership offer?

To create an alternative it is necessary to develop the different approach from below that real socialists have always argued for. But this alternative has to be built around fighting oppression and exploitation wherever they exist. Real unity can never come about from the denial of real grievances. Even less can it come about if those grievances are merely treated with fine words and gestures. Building the confidence that can overcome national hatred will not be easy. It requires workers and socialists in the oppressing country to fight for and make real sacrifices for workers and socialists in the oppressed country, otherwise they will be swept aside by the forces of national hatred. They too must respond in kind, but the burden falls overwhelmingly on those in the oppressor country, for it is there that the root of the problem lies and it is there that a solution can be found. This means in the West and in Europe there is a need to attack the very basis of NATO's power. In local oppressors like

Serbia it means an opposition that is not seduced by nationalism but resolutely attacks it in all its forms to the extent of being prepared to argue for self determination—only then can the foundations of an alternative be laid.

There is always the temptation to hope that someone else will do this hard work for us. But what NATO's Balkan War shows is that more than ever it is necessary to develop this alternative in the West, for it is here that the power lies for our rulers to create global chaos and it is here that the power lies to reverse the process by reining them in and overturning them. Only this can create an opportunity to use the wealth of the world for the people of the world—it is this that is the real and only humanitarian policy.

APPENDIX 1: MAKING AND REMAKING THE BALKANS —
NATIONALISM, WAR AND GREAT POWER INTERVENTION[57]

	Gained from	Lost to
Greece		
1830	1821-1829 independence war. 1827 by Treaty of London England, France, Russia support autonomy and defeat Turkish-Egyptian fleet. 1828-1929 Russo-Turkish War leads to 1829 Treaty of Adrianople and 1830 London Conference which recognises and protects a limited Greece consisting of what is today Southern Greece	
1864	Ionian Islands ceded by Britain	
1881	Thessaly and Arta region of Epirus ceded by Ottoman Empire under pressure from Great Powers	
1897	Loses war with Ottoman Empire over union with Crete. Despite displeasure of Great Powers they still guarantee Cretan autonomy	
1912-1913	Two Balkan wars increase land area by 70 percent and population from 2.8 to 4.8 million. Gains include Aegean Islands, Salonica, Crete and part of 'Macedonia'. Denied Northern Epirus by Great Power decision to recognise it as part of new Albania	
1914-1918	Ruling class splits pro-Entente v pro Central Powers. Allies blockade and attempt landing to support pro-Entente section	
1919	Allies reward pro-Entente government with support for Greek troops taking Smyrna (in part to thwart Italian occupation)	
1920	Treaty of Sèvres: (i) recognises sovereignty of Aegean islands; (ii) awards most of Western and Eastern Thrace; (iii) awards Smyrna for five years to be followed by referendum. Greece exists as a Greece	

	of 'the two continents and the five seas'	
1920-1922	*Turkey rejects Treaty of Sèvres. War*	*Turkey*
	leads to Greek humiliation and	*regains*
	recapture of Smyrna but Britain	*Smyrna*
	opposes too great a Turkish victory	
1923	*Treaty of Lausanne recognises Turkish*	
	victory but also limits gains. Leads to	
	huge officially endorsed population	
	exchange	
1940	*Italy invades Greece*	
1940	*Greece counter-attacks and pushes*	
	into Albania	
1941-1945	*German invasion leading to tripartite*	
	division. German, Italian and	
	Bulgarian occupation	
1944-1949	*Greek Civil War. Stalin stands by while*	
	left defeated by Western supported	
	forces	
1947	*Dodecanese Islands from Italy*	
1960	*Separate independence for Cyprus in*	
	part to forestall union with Greece	
	supported by pro-Greek forces	
1974	*Failed Greek sponsored coup*	
	precipitates Turkish invasion of	
	Cyprus and division of island	

Serbia

1804-1813	*First Serbian revolt leads to*
	independence backed by Russia in
	1807 as part of Russo-Turkish War
	1806-1812
1813-1815	*Turkish reconquest*
1815-1817	*Second Serbian revolt leading to*
	autonomy within Ottoman Empire
1830	*Treaty of Adrianople (as a result of*
	Russo-Turkish War 1828-1829) further
	defines autonomy within Ottoman
	Empire
1876-1878	*War with Turkey*
1878	*Fully Independent Kingdom under*
	Treaty of Berlin
1885	*Failed Serbo-Bulgarian War for*
	territory and restoration of local

	balance of power after Bulgarian union with Eastern Rumelia	
1912-1913	*Balkan Wars—large territorial gains, including Kosovo*	
1918	*Core of new Kingdom of Serbs, Croats and Slovenes (from 1928 Yugoslavia)*	
1941-1945	*German invasion and puppet government sponsored by Axis powers*	
1991	*Independent state following breakup of Yugoslavia*	

Yugoslavia

1918	*Formed as Kingdom of Serbs, Croats and Slovenes*	
1919	*Loses Fiume to Italy (annexed finally 1924)*	*Italy*
1922	*Rappalo Treaty awards Nettuno to Italy*	*Italy*
1941	*Conflict in ruling class over whether to support Allies or Axis*	
1941	*Italian, German, Hungarian, Bulgarian division*	
	Dalmatia annexed by Italy	
	Puppet Croatian state	
1945	*Reconstitution of Yugoslavia*	
1991	*Breakup of Yugoslavia*	

Croatia

Pre-1918	*Part of Hungarian part of Austro-Hungarian Empire*	
1918	*Part of Kingdom of Serbs, Croats and Slovenes/Yugoslavia*	
1941	*Following German invasion puppet fascist kingdom*	
1944-1945	*Reintegration into Yugoslavia*	
1991	*Independence*	

Slovenia

Pre-1918	*Part of Austro-Hungarian Empire*	
1918	*Formed from Lower Styria, Carniola and part of Carinthia as part of Kingdom of Serbs, Croats and Slovenes—Yugoslavia*	
1941-1945	*Fascist occupation*	

| 1945 | *Federal republic of Slovenia part of new Yugoslavia. Includes 1918 lands plus parts of Istria, Venezia, Giulia* |
| 1991 | *Independence* |

Bosnia-Hercegovina
1878	*Autonomy within Ottoman Empire but under Austrian administration*
1908	*Annexed by Austro-Hungarian Empire*
1918	*Part of Yugoslavia*
1945	*Federal Republic in new Yugoslavia*
1991	*Independence*
1995	*Division under Dayton agreement*

Macedonia
	Historical concept of a Macedonian land highly controversial
1903	*Special province of Ottoman Empire under European powers*
1912	*As a result of First Balkan War much of land taken by Bulgaria*
1913	*As a result Second Balkan War redivided Greece, Serbia, Montenegro*
1944	*Yugoslavia includes 'Macedonia' and recognises language*
1991	*Independence of ex-Yugoslav version of 'Macedonia'*
1994-1995	*Blockade by Greece*

Montenegro
1878	*Independent under Treaty of San Stefano*
1910	*Kingdom*
1912-1913	*Balkan Wars—allies first with Bulgaria, Greece and Serbia against Turkey and then in 1913 with Serbia and Greece against Bulgaria, Turkey, Romania*
1918	*Incorporation into Yugoslavia*
1991	*Independent*

Albania
| 1913 | *Created from Ottoman Empire Independent principality under International Control Commission* |

1914	*Invasion by Austria and allies*	
1917	*Italian protectorate*	
1920	*Independent but Italian supervision*	
1940	*Greek counter-attack against Italy leads to invasion*	
1941	*Italian invasion. Part of Greater Italy*	
1944-1945	*Partisan led liberation*	

Romania

1831-1832	*Russia writes Organic Statutes of Wallachia and Moldavia to create autonomous principalities within Ottoman Empire*	
1848	*Revolt suppressed by actions of Russia and Ottoman Empire*	
1853	*Russian occupation of principalities helps precipitate Crimean War*	
1856	*Paris Treaty puts control of two principalities under International Commission. Russian influence weakened*	
1859	*Principalities elect Cuza as joint Prince*	
1861	*Union recognised by Ottoman Sultan*	
1878	*Romanian independence as a result of Russo-Turkish War and Congress of Berlin*	
1881	*Kingdom*	
1916	*Joins First World War on Entente side*	
1918	*Seizes Bessarabia from Russia*	
1919-1920	*Rewarded under Treaties of St Germain, Trianon, Neuilly nearly doubling size by acquisition of land from Hungary (including Transylvania) and Austria plus recognition of seizure of Bessarabia.*	
1940	*Loses Bessarabia and Northern Bukovina to Stalin's Russia*	
1940	*Loses Southern Dobrudja under Treaty of Craiova*	*Russia*
1940	*Loses part of Transylvania to Hungary under Vienna Award*	*Bulgaria*
1941	*Allies with Hitler hoping to regain land*	*Hungary*

1944	Switches to Allied side to maintain position—regains Transylvania	
Bessarabia		
1812	Taken from Ottoman Empire by Russia	
1918	Seized from Russia by Romania	Russia
1940	Seized back by Russia	Romania
1991	Part of independent Moldova following breakup of USSR	Russia
Bulgaria		
1878	Under Treaty of San Stefano huge principality dominating Balkans	
1878	Within months reduced in size by Treaty of Berlin	
1885	Incorporation of Eastern Rumelia	
1885	Serbo-Bulgarian War	
1908	Independent	
1912-1913	First Balkan War—huge gains. Second Balkan war—huge losses	Greece,
1915	Joins First World War on German side	Serbia
1919	Treaty of Neuilly cedes territory to Greece, Romania & Yugoslavia	Greece, Romania,
1940	Gains Dobrudja from Romania under Treaty of Craiova	Yugoslavia
1941-45	Invades Greece and Yugoslavia in support of Germany. Occupies Thrace and 'Macedonia'	
1944	Brief war with Russia (September)	
1944	Switches sides to attack German forces	
Eastern Rumelia		
1878	Autonomous province of Ottoman Empire	
1885	United with Bulgaria	

APPENDIX 2: FORCED MIGRATIONS IN THE 20TH CENTURY BALKANS[58]				
Dates	Who	From	To	Numbers
Balkan Wars	'Tens and hundreds of thousands ran in all directions' (Sola)			
including				
1912	Turks	'Macedonia'	Turkey	100,000
1912	Macedonians	Macedonia	Bulgaria	15,000
1912-1913	Greeks	Western Thrace	Greece	70,000
1912-1913	Turks	Bulgaria	Turkey	50,000
1913	Greeks and other groups	war areas	Greece	90,000?
1913	Turks	Western Thrace	Turkey	40,000-50,000
1913	Treaty of Adrianople between Bulgaria and Turkey— first interstate treaty to provide for transfer of peoples			
1913-1914	Bulgarians	Greece, Serbia, Turkey	Bulgaria	250,000
1913-1914	Greeks	post-war forced movement by Greek-Turkish agreement from Turkey— interrupted by 1914 war	Greece	?
World War One	even larger movements similar to Balkan Wars			
including				
1914-1918	Serbs	internal and external displacement of over one third population including	all directions	750,000-1,000,000?
1914-1918	Serbs	Serbs as forced labour, about 10 percent of population	Bulgaria/ Hungary	250,000-300,000?
1914-1918	Serbs	march to Adriatic— Serb army and civilians (huge death toll)	Adriatic	200,000-500,000?
1914-1918	Bulgarians	former 'Bulgarian lands'	Bulgaria	300,000?
1916-1918	Romanians	Dobrudja (taken by Bulgaria)	Romania	?
post-war				
1918-1924	Hungarians	Romania (Transylvania)	Hungary	200,000
1918-1924	Hungarians	Yugoslavia and Czechoslovakia	Hungary	200,000
1918-1926	Bulgarians	Greece (Greek Macedonia and Thrace)	Bulgaria	120,000
1918-1928	Greeks	Bulgaria	Greece	50,000
1922-1923	Greeks	forced exchange from Turkey under Treaty of Lausanne	Greece	1,200,000
1921-1928	Turks	Greece	Turkey	400,000
1921-1939	Turks	Romania, Bulgaria, Yugoslavia	Turkey	200,000

World War Two				
1939-1940	Romanians Germans Hungarians	Bessarabia and Northern Bukovina taken by Russia	Romania/ Germany/ Hungary	40,000 plus
1939-1940	Jews	Romania	Russia	70,000?
1939-1941	Romanians	suspect population Bessarabia	Russian camps	100,000?
1940-1941	Yugoslav (Serbs- Jews)	flee before invading German/ Hungarian armies	Yugoslavia	300,000?
1940	Romanians	Transylvania (ceded to Hungary)	Romania	220,000
1940	Hungarians	Romania	Hungary	160,000
1940	Romanians	Dobrudja annexed by Bulgaria	Romania	100,000
1940	Bulgarians	resettled Bulgarian Dobrudja	Bulgaria	60,000
1941	Greeks	'Greek' Macedonia and Western Thrace occupied by Bulgaria	Greece	90,000- 100,000
1940-1944	Ethnic Germans	Romania, Croatia, Bulgaria, Serbia	German areas	300,000?
1940-1945	Serbs	'Yugoslav' Macedonia occupied by Bulgaria	Serbia	500,000?
1940-1945	Serbs	Banat taken by Hungary	Serbia	?
1940-1945	Slovenians	Slovenia taken by Italy/Germany	Southern Slovenia/ Serbia	120,000
1940-1945	Serbs	Croatia	Serbia	120,000
1940-1945	Croatians Hungarians	Serbia	Croatia and Hungary	70,000
1941-1945	forced labour	18,000 Bulgarians, 9,000 Romanians, 103,000 Yugoslavs	Nazi Germany	130,000
1941-1945	Jews	Romania 270,000-400,000, Greece 60,000, Bulgaria 10,000 Yugoslavia 55,000-60,000	Nazi camps/ death	400,000 500,000
1943-1944	Italians	Albania and Dodecanese	Italy	40,000
1944-1945	Germans	Romania to west fleeing ahead of army	West	100,000
1944-1945	Germans	Yugoslavia to west fleeing ahead of Partisans Red Army	West	35,000
1944-1945	Hungarians	ahead of Red Army and return of Transylvania to Romania	Hungary	?
1944-1945	Balkan captives	Balkans	Russian camps	?
1944-1945	ethnic Germans	deportation from Romania, Yugoslavia	Germany	170,000?

1944-1945	ethnic Germans	deportation of those left behind from Hungary, Yugoslavia, Romania	Russia	200,000?
1945 on	Bulgarians	Greek and Yugoslav territories occupied in war	Bulgaria	120,000
1945 on	Hungarians	Romania, Yugoslavia (and Czech lands)	Hungary	185,000
1944-1947	Poles	Bosnia (community from 1890s)	Poland	17,000
1945-1946	Italians	New Yugoslavia	Italy	130,000
1946	Hungarians	New Yugoslavia	Hungary	40,000
1946	Serbs and Croats	Hungary	Yugoslavia	40,000
1945-1948	Jews	Bulgaria	Israel/West	50,000
1945-1948	Jews	Romania	Israel/West	40,000
Greek Civil War				
1946-1949		(a) 600,000 plus displaced from Greek Macedonia to Athens —Salonica (b) 90,000 cross borders (c) Albanians of South Epirus	Yugoslavia and Balkan states Albania	700,000 plus 25,000
Communist Era				
1949-1950	Turks	Bulgaria	Turkey	150,000-250,000
1970-1989	Turks	Bulgaria	Turkey	300,000
post-1989				
Croatian War 1991				
1991	Croats	Eastern Slavonia	Croatia	77,000
1991	Serbs	Croatia	Serbia and Montenegro	120,000
Bosnian War 1992-5				
	all but especially Muslims	internal displacement	Bosnia	1,000,000
	all incl.	external displacement	25 countries	1,000,000
	Muslims/ Croats	Republika Skrpska	Croatia	45,000
	Bosnian Serbs	Bosnia	Serbia/ Montenegro	250,000
1995	Croatian Serbs	Croatia/Krajina	Skpska/ Serbia	180,000

Notes

1   D K Fieldhouse, *The Colonial Empires: A Comparative Survey From the Eighteenth Century* (London, 1982).
2   Indeed those who bother to read what Lenin said will see that he dates the imperialist era from the time when the process of colonisation had been completed.
3   See M Haynes, 'The Rhetoric and Reality of Western Aid to Eastern Europe', *European Business and Economic Development*, vol 1 no 2 (September 1992), pp13-18.
4   World Bank, *World Development Indicators Report*, quoted in *The Guardian*, 27 April 1999.
5   OECD, *Development Cooperation 1998 Report* (Paris, 1999).
6   This is Arthur Schlesinger's famous characterisation of the liberal view of the Cold War—see his 'Origins of the Cold War', *Foreign Affairs* (1967).
7   There are several McDonald's restaurants in Belgrade.
8   I have drawn these quotations from an essay by Noam Chomsky circulated on the internet.
9   *The Guardian*, 6 April 1999.
10 Quoted in R de Wijk, 'Towards a New Political Strategy for NATO', *NATO Review* (Summer 1998), p15.
11 Ibid, p15.
12 And in so far as small powers ally with Security Council members the veto then operates. The Security Council has 15 members, ten of which rotate. Power lies with the five permanent members, each of which has veto powers. There is therefore no real accountability to the General Assembly. It is not often appreciated that the most frequent users of the veto in the Security Council have been the US and the UK. In the period from 1976 to the start of the Kosovan crisis in March 1999 the US used its veto 60 times, Britain 19, France 11, Russia 8 and China twice.
13 J Solano, 'The New NATO', *The Guardian*, 22 April 1999. Solana saw the 50th Anniversary NATO Summit as putting 'the finishing touches to the new NATO: an Alliance committed and designed for enhancing stability and security for the entire Euro-Atlantic area through new mechanisms, new partnerships and new missions, well into the 21st century.' J Solana, 'The Washington Summit: NATO Steps Boldly into the 21st Century', *NATO Review* (Spring 1999), p6.
14 H Schmidt, 'The Transatlantic Alliance in the 21st Century', *NATO Review* (50th Anniversary Commemorative Edition, 1999), p23.
15 Ibid, p23.
16 J Zametica, *The Yugoslav Conflict* (International Institute of Strategic Studies, Aldelphi Papers, London, 1992), p25.
17 This is according to the *New York Times* as reported in *The Guardian*, 26 April 1999. The warning was issued on 24 December 1992.
18 In interview on US television on 24 March as reported on *Panorama*, BBC1, 19 April 1999.
19 Veran Metic, editor of the opposition radio station B92, banned by Milosevic at the start of the war, illustrated the dilemma of the Serbian opposition by quoting the opposition mayor of Nis: 'Twenty minutes ago my city was bombed. The people who live here are the same people who voted for democracy in 1996, the same people who protested for 100 days after the authorities tried to deny them their victory in the elections. They voted for the same democracy that exists in Europe and the US. Today my city was bombed by the democratic states of the US, Britain, France, Germany and Canada! Is there any sense in this?' Matic commented, 'NATO's bombs have blasted the germinating seeds of democracy

out of the soil of Kosovo, Serbia and Montenegro and ensured that they will not sprout again for a very long time' (*The Guardian*, 14 April 1999). Earlier he had speculated that NATO plans did not see the Serbian opposition as an ally—it preferred there to be no opposition since this allowed demonisation. NATO's aim was 'to destroy and silence all alternative democratic voices and peace initiatives in order to make Yugoslavia a European Iraq and a pariah state for the next ten years' (*The Guardian*, 5 April 1999). Whether or not NATO was quite this cynical in intention, this was certainly the immediate result of its policy.

20 *The Economist*, 3 April 1999.

21 Several off target NATO bombs had fallen in rural Bulgaria, for example, but the government nevertheless fought off local opposition to get agreement to open Bulgarian air space to NATO. This decision had just been obtained when, to the government's consternation, a NATO missile dropped into a suburb of Sofia.

22 *The Observer*, 18 April 1999—the phrase is that of Johnathan Eyal.

23 United Nations, *Report of the Secretary General relating to Resolution 1160 (1998) of the Security Council*, 21 September 1998. My emphasis.

24 Quoted in *The Guardian*, 13 April 1999.

25 Despite their technological sophistication planes are vulnerable at low levels to the low technology fire of anti-aircraft guns. Four British Tornados were lost this way in the Gulf War.

26 Bombs are tipped with depleted uranium because it is heavier than lead or steel and can stand high velocities but it is also suspected of leaving a legacy of post-war civilian ill health from radioactive dust.

27 The bombing of the Chinese embassy in Belgrade has made this obvious but it is worth recalling that previous US intelligence failures include the 1998 bombing of a Sudanese pharmaceutical factory wrongly identified as a chemical warfare factory. In 1991, in the Gulf War, the Al-Amiriyah civilian bomb shelter in Bhagdad was wrongly identified as a military command post and destroyed with the loss of several hundred lives. In 1988 the USS *Vincennes* identified an Iranian airliner as hostile and shot it down with the loss of all 290 lives of those on board.

28 Quoted in *The Independent*, 16 April 1999. For what it is worth we should remind readers that refugees with a well founded fear of persecution under the UN convention have a right to demand safety in any other country. The talk of quotas, however large, is not therefore an act of 'generosity' but a violation of international refugee law.

29 See Rakovsky's autobiographical essay in C Rakovsky, *Selected Writings On Opposition in the USSR 1923-1930* (Alison & Busby, 1980), p70.

30 J Micklejohn, *A New Comparative Geography* (London, 1889), p184.

31 Historical debate has raged over such conversions, because for nationalist historians they are central to the history of the 'oppressed nation' and therefore must have been forced. English relations with the Ottoman Empire in the 16th and 17th centuries throw an interesting light on the issue and perhaps reveal the real state of affairs because in a number of instances Englishmen abroad found the empire an attractive home compared to the England of their day—a powerful 16th century Ottoman eunuch, Hasan Aga, was Samson Rowlie of Great Yarmouth; in the Algerian part of the empire one Moorish king's executioner turned out to be Abd-es-Salaam or Absalom, a former Exeter butcher; one General of the Janissaries was an Islamic convert known as Ingliz Mustapha (he had been born in Scotland). In 1606 the English consul in Egypt found Ottoman ways sufficiently attractive to convert to Islam. A half century later when Charles II attempted to pay the ransom for a group of enslaved sailors, his emissary found that they all refused to return to Restoration England. Having themselves converted to Islam they were now happily 'partaking of the prosperous Successe of the Turks'. The positive toleration which continued to exist alongside the more negative aspects of

the Ottoman Empire was reflected in the argument in 1798 of an Orthodox
Patriarch of Jerusalem who suggested that the Ottoman Empire was a divine
creation of god to protect Orthodoxy from contamination by the Catholic west.

32   See C Harman, 'The Return of the National Question', in J Rees (ed), *Marxism
      and the New Imperialism* (London, 1994).

33   See the excellent discussion in L S Stavrianos, 'Antecedents of the Balkan
      Revolutions of the Nineteenth Century', *Journal of Modern History*, vol xix
      (December 1957), pp335-348. The first Greek newspaper was published in Vienna
      in 1790; a Serbian paper was also published there in 1791; the first printed book in
      Bulgarian was published in Wallachia in 1806. Novi Sad, then in the Hungarian
      part of the Austro-Hungarian Empire, was known as the 'Serbian Athens'.
      Expatriate groups in the US and Europe today still exert a direct influence on
      internal Balkan politics.

34   Largely illiterate peasants with local visions—even their leaders often lacked the
      capacity to identify with the national cause and its myths, though the intellectual
      leaders of nationalism were happy to try to use them. In the Greek struggle for
      independence in the 1820s one scholar told the prominent peasant outlaw leader
      Nikotsaras that he was the equal of Achilles only to report that 'Nikotsaras was
      deeply offended that he should be compared to an unknown. "What nonsense is
      this," he replied indignantly, "and who is this Achilles? Did the musket of Achilles
      kill many?"'—quoted ibid. Subsequently state education would make sure that
      national myths were commonly known. As one British source put it at the end of
      the 19th century (with considerable exaggeration given the actual spread of
      education in Greece at this time), 'Schools have been established in nearly every
      village; and the little Greek boy learns whole passages of Homer by heart every
      week' (J Micklejohn, op cit, p189).

35   See the discussion in M Haynes and R Husan, 'The State and Market in the
      Transition Economies: Critical Remarks in the Light of Past History and the
      Current Experience', *Journal of European Economic History*, vol 27 no 3 (Winter
      1998), pp609-644.

36   D Aldcroft, 'Europe's Third World? The Peripheral Nations', in his *Studies in the
      Inter-War European Economy* (Ashgate, 1997), pp196-197.

37   Our concern here is with the Balkan question but the Ottoman Empire at its height
      arched around the eastern Mediterranean including much of the Middle East and
      North Africa. Nearly 50 modern states emerged from its fragmentation—a process
      which everywhere involved the balancing of the competing interests of the Great
      Powers and the local leaders. For a full listing see G Barraclough (ed), *Times
      World History Atlas* (London, 1978).

38   Russia was at war with the Ottoman Empire in 1735-1739; 1768-1774; 1787-
      1792; 1806-1812; 1828-1829; 1853-1856 (part of Crimean War); 1877-1878,
      1914-1917 (part of the First World War).

39   E Durham, 'The Balkans as a Danger Point', *International Affairs* (May 1924),
      p139, emphasis in the original.

40   At the end of the Second Balkan War Izvolsky, the tsarist Russian minister and
      diplomat, wrote from Paris in August 1913 of the defeated Bulgaria, Russia's
      supposed pet Balkan state, 'Events have taken a favourable course for us... Had
      Bulgaria come out victor it would have been very disadvantageous and dangerous
      for us... A great Bulgaria might have served as a base for ulterior Bulgar plans
      against Constantinople' (quoted in E Durham, op cit, p143).

41   One term used to describe this is 'irredentism'—the advocacy of the 'restoration'
      of territory. The idea involves a 'restoration' since nationalists believe the land
      was always part of their 'nation'. Irredentism derives from the Italian word
      irrendenta—unredeemed—and reflects the way in which Italian nationalists too

laid claim to the restoration of what they believed to be Italian land on the other side of the Adriatic.

42   'Greece...is the young rising power in the Balkan peninsula, and the one which has the greatest future before it', a late 19th century British audience was told. 'Turkey is the old, sinking, despairing, and dwindling power on the Peninsula; Greece the young, hopeful, and growing' (J Micklejohn, op cit, p186, p188).

43   In the Ottoman Empire the lands of the now disputed area of Macedonia were considered to be incorporated into the three vilayets of Salonika, Monastir and, ironically, Kosovo.

44   1992 saw huge nationalist protests in Greece about the creation of a separate state in the former Yugoslavia calling itself Macedonia. In March 1992 possibly a million marched in Salonica. In December 1992 another million or so were on the streets of Athens around slogans like 'Macedonia has been Greek for 3,000 years.' Socialists who stood out bravely against this hysteria were arrested.

45   J Weber, 'The Balkans', *Fourth International* (June 1941), p145.

46   The Balkan Communist parties were often soon forced underground but in Yugoslavia, for example, in 1920, the Communist Party had some 60,000 members and in electoral terms was the third largest party with 12 percent of the vote.

47   See D Hallas, *The Comintern* (London, 1985) for a brief discussion of these errors.

48   W Churchill, *The Second World War*, vol vi (London, 1954), p198.

49   See, for example, J M van Brabant, *Socialist Economic Integration* (Cambridge, 1980), ch 1 passim.

50   D Aldcroft, op cit, p197.

51   For an analysis of some of the components of this process see M Haynes, 'The European Union and Its Periphery: Inclusion and Exclusion', *Economic and Political Weekly*, vol 33, no 35 (1998), ppPE87-PE97.

52   M Glenny, 'Yugoslavia: The Revengers Tragedy', *New York Review of Books*, 13 August 1992, p38—even more ironically for Serbia two thirds of these industries were located in the Moslem and Croat areas of Bosnia-Hercegovina.

53   D Stola, 'Forced Migrations in Central European History', *International Migration Review*, vol xxxi no 2 (1992), pp324-341. It should be stressed also that this pattern is quite independent of the normal migration pattern.

54   R Fisk in *The Independent*, 26 April 1999.

55   The refusal to allow larger numbers of refugees to leave the area is clearly not explained by the reluctance to 'play Milosevic's game' so much as Western governments bowing to racist immigration agendas. There is also a fear that not only might the refugees not return from Western Europe but once there they might use it as a base for opposition to any settlement that failed to meet their hopes. As one Italian critic has put it, what governments fear is that 'Kosovo's "refugee bomb" can explode twice: creating within the European states the "Kurdisation" of the Albanians and a new disintegration within the Balkan countries' (A Ferrari in *Corriere della Serra*, 7 April 1999, quoted in *The Guardian*, 10 April, 1999). Details of the continuing plight of all refugees in the former Yugoslavia can be found on the UNHCR website.

56   'Defence spending levels below 3 percent of GDP are not adequate for Europe to play an important role in a system of collective defence', L Maria de Puil, 'European Security and Defence Identity Within NATO', *NATO Review* (Summer 1998), p8.

57   For an overview of the competing claims in the Balkans see H L Kostanick, 'The Geopolitics of the Balkans', in B and C Jelavich (eds), *The Balkans in Transition: Essays on the Development of Balkan Life and Politics Since the Eighteenth Century* (Berkeley, 1963). Kostanick's account includes details of some more minor territorial disputes that I have excluded from this table for the sake of brevity.

58   This table focuses on the Balkans defined as Greece, Yugoslavia, Albania, Bulgaria, Romania and the lands disputed by them. Lest readers fall into the trap of thinking that 'ethnic cleansing' is a peculiar Balkan disease we should remind them that in the Second World War forced Balkan migrations were perhaps only 10 percent or more of total forced migrations. All figures are approximate. Those followed by a ? are even less certain than the others. The fact that none of these figures is known with any accuracy is itself a reflection of the way that victims literally 'do not count'. They are what one historian calls the 'unwanted' of Europe in the 20th century. The table is drawn from D Stola, op cit; D Kirk, *Europe's Population in the Inter-War Years* (Geneva, 1946); E M Kulischer, *Europe on the Move. War and Population Changes, 1917-1947* (New York, 1948); M Marrus, *The Unwanted. European Refugees in the Twentieth Century* (Oxford, 1985); R P Magocsi, *Historical Atlas of East Central Europe* (Washington, 1993); UNHCR website.

Into slavery: the rise of imperialism

A review of Nicholas Canny (ed), **The Origins of Empire: The New Oxford History of the British Empire Volume I** *(Oxford University Press, 1998), £30*

ANGUS CALDER

At the start of the 20th century people in Britain were very proud of Queen Victoria's mighty empire, which was still expanding in Africa and would reach its furthest extent in the 1920s. Yet very few knew much about it. When public opinion polls got going towards the middle of the century, they disclosed that most electors found it hard to name colonies, let alone know where they were. The British retreat from the Indian subcontinent in 1947 was presented as a noble and generous renunciation—few realise even now that India had been on its way to home rule with dominion status in 1939 and only Churchill's stubbornness had prevented recognition of independence during the war, when India had voluntarily poured men and munitions into the fight against Hitler. The House of Commons had habitually emptied when Indian and other imperial questions had been discussed.

Empire had been taken for granted, except in those middle and upper class circles which had provided soldiers and administrators for the Raj and its equivalents elsewhere in the tropics, sent professionals and missionaries to far places, or imported and exported goods to the colonies. Shanghai and Argentina, not formally 'owned' or garrisoned by Britain, were hugely more important to the metropolitan economy than the vast tracts of Arctic North America and the far flung archipelagos of the Pacific which were painted or marked with red on the map. Attlee's postwar Labour administration was committed to self rule for imperial peoples, yet it presided over a spate of emigration which vastly increased white settler populations in British Africa and so provided the human basis for Ian Smith's Unilateral Declaration of Independence. The 'absence of mind' which the Victorian historian Seeley had seen as typical of Britain's acquisition of an empire persisted down to that moment in the 1960s when Harold Wilson's government presented the Indian Ocean island of Diego Garcia to the US as a base, wholly irre-spective of the wishes of its contented inhabitants, who were kicked out, and beyond that to the war launched in 1982 by Margaret Thatcher to defend the Falklands, which British administrations, Labour and Tory, had been trying to hand over to Argentina for many years.

The devoted geographers and historians who tried to interest univer-sity students and school children in the empire had support from jingoistic headmasters and the more bone-headed teachers of 'English literature', but knew that they faced an uphill struggle. We should be clear that the general tenor of British education, and public life, was imperialistic right through to the 1950s—Empire Day and the monarch's broadcasts to the empire, along with huge empire exhibitions, did make an impression on the public, and the Queen of Tonga's appearance at Elizabeth II's coronation was a popular stroke of pageantry in time hon-oured style. But bright university students of history would mostly be more interested in the medieval origins of parliament and 'English liberty', or in that splendid industrial revolution which the British had somehow, it was insinuated, engineered all by themselves, or in Wellington's peninsular campaigns, than in the awkward tale of empire which included quasi-genocidal activities in Ireland, slave colonies in the Caribbean, defeat in the war of American Independence, and not too savoury deployment of rapid fire guns against Africans. Even the extremely noble British Raj in India had unmistakably sordid origins, and the Amritsar Massacre of unarmed Pubjabi demonstrators in 1919 hardly supported the case of idealistic imperialists who believed that wise and benevolent British rule was leading the world towards peace and justice.

I have in my hand a school prize awarded to Duncan Stuart of Alloa Academy—'3rd in Mathematics, 3rd in Drawing'—in *1915: Deeds that Won the Empire*, by W H Fitchett, BA, LLD. Dr Fitchett's preface com-mences in the characteristically paranoid mode of embattled imperialist scholarship:

The tales here told are written, not to glorify war, but to nourish patriotism. They represent an effort to renew in popular memory the great traditions of the imperial race to which we belong. The history of the empire of which we are subjects—the story of the struggle and suffering by which it has been built up—is the best legacy which the past has bequeathed to us. But it is a treasure strangely neglected. The state makes primary education its anxious care, yet it does not make its own history a vital part of its education.

War, Dr Fitchett concedes, 'has a side of pure brutality. But it is not all brutal.' In this book young Duncan Stuart, who was quite likely soon conscripted for the horrors of the Western Front, would have found inspiring tales of battles on sea and land against Napoleon—no Indian heroics, no Caribbean derring-do, no mayhem in the Sudan—only, to represent all far continents, Wolfe's conquest of Canada from the French in 1763. In fact, the idea that Britain's world hegemony derived from the victory over France which was sealed in 1815, and which for a while gave the island a virtual monopoly of overseas colonies, could be sustained by solid scholarship. But Fitchett's book represented a typical evasion of the violent and controversial history of British intercontinental expansion, in favour of exploits against 'civilised' European adversaries, even though these happened just now to be Britain's gallant allies against the bestial Hun.

Britain's Story: a History for Seniors—Book 11: Britain, the Empire and the USA, published in 1949—20,000 copies in its first three impressions—represented the more relaxed view of empire after the Second World War, in which Britain's mighty dominions had fought alongside it, and the rhetoric of the Atlantic Charter had advertised a 'special relationship' with the US and promised freedom and human rights to all the earth's peoples. Through the empire, as H Bellis, LLA (Hist Hons), told 'boys and girls', ordinary folk like themselves had 'helped to make the world a better place to live in... Now it is up to you to continue the good work of these older folks and to put right the mistakes they made.' Such mistakes, apparently, included those of the 'wild, barbarous' Scots who in the 14th century rejected England's offer of 'wealth, culture and an ever-developing civilisation' and plunged themselves into desperate poverty and constant warfare, those mistakes of Elizabeth I and Cromwell which sowed 'seeds of enmity and hatred' in Ireland, and that of the 'officer in charge' whose issue of cartridges greased with pig's fat to Mohammedan sepoys precipitated, so the boys and girls learnt, the Indian Mutiny of 1857—though after its suppression 'much fine work' was done by Britain for the benefit of India's 'helpless millions'. This feeble textbook, full of elementary mistakes and outright howlers, represents the lowest depths of the historiography of the British Empire.

Its peaks half a century ago included the two volumes of J A Williamson's *Short History of British Expansion*, first published in 1922, and frequently revised thereafter. Williamson was a sturdy imperialist of the 'blue water' school who believed that the Royal Navy was the key to Britain's sublime greatness. He was, however, a sedulous and accurate scholar who may still be used safely for basic reference. His first volume covers the 'Old Colonial Empire' down to the breakaway of the US. This is the subject of the first volume of the *Cambridge History of the British Empire*, edited by Rose, Newton and Benians, which appeared in 1929, along with the fourth volume, on British India 1497-1858, and edited by the redoubtable H H Dodwell (volumes two and three took the general narrative down to 1919, and the remaining four dealt with India after 1858 and the white dominions).

These remained standard works after the historians who had produced them had gone to exchange opinions with Drake and the Elder Pitt in the great smoking room in the skies. The last and finest product of the imperialist school was V T Harlow's monumental *The Founding of the Second British Empire 1763-1793* (1952-1964) which the author left unfinished at his death.

By the 1960s almost all sensible politicians and academics were embarrassed by the British Empire. They preferred to talk and write about the Commonwealth of Nations. Chairs of imperial history, in the few places where they existed, were renamed accordingly. C A Carrington, a good enough scholar to write very well about Rudyard Kipling, contributed an evasive overview of 'Commonwealth' history, first published in 1950, archly entitled the *British Overseas: Exploits of a Nation of Shopkeepers*. It makes one yearn for the candid triumphalism of J A Williamson and, indeed, for the stern elegiac and epic tones of Kipling. Like Philip Woodruff's widely read apologia for the Raj, *The Men Who Ruled India*, and certain later sanitised overviews aimed at general readership (J A Bowle, Lawrence James), it present the Brits overseas as basically well meaning chaps, out to earn an honest bob or two and turn the natives into Christians with clean white shirts. Plantation slavery was a bad business, but then the Brits led the world in abolishing it— Wilberforce, not Clive, was the prime imperial hero. One was to suppose that Africans were better off under British DOs (carefully recruited by the Colonial Office on the criterion that thickos from feepaying schools who liked field sports were preferable to state school oiks with brains) than governed by degenerate Portuguese, snail eating Amphibians or brutish Germans. No matter that D K Fieldhouse in *The Colonial Empires: A Comparative Survey* (1966) showed that all European powers went about colonisation and administration in much the same way.

In the 1960s historical writing about the British Empire began to make some headway towards truth because its subject area was invaded by scholarship from other fields. The 13 colonies rose again into contestation. Americans had been as vague and selective about the early history of their own country as Brits had been about Francis Drake and All That. The revolution and still more the civil war dominated their sense of their past, if they had any, and neither of these particularly clawed at the heartstrings of recent immigrants from eastern and southern Europe. Hollywood recreated the 19th century in lavish productions, but even now the reconstruction of early colonial life in the fine film of Arthur Miller's *The Crucible* is startling because it is so exceptional. However, after the Second World War the immense array of American universities began to churn out vast numbers of monographs and surveys of 17th and 18th century colonial history, led by such mighty scholars as Perry Miller and Bernard Bailyn. These often developed quasi-Marxist class analyses and this in turn was 'colonised' from the 1960s by new concerns with race and gender.

'The old colonial empire' is still inspected by relatively few students. The more thoughtless devotees of Edward Said's *Orientalism* and the prattling theorists of post-colonialism are satisfied with a lego model of imperialism which travesties its complicated origins. But the first volume of the *New Oxford History of the British Empire*, designed to supersede the Cambridge history at last, can draw on half a century of scholarship which has produced a sophisticated consensus, steady now for 20 years or more, about early British expansion and its place in the early modern history of the north west European archipelago, and in world history.

To itemise the scholarly thrusts which produced this new consensus... The West began to pay serious attention to the history of East Asia— China and Japan. The massive Cambridge survey of science and civilisation in China directed by Joseph Needham from the late 1940s onwards established that the East was technologically ahead of Europe down to and after the pioneering voyages of the Portuguese. Nevertheless, modern capitalism, imperialism and 'world history' had to be explained by developments in Europe. Historians of naval and military technology were activated to examine European innovations in cannon fire and tactics. The study of the origins of capitalism in late medieval and early modern European history, already provoked by the theories of Marx and Weber and given impetus by famous studies by Tawney, bore its richest fruit in Fernand Bradley's massive labours after the Second World War, which employed the perspectives of the French *Annales* school. Certain British historians, notably C R Boxer, J H Elliott and J H Parry, looked exhaustively in to the overseas 'expansion' of Britain's Portuguese, Spanish and Dutch competitors. Early modern English overseas trade was anatomised by Ralph Davis, whose statistics still seem to be standard. The Communist Party Historians' Group in Britain after the Second World War supported Christopher Hill in his seminal reinterpretation of the English Revolution of the 17th century. Hill was neither curious nor particularly well informed about the details of colonial history but his acclaim for Cromwell's successful naval forays against Holland and Spain in the 1650s aligned him, quaintly, with 'blue water' J A Williamson. His rather mechanical Marxist overview was that the English Revolution, and the aggressive 'mercantilist' imperialism which accompanied and followed it, were indispensable to the development of capitalism, and therefore splendidly progressive. More usefully, he explored with erudite subtlety the complex relationships between Puritanism in religion, the scientific revolution of Bacon and Galileo, the imaginative writing of Shakespeare and Milton, the political theory of Hobbes and Locke, and the ultimate triumphs of toleration, commerce, industry and Whiggery.

Meanwhile, Indian history was revitalised by scholars from the subcontinent itself, of whom K N Chaudhuri has been particularly influential. It is now abundantly clear that the Europeans were far from dominating Eastern trade after the Dutch and then the English had followed the Portuguese to the Indian Ocean and China Seas. In fact, the Europeans became, till the mid-18th century, merely a minor, often piratical, component in a vast and thriving system of commerce. The serious study of the African past began, with black scholars to the fore, as the continent was officially 'decolonised' from the 1950s. In the understanding of the slave trade, though, the most potent, indeed revolutionary, contribution came from the West Indies via the US, where Eric Williams, who later became prime minister of Trinidad, published his *Capitalism and Slavery* in 1944. Williams's argument was that the profits of slave trading and sugar were the basis of the Industrial Revolution in Britain, and that Wilberforce had his pious way only because the bloated man-owning planters of the Caribbean, for a long time dominant in British politics, were outweighed by the new economic importance of manufacture by steam. This point was particularly disliked by the new Commonwealth-minded apologists for empire, since it deflated the notion that British imperialism was especially virtuous. Williams did not give full acknowledgement to CLR James, once his teacher at Queen's Royal College, Port of Spain, whose Marxist *The Black Jacobins* (1937), was a history of the Haitian Revolution and contained the essence of what became known as the Williams Thesis. And the trenchancy of his argument was undermined by the crudeness of his methodology, so that for several decades his challenge could be shrugged off. But, as refined by subtler economic historians, the Williams Thesis has become central to our understanding of British and world history.

The consensus expressed, overtly or tacitly, by contributors to the *New Oxford History* may now be summarised. For reasons which would repay further study, a mighty outward thrust of trade and exploration by the Chinese Ming Empire, which might have made 'world history' utterly different had it been sustained, faltered coincidentally with the little probes made by Portuguese voyagers to the Atlantic Islands, around the African coast, then as far as India, in the 15th century. The conquest of Christian Constantinople by the Ottoman Turks in 1453 gave ideological urgency to the aim of replacing trade in exotic products via Muslim intermediaries with direct access to their Eastern sources. Columbus, sailing for the Spanish monarchs, aimed to establish a direct trade route westwards to China, but found the New World instead. While the rich cod fisheries of Newfoundland lured many little ships from Europe, Spanish Conquistadors prevailed in land rich in gold and silver. The bullion which returned to Europe gave traders there for the first time a cargo attractive to Eastern providers of spices and silks, who despised the woollens and other clumsy trade goods which were all that Vasco de Gama and those who followed him had to offer. Since New World 'Indians' died like midges in autumn from commonplace European diseases, and those who survived were largely averse to coercive field labour, the importation of Africans to the New World as slaves began, and the Portuguese began to profit from slave cultivated sugar plantations in Brazil. The French crown took an interest in the New World, and Canada was eventually colonised from France.

Enter the Protestants Northerners. The triumph of Protestantism in parts of Europe was associated with the creation of 'modern' nation states—'empires' as they were then called. (Down to the mid-19th century the term 'British Empire' applied primarily to the British Isles.) Thus Scottish kings 'colonised' successfully in the Norse Northern Isles and unsuccessfully in Lewis, while England's Tudor monarchs sorted their deviant Welsh compatriots out and strove by persuasion and sword to make good their claim to the whole of Ireland. This effort was as much as Elizabeth I's hard up crown could stand, especially as it was accompanied by heavy military support for the Dutch in their revolt against Philip of Spain, during which canny skippers from the Netherlands began to intrude everywhere in world trade. The accounts of far Tudor voyages collected by Richard Hakluyt, which eventually mesmerised imperialist historians, who grossly exaggerated their significance, represented little more than abortive searches for north east and north west passages to China and piratical incursions into the Spanish sphere in Central and South America. Official war with Spain towards the end of Elizabeth I's reign at least permitted some English ship owners to make large profits out of privateering (legalised piracy), and these, aggregated in the City of London, helped to sustain the East India Company born with the new century. Meanwhile, the conquest of Ireland and the exploitation of its resources by 'plantation' provided precedents for colonisation in the New World.

James VI and I, unlike his royal predecessor, was very interested in colonisation. His fellow Scots were lured in disproportionate numbers into the newly conquered province of Ulster. He took over the struggling colony of Virginia, the first English settlement in the New World to survive, and his son Charles I rather absent mindedly permitted Puritan politico-religious dissidents with influential backing to set up the godly colony of Massachussetts and a base for slaving and piracy on Providence Island off Central America. The latter disappeared so thoroughly in the turmoil of the civil war years that most historians of empires have forgotten about its brief and sordid existence, though it was a major focus of interest and activity for the parliamentary opposition to Charles I. Massachusetts survived and generated further colonies in New England where communities of farmers and fishermen, neither rich nor poor, survived by building ships with the abundant local timber and using them to sell cod to Europeans and farm produce to the West Indies.

South of New England, colonies survived only through the cultivation of 'staple' crops. The squabbling Virginian pioneers round Chesapeake Bay found that the vast Old World market for tobacco was enough to keep their settlements solvent. A unique society without towns developed, where planters expanded the cultivation of the weed into land cleared of Indians and sold their produce direct on their own waterfronts to English merchants. Tobacco was everything, functioned as a currency, and provided the wherewithal to buy increasing numbers of black slaves. Chancers who settled various Caribbean islands moved from tobacco to sugar, with the help of Dutch merchants after the Dutch had temporarily conquered Brazil and seen how the Portuguese cultivated that lush and sinister crop. Cane sugar, formerly a luxury, had, like tobacco, a market which seemed almost infinitely elastic. White 'servants' under indentures proved insufficient in health, supply and tractability and by the end of the 17th century the British Caribbean Islands were petty but prodigiously profitable arenas where Englishmen, Welshmen and Irishmen with strong constitutions, doughty livers and flexible moral standards could make vast fortunes from driving black slaves to early death and replacing them from the ships which flocked in with human cargoes from Guinea.

Superimposing the geopolitics of late Victorian empire on the 17th century pattern of English trade led the imperialist historians to gross imbalance. Even before the final abolition of slavery throughout the British Empire in 1838, the West Indian sugar islands were becoming inefficient economic backwaters. The North American colonies, in contrast, had been the germ of a second English speaking empire and clever imperialists explored the vision of a world under joint Anglo-Saxon domination, as when Kipling implored the Yankees to 'take up the white man's burden'. Thus, imperialist historians devoted considerable atten-

tion to the rumbustious daredevil Drake and the pious, genuinely virtuous Pilgrim Fathers, who had established Plymouth Colony in New
England as a religious haven without consideration of profit. On the
other hand the energetic traders of Bristol and Liverpool who risked their
lives on the unhealthy middle passage and made Britain in the 18th
century by some distance the pre-eminent slaving power received less
attention, as did the North Americans who traded salt meat and fish in
the West Indies for rum which they used to fuddle and debauch simple
white fisherfolk and the Native Americans who traded furs with them.
The same was true of the Glasgow tobacco merchants who ventured
beyond the Chesapeake waterfront to new tobacco plantations up
country and by the mid-18th century gave their city a virtual monopoly
in that much prized commodity Virginia tobacco.

The crucial point which Eric Williams spotted is that gross statistics
of industrial production and commerce did not account for the primacy
of Britain in 'Industrial Revolution'. Newcastle coal proved very handy
when that revolution came along, but Britain's copious coal deposits
would not in themselves have generated modern industrial capitalism. At
the end of the 17th century, as at the beginning, woollens were still
England's chief export commodity, as they had been for centuries—so
what? The crucial conjuncture was the proximity of Liverpool and
Glasgow to centres where cotton goods could be produced. The central
event in the 'revolution' was the application of steam power to cotton. A
riot of technological innovations meanwhile applied ideas which would
not have surprised the ingenious Chinese to all manner of industries. The
development of Wedgwood's potteries and the burgeoning of Sheffield
plate cannot be very directly related to sugar production in Jamaica or
the British conquest of Bengal. But they did react to the growth of a relatively vast new middle class market generated by the prosperity brought
by intercontinental trade and its spin offs into banking, brewing, agricultural improvement, and even book publishing. 'Calico' and 'tea' are the
world which sum all this up.

Elizabeth I's court knew little of cotton. The very expensive alternative to heavy, smelly woollens was bug excreted silk. The arrival of
calicoes from the East, where Indian workmen who were at least as prosperous as their counterparts in the English textile manufactures produced
them most attractively and efficiently, preluded the liberation of affluent
folk from sweaty wool. Cotton could not be grown in Britain, but it
could be imported from the New World. The colonial empire therefore
provided the raw material for mass production for another very elastic
market. The slowish but ultimately explosive rise of Manchester and
West of Scotland cotton manufacture marked the sudden reversal of the
age old East-West imbalance. Manchester textiles invaded markets

everywhere in the world, including India. Opium grown in India for the
British was the means for aggressive penetration at last of the mighty
Chinese market.

Imperialist historians were, of course, clear that British involvement
in India had been of paramount importance. What could they make of its
early history? Small English trading settlements at Surat (later usurped
by Bombay), in Madras, and finally in Calcutta, had dealt in Indian
cottons and eastern spices to the great profit of investors back home, but
with negligible effect on the overall pattern of Asian trade. An Indian
gravestone reads, 'The Dutch and the English, they were here/They
drank toddy instead of beer.' Survivors of gross feasting, unwise compu-
tations and violent tropical diseases could make excellent profits by
fitting out ships for the local trade, manned by local sailors. 'Necessity
was the mother of invention and the father of the Eurasian.' Haughty
racial exclusiveness came much later, deep in the high minded evangel-
ical 19th century. When the East India Company presumptuously
declared war on the Mughal Empire late in the 17th, the result was a
mouse-that-roared debacle. As in Africa, where European forts on the
Guinea Coast existed by sufferance of native rulers, the Brits in India
usually tried to keep out of trouble. Tea was an increasingly valuable
commodity, not least prized by those smugglers whose activities in 18th
century Britain corresponded in extent and collateral violence to those of
late 20th drug dealers. Like sugar and cotton cloth it gravitated down-
wards inexorably from luxury to mass market. Brits, like other
Europeans, acquired it in the one port, Canton, which the Chinese
emperors opened to the trade. Of no great consequence to the Sons of
Heaven, this leaf, too, helped create world history.

Your Williamsons and Dodwells, reading away, cheered up when the
arrogant Amphibians began to intervene in the politics of India as the
Mughal emperors lost their grip. The series of wars against France from
the 1690s through to 1815 became a contest for world hegemony, and
gave a context, as Linda Colley has brilliantly shown, to the development among English, Welsh, Scots and many Irish, of a composite and
bellicose common 'British' identity—Protestant, libertarian and deeply
averse to the eating of garlic and snails, let alone poncy French gallantry
and sexual licence. As the East India Company responded to French
aggression in India, that remarkable man Robert Clive was positioned to
win the victory over the Nawab of Bengal at Plassey in 1757 which preluded British conquest of the subcontinent. Imperialist historians felt
able to justify the cynical plundering of Bengal which followed,
reducing India's richest area to the poverty which prevails to this day, by
working up the long forgotten incident of the Black Hole of Calcutta.
The East India Company had defied the Nawab. He had, quite within his

rights, conquered their fort. Like every British garrison from Inverness to Jamaica, it had a 'Black Hole' in which disorderly soldiers were deposited to rue their mischievous deeds. The Nawab quite sensibly commanded that the vanquished Brits should be put into their own prison. It was a hot night, some were wounded, water was in short supply, and numbers died—though nothing anywhere near the number later alleged. So Plassey was a valid 'revenge' for fiendish Asiatic cruelty. And it followed that the barbaric ferocity with which the British suppressed the Sepoy mutiny of 1857 was justified by the intrinsic viciousness of Indian natives who would rape every white woman in sight if they weren't kept severely in their place.

Gender studies have not made much impact yet on imperial historiography, except in the crazier reaches of 'theory'. The study of family history and intricate demography since the Second World War confirms unsurprisingly that colonial societies in North America were resolutely patriarchal, though wives and widows of farmers and traders often had independent influence. One remarkable Puritan, Anne Hutchinson, who was expelled from Massachussetts for openly preaching heterodox Calvinist doctrines, and helped found the deviant, because tolerant, new colony of Rhode Island, is an exception proving the rule that the chief role of women in early English speaking America was to assist in remarkably rapid population growth made possible by the basic prosperity of the fertile frontier, where land and firewood were abundant. Conversely, in slave communities, where men were overworked and susceptible to raw rum and early death, the minority of black women probably played a disproportionate part in the upbringing of children and the preservation of African traditions.

The main point to make about the *New Oxford History*'s first volume is that, while it represents solid recent consensus (albeit, one getting stale and in need of fresh challenge) and so makes sense for readers of the New Millennium that Old Cambridge can provide, it is not organised so as to do justice to all major areas of interest, and it culpably perpetuates old imperialist neglect of plantation slavery. The series editor Wm Roger Louis is a Texan best known for his studies of Anglo-American rivalry in the 20th century. We must be grateful to the volume editor, Nicholas Canny, for his revelatory work two decades ago on 17th century Ireland. Between them they have employed the veteran Richard S Dunn to write, not about the Caribbean, where he has published brilliant work on sugar and slaves, but on the reorganisation of the North American colonies under James II and William III, a topic which he covered admirably three and a half decades ago. The African slave trade gets no more space than it did in the old *Cambridge History*. Unbelievably, the rackety era of the

Buccaneers in Jamaica gets no mention at all, and that remarkable rogue Sir Henry Morgan does not appear in the index. But then, after all, he was Welsh. Though Professor Canny pays editorial tribute to the current, post-Colley, fashion for integrating the histories of the Celtic nations with those of England, and Ireland gets what is probably its full due, attention to Scotland is very patchy (much about settlement in Ulster and the interesting Quaker venture which created in East New Jersey what for a while was a distinctively Scottish colony, but little about the internal relations of the administrative centre with the Scottish Gaeltacht), and Wales receives only scant mention.

The Old Cambridge imperialists planned their first volume carefully to avoid overlap and to achieve what to them seemed to be the right proportions. New Oxford, in contrast, seems to have been slung together far too fast, and I am afraid that black scholars in particular will find its disemphases offensive. Why do we get two separate stabs at the topic of European reactions to North American 'Indians' and nothing on the 'images of Africa' so potently opened up for discussion by Basil Davidson and Philip Curtin four decades ago? Why do the trivial slaving voyages of John Hawkins, once so overrated by imperialist historians who worshipped Sea Dogs, still receive attention denied to the origins of the runaway Maroon communities of Jamaica and other islands, which had long term political and cultural consequences? Why do the ineffably petty 'politics' of the unimportant colony of North Carolina get space which could have been devoted to further discussion of the epochal 'sugar revolution' on Barbados in the 1640s? Why, in contrast, is discussion of South Carolina, which soon came to depend heavily on slave labour, allowed to continue deep into the 18th century, where the rest of the volume provides no context for it?

There is a lot of good writing here, some of it by scholars relatively fresh in the field, some by well established experts like N A M Rodger, who contributes a very valuable chapter on the technology of guns and sail. But readers without a good deal of prior knowledge will be baffled, as so often these days, by our modern, or postmodern, distaste for straightforward basic narrative. The English 'Civil War', otherwise 'Revolution', otherwise 'War of Three Nations', preceded by and involving complex struggles in Scotland and Ireland, has to be straightened out as far as possible in chronological sequence before much of the detail here can make sense at all. Out of the civil war and interregnum emerged an English polity armed with Navigation Acts which sought to maximise profit to the state and to English manufacturers and merchants from overseas trade, a serious Royal Navy ready to take on the Dutch and all comers, a metropolitan financial upsurge in London which poised that city to overtake Amsterdam as the commercial hub of Europe, the

conquest from the Dutch of New York, the growth of the slave trade out
of English ports, the systematic colonisation of rich farmland in
Pennsylvania, the opening up of Jamaica and South Carolina, the rudi-
ments of a system of centralised control of the empire, and the makings
of industrial revolution.

Yet this rush of development seminal for world history up to and
including our current globalisation and pregnant with the rise to hegemony of the yet unimagined US is nowhere discussed in terms of the
economic and ideological overview validly suggested by Christopher
Hill, or the broader perspectives provided by Braudel. Sometimes this
volume welters in minutiae and suffers from the tendency of US historians to descry Manifest Destiny and the mighty future in the early
proceedings of tiny townlets—thus Philadelphia is described as a 'city'
at a point when its total population matched that of present day Ullapool.
Around its multiplicity of trees, New Oxford does not clearly map the
wood. There are four further volumes following this. One, bizarrely, will
be devoted to historiography. As I have tried to demonstrate, to separate
historiography as a discrete topic from the revision of imperial history is,
at this moment, impossible. Understanding by serious historians themselves has advanced far beyond the twaddle still accepted by 'general
readers' and producers of TV documentaries. Indifference to what may
be said to have really happened because of the British fighting, slaving
and trading overseas is still almost universal. New history has to explain
old nonsense and stake out clearly the reasons, provided by new perspectives, why chauvinist, racist, patriarchal and anglocentric fables
should be rejected. New narrative—retelling the story, in order—is
another indispensable requirement.

THE BALKANS, NATIONALISM & IMPERIALISM

EDITED BY LINDSEY GERMAN

This new book from Bookmarks Publications contains more than 20 articles covering the development of the Balkan tragedy from the 1980s onwards.

It examines the political economy of Yugoslavia before its disintegration, the economic collapse which provided the background to the rise of rival nationalist leaders like Franjo Tudjman in Croatia and Slobodan Milosevic in Serbia, and details the unfolding of the bloody conflict between Serbia and Croatia which later engulfed Bosnia.

It shows that there was significant opposition from the earliest days, in terms of both strikes and demonstrations, to the leaders who plunged the Balkans into war.

And it examines the role of Western governments, whose intervention in the Balkans throughout the last ten years and more has in some cases precipitated and always added to the conflict. It ends with an analysis of the war in Kosovo. This is a major contribution to an understanding of the Balkan tragedy and the attitude and approach socialists must adopt.

CONTRIBUTORS INCLUDE: Alex Callinicos, Chris Harman, Mike Haynes, Lindsey German and many others.

Bookmarks publication £6.50 + £1 p&p, available from Bookmarks, 1 Bloomsbury Street, London WC1B 3QE. Phone 0171 637 1848, fax 0171 637 3616 email bookmarks_bookshop@compuserve.com

The physiology of barbarism

A review of Donny Gluckstein, **The Nazis, Capitalism and the Working Class** *(Bookmarks, 1999), £9.99*

JIM WOLFREYS

Few historical events have been subject to the same degree of controversy, confusion and mystification as the Nazi rise to power and the
tragedy which unfolded in its wake. Attempts to understand the phenomenon have focused on a variety of explanations, some stressing the
psychology of individual Nazis, others, such as Daniel Goldhagen's
Hitler's Willing Executioners, arguing that the German population shared
Hitler's pathological race hatred and that this mass psychosis made the
Holocaust possible. Various studies have stressed the exceptional nature
of the Nazi regime, and many have therefore tended to minimise the
potential for such atrocities to happen again. Recent trends have seen
earlier social explanations of Nazism challenged by studies which claim
that the Third Reich was above all else a racial hierarchy.[1] Another
increasingly widespread view holds that the Nazi state pursued a programme not of reaction but of modernisation or revolution. Donny
Gluckstein offers a powerful counter to such arguments, and in the
process reaffirms the Marxist analysis of fascism with a clarity and an
authority that make *The Nazis, Capitalism and the Working Class* essential reading.

The book begins with an outline of the development of modern
Germany and takes up the argument that the conditions which gave rise
to the Nazi regime are somehow linked to a unique path of historical
development whereby the 'normal' process of capitalist development
was bypassed, producing an exceptional semi-feudal state. The opening

chapter succinctly describes the specific features of German capitalism
and their consequences for the classes in that society. In most advanced
industrial nations capitalism had emerged with national unification and
the establishment of bourgeois democracy. In Germany national unification was brought about by the Kaiser without any real democracy. This
did not mean that capitalism failed to develop in Germany—in fact it did
so at a great rate. But Germany's status as a 'follower' nation, industrial-
ising after Britain, meant that it emerged with certain distinctive features,
notably a greater concentration of capital in certain sectors, since it
started out with larger production units, greater collaboration between
capital and the state and, as a latecomer to the battle for international
markets, a more prominent role for the state. At the same time, a mass of
smaller, artisanal units continued to prosper, ensuring the survival of a
large middle class.

The development of Nazism was to be shaped by all these factors, but
above all else it was a product of the imperialist stage of capitalism. The
concentration and centralisation of production, the increasing importance
of banks as investors of finance capital, and the intensification of competition in an expanding world market led to a greater role for the state as an
actor in defending and promoting economic interests both domestically
and abroad. The fusion of state and capital under Nazism was therefore
characteristic of an era dominated by finance capital which 'makes the
dictatorship of the capitalist lords of one country increasingly incompat-
ible with the capitalist interests of other countries, and the internal
domination of capital increasingly irreconcilable with the interests of the
masses'.[2] In order to resolve these conflicts Germany's ruling elite turned
to Hitler in much the same way as the French bourgeoisie had turned to
Bonapartism in 1851, giving up its crown 'in order to save its purse'.
Except that, given Germany's status as an advanced industrialised nation,
the Nazis were forced to mobilise the petty bourgeoisie to secure power,
using it as a 'battering ram' against working class opposition.[3]

Rather than transforming existing social relations, Nazism reinforced
them 'by the most brutal and systematic methods imaginable—counter-
revolution at home and, later, world war abroad'.[4] Hitler, then, 'did not
fall from the sky or come up out of hell: he is nothing but the personifica-
tion of all the destructive forces of imperialism'.[5] In the sense that Nazism
reflected the tendency, identified by Marx, for the relations of production
to be constantly revolutionised under capitalism, it may be considered
'modern', but, as the author argues, a regime which bolsters a system that
has 'outlived its usefulness' is not engaged in modernisation.[6]

The origins of Nazism are firmly rooted in the counter-revolutionary
current which developed in Germany after the First World War as a reaction to the revolutionary surge of 1918-1923. During this period Hitler

established himself as a force to be reckoned with and sealed links with industrialists prepared to consider radical means to block the left, like the steel magnate Thyssen, who stated, 'Democracy with us represents nothing'.[7] But although the capitalist class had an interest in promoting Hitler as a means of eliminating obstacles to its domination both at home and abroad, funding of the Nazi Party (NSDAP) did not guarantee complete control over them: 'Connections existed between capitalism and the NSDAP; but this does not mean the Nazis were either robots programmed by the bosses, or free agents making up their own minds and acting as they pleased'.[8] Having failed to win ruling class backing for an armed uprising in 1923, Hitler realised that mass support was necessary to make fascism a serious alternative to democratic forces. The creation of a mass party of a million members with a 400,000 strong armed wing gave the Nazis a degree of autonomy, but their capacity for brutality had to be balanced against the need to keep elite supporters on board by not upsetting ruling class sensibilities.

When the Nazis came to power in 1933 they did so not as the result of a popular uprising, or even an electoral majority, but because they had the backing of a section of the ruling class. How, then, the author asks, did a party acting in the interests of this tiny elite achieve such widespread support among ordinary Germans? The analysis of this question, presented in chapters on the 'Nazi machine' and the Holocaust, is one of the book's great strengths. Central to the explanation developed here is an understanding of the way in which capitalism's capacity to mask the exploitation at its core is refracted through the prism of class:

> *The daily experience of life under capitalism mediates the impact of capitalist ideology. It can reinforce it, contradict it, or still have more complex results, partially reinforcing some points of the ideology and negating others. The general pattern is that with capitalists their life experience serves to reinforce belief in the system; the life experience of workers tends to clash with the received ways of thinking and cause it to be questioned either partially or totally. The middle class has a life experience which leaves it vacillating between both these poles.*[9]

Nazi ideology was less likely to exert an influence over workers living in large towns—whose livelihood was threatened by unemployment and whose experience of work was characterised by a sense of collective solidarity—than over those working in craft or service sectors, less affected by unemployment, or those living in isolated rural communities. Similarly, in terms of middle class support, those whose livelihoods were threatened by the loss of savings—the old middle class 'rentiers'—or whose careers were bound up with the survival of the capitalist state—the civil service bureaucrats—were more likely to identify with Nazism than white collar employees, who remained potential allies of the industrial working class. What determined both electoral support for the Nazis and membership of the party itself were the social relations of capitalism. The more isolated the individual, the more bound up their lives and careers were with the preservation of the status quo, the less resistant they were likely to be to fascism: 'What counts in resisting Nazism are the chances of collective organisation and consciousness, and freedom from the direct influence (and intimidation) of the employer'.[10]

This is not to say that workers were immune to the pull of Nazism, or that no workers joined Hitler's party, but in general it was anxiety about the effects of the crisis which drove people into his arms, rather than rejection of the capitalist system, or even direct experience of unemployment. At the core of the mass movement built by the Nazis was the frustrated petty bourgeoisie which, faced with the disintegration of society and fearful of the prospect of revolution, sought to break free from the domination of the monopolies and cartels. Fusing at the lower end of the social scale with the working class, and with the capitalist bourgeoisie at the other, it is 'no wonder', wrote Trotsky, 'that ideologically it scintillates with all the colours of the rainbow'.[11]

Fascism's capacity to combine counter-revolutionary aims with a mass movement was both its strength and its weakness, a factor identified very early on by Clara Zetkin:

> *We should not regard fascism as a homogenous entity, as a granite block from which all our exertions will simply rebound. Fascism is a disparate formation, comprising various contradictory elements, and hence liable to internal dissolution and disintegration… however tough an image fascism presents, it is in fact the result of the decay and disintegration of the capitalist economy and a symptom of the dissolution of the bourgeois state.*[12]

Although the 'sheer weight of forces at its disposal'[13] would permit a fascist regime to survive for some time, as a movement it was nevertheless vulnerable when confronted, and sections of its support could even be won to a different political project. In the absence of a credible revolutionary socialist alternative, however, the 'countless human beings whom finance capital has brought to desperation and frenzy'[14] were pulled by fascism into a movement in which everything was 'as contradictory and chaotic as in a nightmare'.[15]

Was fascism a middle class movement? Nazi propaganda before 1933 was full of promises to its middle class followers: '100,000 independent cobblers', declared Gottfried Feder, 'are worth more to the economy of the people and the state than five giant shoe factories'.[16] Despite such rhetoric, Nazi rule offered very little to the middle classes. Indeed, once the labour movement had been defeated, ruling class power was immeasurably reinforced, at the expense of all other classes.[17]

If the regime can be seen to have retained the basic features of capitalism in an extreme form, rather than representing a break with it, how can the importance of anti-Semitism to the Nazi project be explained? A common view holds that the Nazis attempted a racial revolution and that their supporters were motivated above all else by pathological anti-Semitism. Here, again, the book underlines the importance of class distinctions. As far as ordinary Germans were concerned, racist attitudes derived from the anxieties and frustrations of everyday existence and provided scapegoats for their various grievances. In contrast, ruling class racism is a means of shoring up existing social relations and forms part of a hierarchical conception of society whereby notions of superiority and inferiority are bolstered by, among other things, the use of racism to legitimise the targeting of certain groups and, by extension, the treatment meted out to all 'inferior' elements in the hierarchy.[18] The reification of existence under capitalism, which turns human beings into objects to be bought and sold, found its most grotesque expression in the Holocaust, when assembly line techniques and a modern transport network were used to commit mass murder, leaving what remained—teeth, human hair, etc—to be treated as industrial 'byproducts'. The distinction between ruling class and popular racism is an important one, not least because it undermines Goldhagen's claim that the Holocaust was a product of a collective German mentality. The shock and repulsion felt by ordinary Germans at Nazi led pogroms such as Kristallnacht (night of broken glass) in 1938, and the revulsion felt even by rank and file Nazis at the euthanasia programme targeted at 'lives not worth living', are evidence of this distinction.[19]

But if ordinary Germans did not share the same outlook as the Nazi leadership, why did so many participate in its crimes? Again, the horrors perpetrated under Nazi rule are best understood not as a reflection of some kind of primordial evil but in relation to the constraints which capitalism imposes on human activity. The dehumanising bureaucratisation of life under capitalism, which strives to subordinate individuals to an external authority, and to control behaviour patterns by imposing deference to a hierarchical social structure, was reinforced and accentuated under Nazism which, by treating genocide as an everyday productive task (to the extent that railway regulations set out a system of fares for those transported to the death camps), imbued it with an illusory normality which helps explain why so many participated in it.[20] Likewise, when leading Nazis boasted of their intention to destroy the individual's private sphere (Robert Ley declared in 1938 that the private citizen had ceased to exist and that hitherto only sleep would remain an intimate affair), such ideas were an extension, rather than a negation, of monopoly capitalism, itself typified by 'the feeling of individual insignificance and powerlessness'[21] as personal autonomy is suppressed by the imperatives of production and the domination of the market.[22]

None of this would have been carried out, however, were it not for the smashing of resistance. This needs to be stressed, because it is an aspect of the Nazi rise to power neglected by writers like Goldhagen who choose to ignore opposition to the Nazis before 1933.[23] In the early 1920s Hitler's attempts to seize power came to nothing. By 1928 electoral support for the Nazis stood at only 2.8 percent. As the crisis deepened and the Weimar Republic became increasingly discredited, society polarised and support for the Nazis grew. Why did the left, the most powerful and organised in Western Europe, fail to eliminate their threat? 'We have been defeated,' wrote the Austrian Marxist Otto Bauer after the fascists took power, 'and each of us is turning over in his mind the question whether we brought the bloody disaster on ourselves by our own political mistakes'.[24]

The tragedy of German social democracy's attitude to fascism was that it repeated the errors made by Italian social democracy a decade earlier in pinning its hopes on legality and the constitution: 'Stay at home: do not respond to provocations,' union leader Matteotti urged Italian workers attacked by fascists, 'Even silence, even cowardice, are sometimes heroic'.[25] The German socialist Hilferding proclaimed 'the downfall of fascism' in January 1933, the month Hitler became chancellor, arguing that 'legality will be his undoing'.[26] This loyalty to the institutions of the German state had led the Social Democratic Party (the SPD) to use violence against Communist opposition and even its own members, sending in the Freikorps to crush the Spartakist revolt in 1919, murdering Karl Liebknecht and Rosa Luxemburg, granting emergency powers to General Seekt to smash the left wing provincial government in Saxony and shooting down 30 Communists taking part in the banned May Day parade of 1929. Instead of attempting to win rank and file socialists to the fight against fascism, the Communist Party simply issued sectarian declarations against the SPD, denouncing it as fascism's 'twin' and calling for a 'united front...against the Hitler party and the Social Democratic leadership' which, as Trotsky pointed out, amounted to nothing more than 'a united front with itself'[27]. Having failed to stop the Nazis before they took control of the state, the left was immediately targeted and crushed by the regime. No amount of heroic resistance, well documented here in a chapter on defiance against Nazi rule, could prevent the imposition of the Nazis' sick 'moral norms' once the labour movement had been wiped out.

In the 1930s Trotsky highlighted the way in which barbaric aspects of medieval society survived alongside the technological advances of modernity. People all over the world could listen to radio and hear the pope talk about water being transformed into wine. Pilots flew the most advanced aircraft that science could produce but wore lucky charms to protect themselves from danger. Fascism drew on this kind of superstition and backwardness. When the Nazis came to power, he described how fascism had 'opened up the depths of society for politics':

Everything that should have been eliminated from the national organism in the form of cultural excrement in the course of the normal development of society has now come gushing out from the throat; capitalist society is puking up the undigested barbarism. Such is the physiology of National Socialism.[28]

Today such contradictions between society's modernity and the persistence of backwardness and superstition are even more marked. Before playing his part in one of the century's most dazzling feats of technology by walking on the moon, the US astronaut Buzz Aldrin sat in his spacecraft and took holy communion; during the 1980s Reagan and Mitterrand, the leaders of two of the world's most advanced industrialised nations, both felt the need to employ the services of astrologers; in the 1990s religious sects announce their suicide pacts over the internet.

In a year when New Labour ministers have used the rhetoric of antifascism to justify the imposition of NATO power in the Balkans, and compared those who oppose their warmongering to appeasers of Hitler, this book is a timely reminder of what fascism is and what it is not. Donny Gluckstein has provided us with an outstanding analysis of the Nazi phenomenon. In its discussion of the Nazi leadership and its anti-Semitism, its analysis of the relationship between the Nazi regime, capitalism and the ruling class, and in its assessment of the aims and actions of both supporters and opponents of Nazism, this book's sensitivity to the interplay between the motivations of individuals and the broader historical and social context sets it out as a model for a dialectical understanding of fascism.

Notes

1   M Burleigh and W Wippermann, *The Racial State: Germany 1933-1945* (Cambridge, 1991).
2   R Hilferding, *Finance Capital*, cited in D Gluckstein, *The Nazis, Capitalism and the Working Class* (London, 1999), p8.
3   In 1931 Trotsky warned that 'considering the far greater maturity and acuteness of the social contradictions in Germany, the hellish work of Italian fascism would probably appear as a pale and almost humane experiment in comparison with the work of the German National Socialists'. See 'Germany, the Key to the

International Situation', in L Trotsky, *The Struggle Against Fascism in Germany* (New York, 1971), p125.

4   D Gluckstein, op cit, p128.
5   L Trotsky, cited ibid, p182.
6   Ibid, pp190-191.
7   F Thyssen, cited in D Guerin, *Fascism and Big Business* (New York, 1973), p35.
8   D Gluckstein, op cit, p44.
9   Ibid, p69.
10   Ibid, p89.
11   L Trotsky, 'What Next? Vital Questions for the German Proletariat', in L Trotsky, op cit, p212.
12   C Zetkin, 'The Struggle against Fascism', in D Beetham (ed), *Marxists in Face of Fascism* (Manchester, 1983), pp104, 109-110.
13   Ibid, p110.
14   L Trotsky, 'What Next? Vital Questions for the German Proletariat', in L Trotsky, op cit, p155.
15   L Trotsky, 'The German Puzzle', in L Trotsky, op cit, p266.
16   G Feder, cited in D Guerin, op cit, p86.
17   D Gluckstein, op cit, p135.
18   Ibid, pp175-176.
19   Ibid, pp173-177.
20   Ibid, pp182-183.
21   E Fromm, *Fear of Freedom* (London, 1942), p188.
22   D Gluckstein, op cit, pp148-149.
23   For a critique of Goldhagen see H Maitles, 'Never Again!', *International Socialism* 77 (1997).
24   O Bauer, 'Austrian Democracy under Fire', in D Beetham (ed), op cit, p289.
25   G Matteotti, cited in D Guerin, op cit, p109.
26   R Hilferding, 'Between the Decisions', cited in D Beetham (ed), op cit, p261.
27   B Fowkes, *Communism in Germany under the Weimar Republic* (London, 1984), p163.
28   L Trotsky, 'What is National Socialism?', in L Trotsky, op cit, p405.

Scenes from the class war: Ken Loach and socialist cinema

A review of G Fuller (ed), **Loach on Loach** *(Faber & Faber, 1998), £11.99; and G McKnight (ed),* **Agent of Challenge and Defiance** *(Flick Books, 1997), £14.95*

JOHN NEWSINGER

For 35 years Ken Loach has been making films about the realities of class society in Britain. From his early days at the BBC, which produced the celebrated 'Wednesday Plays' *Up The Junction* (1965), *Cathy Come Home* (1966), *In Two Minds* (1967) and *The Big Flame* (1969), through to his feature films of the 1990s, *Hidden Agenda* (1990), *Riff-Raff* (1991), *Raining Stones* (1993), *Ladybird, Ladybird* (1994), *Land and Freedom* (1995), *Carla's Song* (1996) and most recently the magnificent *My Name Is Joe* (1998), Loach has maintained a steadfast commitment to working class experience, portraying both the relentless struggle to survive in capitalist society, and the fightback against oppression and exploitation. Over the years he has, in often difficult circumstances, produced a marvellous body of work, culminating in the epic *Land and Freedom*, still going strong with *My Name Is Joe*, arguably his best film so far, and rumoured to be working with writer Jim Allen on a new film about James Connolly and the Easter Rising. After 30-odd years, Loach seems to have been given a new lease of life, playing off against the crass hypocrisies of Tony Blair's New Labour. Paradoxically, his most recent films are better known on the Continent than they are in Britain, where his passions and concerns have, to all intents and purposes, been marginalised and outlawed as Blair and Co have sought to dedicate Cool Britannia to the service of big business.

At last, however, we have two books celebrating Loach and his work: *Loach on Loach*, edited by Graham Fuller, and *Agent of Challenge and*

Defiance, edited by George McKnight. The first is a volume in the Faber & Faber series of extended interviews with notable film directors. Loach joins the likes of Woody Allen, Frederico Fellini, David Lynch, Alfred Hitchcock, Krzysztof Kiéslowski, David Cronenberg, Martin Scorsese and, most recently, John Sayles. This is an indispensable volume that no socialist interested in the cinema should be without. The second, edited by McKnight, is a mixed collection of essays examining different aspects of Loach's work for a primarily academic audience. A number of the contributions are of interest, but taken as a whole the volume lacks bite.

From *Cathy Comes Home* to *Days of Hope*

In his introduction to the *Loach on Loach* volume, Graham Fuller usefully divides Loach's career into four phases: first, the 'Wednesday Plays' period of the 1960s; second, the period of the more overtly political plays and the first feature films in the 1970s; third, the documentary period in the 1980s when Loach was successfully strangled by censorship; and lastly, the succession of powerful feature films that he has made and is still making in the 1990s. Let us look at the first two phases.

Loach directed ten 'Wednesday Plays', of which the best known is undoubtedly *Cathy Come Home*, written by Jeremy Sandford and starring Carol White and Ray Brooks. This powerful drama of homelessness was first broadcast in 1966 and is generally credited with making the homeless a political issue and with inspiring the establishment of the charity Shelter. It successfully highlighted the failure of Harold Wilson's Labour government to seriously tackle a major social injustice.

In retrospect, however, Loach himself is quite critical of the play:

> *Shelter's done some terrific work. It's been an excellent resource for research and has obviously helped a lot of families find homes and that's a very positive thing. What's inadequate is the idea that homelessness is a problem that should be solved by a charity. It boils down to a structural problem within society. Who owns the land? Who owns the building industry? How does housing relate to unemployment? How do we decide what we produce, where we produce it, under what conditions? And housing fits into that. You can't abstract housing from the economic pattern. So it is a political issue; the film just didn't examine it at that level.*

He goes on to describe how the Labour minister of housing, Anthony Greenwood, met with him and his producer, Tony Garnett, to express his appreciation of the play. When they tried to discuss with him what the Labour government was actually going to do about homelessness, 'He ummed and ahhed and talked around it.' Even Edward Heath, the then leader of the Conservative Party, expressed concern. Of course, by the standards of New Labour, Greenwood would be a dangerous red— indeed so would Edward Heath—and even an expression of concern would be most unlikely. Nevertheless, is Loach being too hard on himself here? Certainly, *Cathy Come Home* had limitations which meant that the likes of Greenwood and Heath never felt threatened by it, but this particular viewer can still remember the feelings of anger and outrage with which the play left him. These feelings were not contain- able within the parameters of British Labourism. This seems to have been Loach's own experience.

Cathy Come Home was a step, perhaps a necessary step, on the way to a more explicitly Marxist stance, to a determination to make more overtly socialist films. If the likes of Greenwood and Heath could respond favourably to the play then the conclusion that Loach and Garnett drew was that it 'couldn't have been very political. As a result, we said to ourselves that if we were to do a film like that again, we'd somehow have to tackle the ownership of land, the building industry and the financing behind it. Otherwise you're not really challenging any- thing'.[1] In a period of increasing class conflict, when first Wilson's Labour government and then Heath's Conservative government con- fronted the trade unions, Loach and Garnett were to find themselves with a growing audience, moving from drama exposing the victimisation of the poor to drama celebrating working class resistance.

In 1969 Loach directed *The Big Flame*, in 1971 *The Rank and File* and in 1975 the epic *Days of Hope*, all written by the Trotskyist play- wright Jim Allen.[2] These were a response to and celebration of the great class battles that saw the defeat of Labour's 'In Place of Strife' and of the Conservatives' Industrial Relations Act, that saw first the defeat of Heath's government by the miners in 1972 and then its destruction at their hands in 1974. As far as we know, this was not drama that the likes of Greenwood or Heath found the least bit congenial.

It is perhaps a mistake to describe the Loach-Allen dramas as merely celebrating working class resistance, because they were also very much concerned with explaining betrayal and defeat. They were determined to show not just working class men and women fighting back, displaying their creativity, courage, intelligence and humanity in battle with the bosses, but also how they were sold down the river by the official leaders of the labour movement, whether it was the trade union leader or Labour government minister. This is a crucial dimension of *The Big Flame*, with its occupation of the Liverpool docks, of *The Rank and File*, a dramatic account of the 1970 Pilkington's strike (the firm was cunningly disguised as Wilkinson's), and, lastly, of *Days of Hope*, their epic four part dramatic reconstruction of working class experience from 1916 through to the defeat of the General Strike in 1926. In some ways, this particular emphasis on betrayal can be seen as deriving from Jim Allen's orthodox Trotskyism. He was for a period a member of the Socialist Labour League and has tended ever since to continue that organisation's tendency to reduce all the problems confronting the working class to 'a crisis of leadership', and Loach has fallen in with this approach.

The danger of the 'crisis of leadership' notion is that abstracted from a more general appreciation of the balance of class forces, of the relative strengths and weaknesses of both the working class and the capitalist class, it can become a variant of conspiracy theory, whereby all that is necessary is to expose what is going on, to show the reformist or Stalinist leadership for what they are and, hopefully, replace them with a revolutionary leadership that will lead the working class to victory. In a revolutionary situation, the decisive moment can, indeed, be reduced to the question of leadership, but, short of that, other considerations require attention. It is necessary to consider the level of organisation and consciousness of the working class, the state of working class morale, the degree of confidence, the strength of traditions of solidarity, the willingness to engage in struggle, how angry people are, and how confident they are that they can do something about it. And, moreover, it always has to be remembered how quickly all this can change, so that an apparently cowed workforce, stitched up by a corrupt alliance of union leaders and management, can suddenly explode into action, as happened at Pilkington's. The question of leadership has to be placed in this context. Interestingly enough, I would argue that this is exactly what Loach and Allen do in *The Big Flame* and *The Rank and File,* where the drama remained at ground level, focusing on working class people organising and fighting back. It is lost in *Days of Hope.*

Days of Hope is a working class saga that follows Philip, his wife Sarah, and her brother Ben through the tumultuous years of war and class struggle from 1916 to 1926. The first two episodes, '1916—Joining Up' and '1921' are magnificent socialist dramas that successfully use individual experience of historical developments to illuminate the meaning of those developments. By the disappointing fourth episode, '1926—The General Strike', however, the drama has abandoned this necessary grounding. Instead, it has become an overly didactic history lesson intent on showing how the General Strike was betrayed. Loach and Allen were concerned to 'prove', beyond any shadow of doubt, that it was betrayed by showing how the sell out was contrived at national level. It was as if showing that union leaders betray strikes was enough to make them magically disappear, or at the very least obliterate their influence. Unfortunately, one of the problems with merely proving betrayal is that it can fulfil working class expectations of the inevitability of betrayal, producing resignation and hopelessness rather than anger and increased determination. From the shop steward who becomes a foreman to the union leader who joins the ermine vermin in the House of Lords, traitors are very much part of working class folklore.

What was crucially missing from the last episode of *Days of Hope* was how the General Strike, the most momentous act of solidarity in British working class history, was actually experienced by the rank and file, of how they reacted to the betrayal and the conclusions that the most politically advanced of them drew. Working class experience and its articulation, Loach and Allen's great strength, was abandoned in order to prove the betrayal of the General Strike. The final episode seemed almost to be intended to satisfy professional historians rather than a working class audience. The drama had lost its way, had become boring just at the moment where it attempted to make its big point. *Days of Hope* ended on the wrong note. It has to be accounted a heroic failure.

Subsequently, this dramatic failure was put down by some to the Trotskyist politics that informed the series. This is not so. *Days of Hope* did not fail because of its Trotskyist politics, but because Loach and Allen failed to successfully dramatise those politics. This was not a mistake they were to make with their later epic, *Land and Freedom*, where the temptation to have scenes showing the Stalinist apparatchiks actually planning the downfall of the Spanish Revolution is firmly resisted.

One interesting point worth briefly considering is the response of a section of the academic left to *Days of Hope*, in particular the journal *Screen*. There was a brief furore around the notion of 'the classic realist text', occasioned by Colin McCabe's indictment of Loach's failure to develop a revolutionary cinematic form that would somehow endow the audience with a revolutionary awareness of contradiction. Two problems arose from this scholasticism, problems that, it must be said, never seemed to trouble Loach: first, those few films that ever attempted to fulfil McCabe's ambitions proved incomprehensible and, second, far from advancing working class struggle, the whole exercise proved more adapted to advancing academic careers.[3]

The year 1967 saw the appearance of Loach's first feature film, *Poor Cow*, based on the Nell Dunn novel. This was followed in 1969 by *Kes*, based on the Barry Hines novel. Both these films explored a very different dimension of working class experience from his class war dramas. They focused on working class people surviving in capitalist society and on the costs and consequences involved. *Kes* in particular is a magnificent achievement. Similar themes were explored in subsequent feature films: *Family Life* (1971), *The Gamekeeper* (1980), and *Looks and*

Smiles (1981). *Looks and Smiles* has been described by Loach as being in some ways a sequel to *Kes*. Whereas in *Kes* the tragedy was of the working class lad being sentenced to a life of working down the pit, by 1980 in *Looks and Smiles* the tragedy was of the working class lads being sentenced to life on the dole! Times change.

Censored

Loach had lost any illusions he might have had in the Labour Party and Labour governments during Harold Wilson's first term in office from 1964 to 1970. Wilson's support for the US war in Vietnam and his notorious attack on the National Union of Seamen in 1966 all helped convince Loach, along with thousands of other socialists, that there was no place for them in the Labour Party. The conclusion he drew was that Labour 'was the enemy in another guise'. He acknowledged that there were still socialists in the Labour Party, but 'as far as the leadership goes, it's still the enemy'.[4] The election of Margaret Thatcher and the Conservatives to power in 1979, however, was to herald a dramatic intensification of the class struggle, at least on the part of the ruling class. The deliberate creation of mass unemployment, the calculated wrecking of the lives of millions of working class men and women, was accompanied by an unprecedented assault on the trade union movement.

In these circumstances Loach decided that it was not enough to direct plays or feature films, no matter how politically informed they might be. He determined to turn his considerable talents to the production of documentaries, made for television, that would put the socialist case. Thatcher would be condemned, her accomplices in the labour movement would be exposed, and the rank and file would be given a voice. The result was the most dramatic and blatant episode of political censorship, the suppression of a major film maker, since the Second World War. Loach describes his own thinking at the time:

> *I'd lost direction as regards feature films. But I also wanted to try to make a contribution, however minimal, to the political struggle that was going on...by the early 80s working people were getting hammered right, left and centre. Margaret Thatcher had embarked on her catastrophic project of revitalising the economy in the way she saw fit—restoring the profit margins by attacking the working class. Unemployment went up from half a million to over 3 million in a year or so. Factories were closing. Families were being destroyed. With that in mind, the idea of making a feature film which took three years to finance and another year to come out and then got shown in an arthouse to ten people and a dog just seemed a crazy thing for me to be doing.[5]*

Out of these concerns came the four part documentary *Questions of Leadership* (1983), subtitled, 'Problems of Democracy in Trade Unions: Some Views from the Frontline'. According to Loach, the series told how:

> *In the first three years of the Thatcher government there had been a whole series of major strikes and the possibilities of more by an organised work-force that was basically militant, undefeated, and prepared to fight closures, prepared to fight wage cuts, prepared to fight all the things that we now take for granted as an act of god. The response of the union leaders to this mili-tancy was to make certain that each strike happened on its own; not to call out other sections of the union in support; to do a deal before the goal was achieved so that the people out on strike were constantly confused; not to challenge the employers or the government in the way the workers who were prepared to take action wanted. As a result, all the strikes were defeated. So that's what the films said.*[6]

The first episode looked at the Lawrence Scott and Electromotors closure, the steel workers' strike, British Leyland, British Rail and the NHS. The second looked at democracy, or rather the lack of democracy, in the electricians' union, the EETPU, including an interview with union leader Frank Chapple, who cut it short by walking out. The third dealt with the victimisation of Derek Robinson at British Leyland. And the fourth and last was a film of a day's discussion and debate of the issues raised that included contributions from both critics and supporters of the union leaderships. The four programmes provided a unique opportunity for a number of left wing and rank and file trade unionists to criticise the conduct of the trade union leaders and the lack of democracy in the trade unions. These criticisms were explicitly endorsed by the commentary, which at one point stated quite bluntly that, in a very real sense, 'the leaders of the trade unions have kept this Conservative government in power'.[7]

There is an excellent discussion of *Questions of Leadership* and its fate in the McKnight volume—Julian Petley's chapter, 'Ken Loach and Questions of Censorship'. Loach was eventually informed that the series was too unbalanced to be broadcast and required substantial changes, with Channel 4 and the Independent Broadcasting Authority blaming each other for the decision. The series was to be reduced to three pro-grammes, with each programme followed by a half hour discussion made by another director. The fourth programme that concluded the series was also to be made by someone else. This began a protracted process of negotiation and delay that dragged on into 1984 and the start of the Great Miners' Strike. By now the stakes were such that any chance of the programmes being broadcast in any shape whatsoever had vanished. As Loach himself observed, the union leaders criticised were the very men that 'the government and the Coal Board are relying on to leave the miners isolated. Anything which criticises them is really too sensitive to broadcast now'.[8] *Questions of Leadership* was killed. Legalistic pretexts were found to mask what was in reality straightforward political censorship.

Once the Great Miners' Strike was under way, Loach was commissioned by Melvyn Bragg's *The South Bank Show* to make a documentary looking at the songs and poems that were being written by the strikers about their experiences. The film included scenes of police violence against the pickets, and somewhat predictably it was decided not to show it due to lack of balance. Eventually it did appear on Channel 4 in January 1985, but with a balancing programme providing an opportunity for the former Communist Jimmy Reid to join the chorus attacking Arthur Scargill. It is worth remembering that coverage of the strike produced such breakthroughs in creative television as the celebrated filming of a mounted police charge at Orgreave provoking the miners into throwing anything they could lay their hands on at their attackers. This was shown on television the other way round to create the impression that the police charge was a response to attacks made on them. So much for balance.

The overall consequence of all this was, as Julian Petley points out, that 'one of Britain's most radical film makers was either marginalised or completely silenced during one of the most momentous, not to say catastrophic, decades in British political history'.[9]

Fighting to survive

The late 1980s saw Loach make a return to political film making. In 1986 he directed *Fatherland*, which prepared the way for a remarkable sustained period of creativity that is still going strong. The year 1990 saw the appearance of his underrated thriller *Hidden Agenda*. Set in Northern Ireland, the film combined the John Stalker and Colin Wallace affairs effectively enough to be described as 'the IRA entry at Cannes' by one Tory MP. It is a grim tale of conspiracy and assassination, involving a secret state that is running out of control, and ending with the police investigator, Kerrigan, walking away from what he knows has gone on. This is a fitting metaphor for the conduct of the liberal establishment throughout the whole war. The film impresses more with every viewing.

After *Hidden Agenda* Loach went on to make three films that explored working class experience in a period of defeat. *Riff-Raff* (1991) and *Raining Stones* (1993) are films about ducking and diving as class struggle, of guerrilla war and individual resistance within the capitalist system. The first, *Riff-Raff*, looks at a group of building workers, all fiddling the dole, converting a disused hospital into luxury flats, a symbolic rendering of the triumph of Thatcherism. Low pay, dangerous conditions and personal abuse are their everyday experience. They respond by taking as many liberties as possible while dreaming of something better. The only one of them who is politically aware, Larry, attempts to interest them in the union and even goes to the site manager to complain on behalf of his mates. His victimisation goes unopposed. This is a working class that has been defeated. The corrosive effects of this defeat are highlighted by the young Glaswegian, Stevie, who catches someone breaking into his squat (the poor robbing the poor) and discovers that his girlfriend is using heroin. Resistance does come in the end, however, although it is individual, not collective. After a fatal accident on the site, Stevie and one of his mates torch the building and bring the whole lot down. The end of the film is immensely satisfying, even if it does not point the way forward politically.

The harsh reality is that for millions of people at that time the collective response to oppression and exploitation did not seem a realistic prospect. Sticking your neck out has been replaced by ducking and diving. Nevertheless individual victories, small triumphs, can still be achieved even in the context of defeat. Loach celebrates these small scale victories, while recognising the larger picture of retreat and downturn. There is, however, always a voice in these films arguing for a collective response, advocating class politics. The only exception to this is the recent *My Name Is Joe*. How significant is this? Has the triumph of Blair's New Labour somehow demoralised Loach? My own view is that there are no real grounds for regarding this absence as ominous, as indicating a depoliticisation of his work. Instead, one can be confident that the voice advocating class politics will undoubtedly reappear and move centre stage when the working class once again moves into action as a class, and resistance becomes generalised.

Raining Stones follows the attempt of a working class family to retain their dignity and self respect in circumstances of poverty and unemployment. Bob wants his daughter to have a new dress for her first communion. He tries to raise the money by various means (rustling a sheep and stealing the turf from the Conservative Club's bowling green), but in the end has to go into debt, a debt he has no chance of paying. What Loach and writer Jim Allen show us are working class men and women trying everything to survive, while being preyed on by loan sharks, the purest exponents of Thatcherism. Once again, Bob is driven to lash out in an act of individual, not collective, resistance, and once again it is tremendously satisfying.

Loach's next film was *Ladybird, Ladybird* (1994), an almost unbearable experience. He acknowledges this as a film he personally 'feels very warmly toward', although, 'I can see it's quite a tough film for people to take'.[10] This is something of an understatement. Once again, it is a story of working class men and women surviving, but only just.

At one point in the *Loach on Loach* book, Graham Fuller asks him what has driven his work in the 1990s. His reply is most instructive:

As Britain emerged from the spell that Thatcher had put on it, I and perhaps some other film makers, felt very dissatisfied with ourselves. We felt we hadn't really put on the screen the appalling cost in human misery that aggressive Thatcherite politics had brought on everybody. We should have made films in the early 80s that really showed what was happening, but I know that I didn't. I think the last few years have been an attempt to remedy that.[11]

His most recent film, the outstanding *My Name Is Joe* (1998), continues in that vein, with its central character a reformed alcoholic fighting to survive in a community devastated by unemployment, drugs and crime.

Very different is *Carla's Song* (1996). Here we have a Glasweigian bus driver who refuses to knuckle down at work and be a 'good employee' confronting the realities of the US war on the Sandinistas in Nicaragua. George—standing in, one suspects, for the British working class—knows nothing of what is going on in Central America, of the brutal war that is being waged by the US backed Contras against the Nicaraguan people. He accompanies the Nicaraguan refugee, Carla, back to Nicaragua to help her search for her missing lover. The search becomes George's journey to understanding as he is forced to confront the enormity of what is being done in Nicaragua. An attempt by the common people to take control over their lives has brought the vengeance of the most powerful country in the world down on them. George cannot deal with this and returns home, hopefully a wiser man, while Carla remains behind to fight for the Nicaraguan Revolution.

One recent discussion of Loach's work, John Hill's 'Every Fuckin' Choice Stinks' that appeared in *Sight and Sound*, has argued that what we see in *Carla's Song* is Loach turning to the 'Hispanic "other"' for an embodiment of 'the purity of political spirit the British working class is increasingly seen to lack'. Certainly there is implicit in *Carla's Song* a lament that whereas the Spanish Civil War was a major issue within the British labour movement and someone like George might well have gone to fight there, today the Nicaraguan war has gone relatively unnoticed. Nevertheless, Hill is exaggerating what he sees as Loach's growing pessimism.[12] Instead, we have to see his films as dramatising what is undoubtedly the experience of an important section of the working class—trying to survive rather than fighting back. As the level of class conflict in Britain rises, as working class confidence increases and the fightback gathers momentum, so, without any doubt, this will be reflected and celebrated in Loach's films.

The Spanish Revolution

What of *Land and Freedom*? This is arguably Loach's masterpiece, one of the great socialist films. Here Loach not only produces a remarkable portrayal of revolution and of the fight against fascism, but also decisively settles the account with Stalinism. The film retells the story of George Orwell's *Homage To Catalonia*, but through the eyes and in the voice of Dave a young, idealistic, working class Communist from Liverpool. He falls in with the POUM in revolutionary Barcelona and becomes a witness to the secret history of the Spanish Revolution. His story is told through the old letters, photographs and newspapers that his granddaughter has discovered after his death.

Dave is a witness to the bravery with which the POUM militia, both men and women, fight the fascists. He fights alongside them and has friends and comrades killed. He is a witness to the carrying out of the revolution—Loach's celebrated scene when the issue of collectivisation is discussed and voted on. Nevertheless, he still supports the Communist Party line of postponing the revolution until after Franco has been defeated (as did Orwell), and eventually prepares to transfer from the POUM militia to the International Brigades (as did Orwell). Dave is in Barcelona recovering from a wound at the time of the revolutionary outbreak of May 1937 and sees the Communist apparatus in action, suppressing the revolutionary left in the interests of Stalin's foreign policy. He realises that what his POUM comrades, including his lover, Blanca, have been saying about the Communists and their counter-revolutionary intentions is true, whereas what the Communists are saying about the POUM being fascist agents and stooges is lies. Dave has fought alongside these people, and he knows they are being slandered. He tears up his party card and rejoins his militia unit. The terrible climax of the film is the enforced disarming and disbandment of the POUM militia and the arrest of its leaders under the guns of Communist troops. In the confusion, Blanca is shot and killed. The revolution is dead, murdered.

The last image of the film is of Dave's funeral with his granddaughter and some old comrades giving the revolutionary salute over his grave. The spirit of revolution lives on. Loach explores an episode of heroic defeat, but succeeds in leaving his audience inspired.

Last word

Let us leave the last word with Loach himself. He is replying to Graham Fuller asking whether his socialist politics were still relevant:

> *It just grows ever more apparent that there are two classes in society, that their interests are irreconcilable, and that one survives at the expense of the other. In the 60s, we didn't have the mass unemployment we have now. We didn't have such alienation. We didn't insist that the workforce should be ever more flexible, ever more exploited. All that was endorsed by Thatcher. Her politics were inverse Marxism in a way: the working class must pay; the organised working class must be disorganised. And that's exactly what she did... In Britain, the recurring themes don't go away. The human cost of the experiment in free market economics that Thatcher inflicted on us is still working itself out because the policy hasn't changed, and it won't change drastically under Tony Blair. The human cost is something that never goes away. Its always in front of your eyes and its always something that draws you to deal with it. You walk through the cities, especially the outskirts of cities, and you see people are not having a good time. The underlying observation of what people are experiencing is that things don't have to be this way. There are better ways to live.*[13]

Notes

1 G Fuller (ed), *Loach on Loach* (London, 1998), p24.
2 Born in 1926 in Manchester, Jim Allen worked in many industries, including the building trade, the merchant navy and as a miner. In January 1965 he became a script writer on *Coronation Street* (Stan Ogden, it is worth remembering, was at one time a former International Brigade member, although any residue leftism was soon eliminated from the programme) where he worked for 18 months. He resigned after writing a script in which the whole cast go on a mystery bus tour from the *Rover's Return* and are all killed when the bus goes over a cliff. Unfortunately this episode was never made. He is one of the most important 20th century British dramatists. For a discussion of his work see P Madden, 'Jim Allen', in G Brandt (ed), *British Television Drama* (Cambridge, 1991).
3 There is a discussion of this controversy in D Knight, 'Naturalism, Narration and Critical Perspective: Ken Loach and the Experimental Method', in G McKnight (ed), *Agent of Challenge and Defiance* (Trowbridge, 1997).
4 G Fuller, op cit, p24.
5 Ibid, p64.
6 Ibid, p66.
7 G McKnight, op cit, p106. Once again, the 'crisis of leadership' thesis is not an adequate explanation of the defeat of the unions at the hands of the Conservatives. This can be demonstrated quite simply: the union leaders had been just as prone to betrayal in the early 1970s but had been carried along, against their will, by a

working class revolt that generalised class conflict whether they liked it or not. This did not happen in the early 1980s when the working class was on the defensive and was defeated in detail. This is not to let the union leaders off the hook. They certainly played their part in the defeats of the time, but their contribution, shameful though it was, has to be put in the wider context of the balance of class forces.

8   Ibid, p109.
9   Ibid, p119.
10   G Fuller, op cit, p94.
11   p111.
12   J Hill, 'Every Fuckin' Choice Stinks', *Sight and Sound* (November, 1998). For a more fundamental critique of Loach, see B Light's letter in *Sight and Sound* (January, 1999).
13   G Fuller, op cit, p113.

The Far Left in the English Revolution

BRIAN MANNING

BRIAN MANNING is one of the foremost historians of the English Revolution. He has defended and extended an explicitly Marxist approach to history. In his latest book, he examines the role of the most radical elements within the English Revolution, which he controversially calls the far left. He demonstrates that this far left foreshadowed the development of working class consciousness and revolutionary socialist politics. This fascinating volume is essential reading for all those who wish to find out about the extraordinary political developments in this most exciting period in English history.

Bookmarks publication £7.95 + £1.20p&p, available from Bookmarks, the socialist bookshop
1 Bloomsbury Street, London WC1B 3QE
Phone 0171 637 1848, fax 0171 637 3616
email bookmarks_bookshop@compuserve.com

The Socialist Workers Party is one of an international grouping of socialist organisations:

AUSTRALIA	International Socialists, PO Box A338, Sydney South
BRITAIN	Socialist Workers Party, PO Box 82, London E3
CANADA	International Socialists, PO Box 339, Station E, Toronto, Ontario M6H 4E3
CYPRUS	Ergatiki Demokratia, PO Box 7280, Nicosia
DENMARK	Internationale Socialister, P0 Box 5113, 8100 Aarhus C
GERMANY	Linksruck, Postfach 304 183, 20359 Hamburg
GREECE	Sosialistiko Ergatiko Komma, c/o Workers Solidarity, PO Box 8161, Athens 100 10
HOLLAND	Internationale Socialisten, PO Box 92052, 1090AA Amsterdam
IRELAND	Socialist Workers Party, PO Box 1648, Dublin 8
NEW ZEALAND	Socialist Workers Organization, PO Box 8851, Auckland
NORWAY	Internasjonale Socialisterr, Postboks 9226 Grønland, 0134 Oslo
POLAND	Solidarność Socjalistyczna, PO Box 12, 01-900 Warszawa 118
SPAIN	Socialismo Internacional, Apartado 563, 08080 Barcelona
UNITED STATES	International Socialist Organisation, PO Box 16085, Chicago, Illinois 60616
ZIMBABWE	International Socialist Organisation, PO Box 6758, Harare

The following issues of *International Socialism* (second series) are available price £3 (including postage) from IS Journal, PO Box 82, London E3 3LH. *International Socialism* 2:58 and 2:65 are available on cassette from the Royal National Institute for the Blind (Peterborough Library Unit). Phone 01733 370777.

International Socialism 2:82 Spring 1999
Lindsey German: The Blair project cracks ★ Dan Atkinson and Larry Elliott: Reflating Keynes: a different view of the crisis ★ Peter Morgan: The new Keynesians: staking a hold in the system? ★ Rob Hoveman: Brenner and crisis: a critique ★ Chris Nineham: Art and alienation: a reply to John Molyneux ★ Paul McGarr: Fascists brought to book ★ Brian Manning: Revisionism revised ★ Neil Davidson: In perspective: Tom Nairn ★

International Socialism 2:81 Winter 1998
Alex Callinicos: World capitalism at the abyss ★ Mike Haynes and Pete Glatter: The Russian catastrophe ★ Phil Marfleet: Globalisation and the Third World ★ Lindsey German: In a class of its own ★ Judy Cox: John Reed: reporting on the revolution ★ Kevin Ovenden: The resistible rise of Adolf Hitler ★

International Socialism 2:80 Autumn 1998
Clare Fermont: Indonesia: the inferno of revolution ★ Workers' representatives and socialists: Three interviews from Indonesia ★ Chris Bambery: Report from Indonesia ★ Tony Cliff: Revolution and counter-revolution: lessons for Indonesia ★ John Molyneux: The legitimacy of modern art ★ Gary McFarlane: A respectable trade? Slavery and the rise of capitalism ★ Paul McGarr: The French Revolution: Marxism versus capitalism ★ Shaun Doherty: Will the real James Connolly please stand up? ★

International Socialism 2:79 Summer 1998
John Rees: The return of Marx? ★ Lindsey German: Reflections on *The Communist Manifesto* ★ Judy Cox: An introduction to Marx's theory of alienation ★ Judith Orr: Making a comeback: the Marxist theory of crisis ★ Megan Trudell: New Labour, old conflicts: the story so far ★ John Molyneux: State of the art ★ Anna Chen: In perspective: Sergei Eisenstein ★ Jonathan Neale: Vietnam veterans ★ Phil Gasper: Bookwatch: Marxism and science ★

International Socialism 2:78 Spring 1998
Colin Sparks: The eye of the storm ★ Shin Gyoung-hee: The crisis and the workers' movement in South Korea ★ Rob Hoveman: Financial crises and the real economy ★ Peter Morgan: Class divisions in the gay community ★ Alex Callinicos: The secret of the dialectic ★ John Parrington: It's life, Jim, but not as we know it ★ Judy Cox: Robin Hood: earl, outlaw or rebel? ★ Ian Birchall: The vicelike hold of nationalism? A comment on Megan Trudell's 'Prelude to revolution' ★ William Keach: In perspective: Alexander Cockburn and Christopher Hitchens ★

International Socialism 2:76 Autumn 1997
Mike Haynes: Was there a parliamentary alternative in 1917? ★ Megan Trudell: Prelude to revolution: class consciousness and the First World War ★ Judy Cox: A light in the darkness ★ Pete Glatter: Victor Serge: writing for the future ★ Gill Hubbard: A guide to action ★ Chris Bambery: Review article: Labour's history of hope and despair ★

International Socialism 2:75 Summer 1997
John Rees: The class struggle under New Labour ★ Alex Callinicos: Europe: the mounting crisis ★ Lance Selfa: Mexico after the Zapatista uprising ★ William Keach: Rise like lions? Shelley and the revolutionary left ★ Judy Cox: What state are we really in? ★ John Parrington: In perspective: Valentin Voloshinov ★

International Socialism 2:74 Spring 1997
Colin Sparks: Tories, Labour and the crisis in education ★ Colin Wilson: The politics of information technology ★ Mike Gonzalez: No more heroes: Nicaragua 1996 ★ Christopher Hill: Tulmults and commotions: turning the world upside down ★ Peter Morgan: Capitalism without frontiers? ★ Alex Callinicos: Minds, machines and evolution ★ Anthony Arnove: In perspective: Noam Chomsky★

International Socialism 2:73 Winter 1996
Chris Harman: Globalisation: a critique of a new orthodoxy ★ Chris Bambery: Marxism and sport ★ John Parrington: Computers and consciousness ★ Joe Faith: Dennett, materialism and empiricism ★ Megan Trudell: Who made the American Revolution? ★ Mark O'Brien: The class conflicts which shaped British history ★ John Newsinger: From class war to Cold War ★

Alex Callinicos: The state in debate ★ Charlie Kimber: Review article: coming to terms with barbarism in Rwanda in Burundi★

International Socialism 2:72 Autumn 1996
Alex Callinicos: Betrayal and discontent: Labour under Blair ★ Sue Cockerill and Colin Sparks: Japan in crisis ★ Richard Levins: When science fails us ★ Ian Birchall: The Babeuf bicentenary: conspiracy or revolutionary party? ★ Brian Manning: A voice for the poor ★ Paul O'Flinn: From the kingdom of necessity to the kingdom of freedom: Morris's *News from Nowhere* ★ Clare Fermont: Bookwatch: Palestine and the Middle East 'peace process'★

International Socialism 2:71 Summer 1996
Chris Harman: The crisis of bourgeois economics ★ Hassan Mahamdallie: William Morris and revolutionary Marxism ★ Alex Callinicos: Darwin, materialism and revolution ★ Chris Nineham: Raymond Williams: revitalising the left? ★ Paul Foot: A passionate prophet of liberation ★ Gill Hubbard: Why has feminism failed women? ★ Lee Sustar: Bookwatch: fighting to unite black and white★

International Socialism 2:70 Spring 1996
Alex Callinicos: South Africa after apartheid ★ Chris Harman: France's hot December ★ Brian Richardson: The making of a revolutionary ★ Gareth Jenkins: Why Lucky Jim turned right—an obituary of Kingsley Amis ★ Mark O'Brien: The bloody birth of capitalism ★ Lee Humber: Studies in revolution ★ Adrian Budd: A new life for Lenin ★ Martin Smith: Bookwatch: the General Strike★

International Socialism 2:69 Winter 1995
Lindsey German: The Balkan war: can there be peace? ★ Duncan Blackie: The left and the Balkan war ★ Nicolai Gentchev: The myth of welfare dependency ★ Judy Cox: Wealth, poverty and class in Britain today ★ Peter Morgan: Trade unions and strikes ★ Julie Waterson: The party at its peak ★ Megan Trudell: Living to some purpose ★ Nick Howard: The rise and fall of socialism in one city ★ Andy Durgan: Bookwatch: Civil war and revolution in Spain ★

International Socialism 2:68 Autumn 1995
Ruth Brown: Racism and immigration in Britain ★ John Molyneux: Is Marxism deterministic? ★ Stuart Hood: News from nowhere? ★ Lee Sustar: Communism in the heart of the beast ★ Peter Linebaugh: To the teeth and forehead of our faults ★ George Paizis: Back to the future ★ Phil Marshall: The children of stalinism ★ Paul D'Amato: Bookwatch: 100 years of cinema ★

International Socialism 2:67 Summer 1995
Paul Foot: When will the Blair bubble burst? ★ Chris Harman: From Bernstein to Blair—100 years of revisionism ★ Chris Bambery: Was the Second World War a war for democracy? ★ Alex Callinicos: Hope against the Holocaust ★Chris Nineham: Is the media all powerful? ★ Peter Morgan: How the West was won ★ Charlie Hore: Bookwatch: China since Mao ★

International Socialism 2:66 Spring 1995
Dave Crouch: The crisis in Russia and the rise of the right ★ Phil Gasper: Cruel and unusual punishment: the politics of crime in the United States ★ Alex Callinicos: Backwards to liberalism ★ John Newsinger: Matewan: film and working class struggle ★ John Rees: The light and the dark ★ Judy Cox: How to make the Tories disappear ★ Charlie Hore: Jazz: a reply to the critics ★ Pat Riordan: Bookwatch: Ireland ★

International Socialism 2:65 Special issue
Lindsey German: Frederick Engels: life of a revolutionary ★ John Rees: Engels' Marxism ★ Chris Harman: Engels and the origins of human society ★ Paul McGarr: Engels and natural science ★

International Socialism 2:63 Summer 1994
Alex Callinicos: Crisis and class struggle in Europe today ★ Duncan Blackie: The United Nations and the politics of imperialism ★ Brian Manning: The English Revolution and the transition from feudalism to capitalism ★ Lee Sustar: The roots of multi-racial labour unity in the United States ★ Peter Linebaugh: Days of villainy: a reply to two critics ★ Dave Sherry: Trotsky's last, greatest struggle ★ Peter Morgan: Geronimo and the end of the Indian wars ★ Dave Beecham: Ignazio Silone and *Fontamara* ★ Chris Bambery: Bookwatch: understanding fascism ★

International Socialism 2:62 Spring 1994
Sharon Smith: Mistaken identity—or can identity politics liberate the oppressed? ★ Iain Ferguson: Containing the crisis—crime and the Tories ★ John Newsinger: Orwell and the Spanish Revolution ★ Chris Harman: Change at the first millenium ★ Adrian Budd: Nation and empire—Labour's foreign policy 1945-51 ★ Gareth Jenkins: Novel questions ★ Judy Cox: Blake's revolution ★ Derek Howl: Bookwatch: the Russian Revolution ★

International Socialism 2:61 Winter 1994
Lindsey German: Before the flood? ★ John Molyneux: The 'politically correct' controversy ★ David McNally: E P Thompson—class struggle and historical materialism ★ Charlie Hore: Jazz—a people's music ★ Donny Gluckstein: Revolution and the challenge of labour ★ Charlie Kimber: Bookwatch: the Labour Party in decline ★

International Socialism 2:59 Summer 1993
Ann Rogers: Back to the workhouse ★ Kevin Corr and Andy Brown: The labour aristocracy and the roots of reformism ★ Brian Manning: God, Hill and Marx ★ Henry Maitles: Cutting the wire: a criticial appraisal of Primo Levi ★ Hazel Croft: Bookwatch: women and work ★

International Socialism 2:58 Spring 1993
Chris Harman: Where is capitalism going? (part one) ★ Ruth Brown and Peter Morgan: Politics and the class struggle today: a roundtable discussion ★ Richard Greeman: The return of Comrade Tulayev: Victor Serge and the tragic vision of Stalinism ★ Norah Carlin: A new English revolution ★ John Charlton: Building a new world ★ Colin Barker: A reply to Dave McNally ★

International Socialism 2:56 Autumn 1992
Chris Harman: The Return of the National Question ★ Dave Treece: Why the Earth Summit failed ★ Mike Gonzalez: Can Castro survive? ★ Lee Humber and John Rees: The good old cause—an interview with Christopher Hill ★ Ernest Mandel: The Impasse of Schematic Dogmatism ★

International Socialism 2:55 Summer 1992
Alex Callinicos: Race and class ★ Lee Sustar: Racism and class struggle in the American Civil War era ★ Lindsey German and Peter Morgan: Prospects for socialists—an interview with Tony Cliff ★ Robert Service: Did Lenin lead to Stalin? ★ Samuel Farber: In defence of democratic revolutionary socialism ★ David Finkel: Defending 'October' or sectarian dogmatism? ★ Robin Blackburn: Reply to John Rees ★ John Rees: Dedicated followers of fashion ★ Colin Barker: In praise of custom ★ Sheila McGregor: Revolutionary witness ★

International Socialism 2:54 Spring 1992
Sharon Smith: Twilight of the American dream ★ Mike Haynes: Class and crisis—the transition in eastern Europe ★ Costas Kossis: A miracle without end? Japanese capitalism and the world economy ★ Alex Callinicos: Capitalism and the state system: A reply to Nigel Harris ★ Steven Rose: Do animals have rights? ★ John Charlton: Crime and class in the 18th century ★ John Rees: Revolution, reform and working class culture ★ Chris Harman: Blood simple ★

International Socialism 2:51 Summer 1991
Chris Harman: The state and capitalism today ★ Alex Callinicos: The end of nationalism? ★ Sharon Smith: Feminists for a strong state? ★ Colin Sparks and Sue Cockerill: Goodbye to the Swedish miracle ★ Simon Phillips: The South African Communist Party and the South African working class ★ John Brown: Class conflict and the crisis of feudalism ★

International Socialism 2:49 Winter 1990
Chris Bambery: The decline of the Western Communist Parties ★ Ernest Mandel: A theory which has not withstood the test of time ★ Chris Harman: Criticism which does not withstand the test of logic ★ Derek Howl: The law of value In the USSR ★ Terry Eagleton: Shakespeare and the class struggle ★ Lionel Sims: Rape and pre-state societies ★ Sheila McGregor: A reply to Lionel Sims ★

International Socialism 2:48 Autumn 1990
Lindsey German: The last days of Thatcher ★ John Rees: The new imperialism ★ Neil Davidson and Donny Gluckstein: Nationalism and the class struggle in Scotland ★ Paul McGarr: Order out of chaos ★

International Socialism 2:46 Winter 1989
Chris Harman: The storm breaks ★ Alex Callinicos: Can South Africa be reformed? ★ John Saville: Britain, the Marshall Plan and the Cold War ★ Sue Clegg: Against the stream ★ John Rees: The rising bourgeoisie ★

International Socialism 2:44 Autumn 1989
Charlie Hore: China: Tiananmen Square and after ★ Sue Clegg: Thatcher and the welfare state ★ John Molyneux: *Animal Farm* revisited ★ David Finkel: After Arias, is the revolution over? ★ John Rose: Jews in Poland ★

International Socialism 2:41 Winter 1988
Polish socialists speak out: Solidarity at the Crossroads ★ Mike Haynes: Nightmares of the market ★ Jack Robertson: Socialists and the unions ★ Andy Strouthous: Are the unions in decline? ★ Richard Bradbury: What is Post-Structuralism? ★ Colin Sparks: George Bernard Shaw ★

International Socialism 2:39 Summer 1988
Chris Harman and Andy Zebrowski: Glasnost, before the storm ★ Chanie Rosenberg: Labour and the fight against fascism ★ Mike Gonzalez: Central America after the Peace Plan ★ Ian Birchall: Raymond Williams ★ Alex Callinicos: Reply to John Rees ★

International Socialism 2:35 Summer 1987
Pete Green: Capitalism and the Thatcher years ★ Alex Callinicos: Imperialism, capitalism and the state today ★ Ian Birchall: Five years of *New Socialist* ★ Callinicos and Wood debate 'Looking for alternatives to reformism' ★ David Widgery replies on 'Beating Time' ★

International Socialism 2:30 Autumn 1985
Gareth Jenkins: Where is the Labour Party heading? ★ David McNally: Debt, inflation and the rate of profit ★ Ian Birchall: The terminal crisis in the British Communist Party ★ replies on Women's oppression and *Marxism Today* ★

International Socialism 2:26 Spring 1985
Pete Green: Contradictions of the American boom ★ Colin Sparks: Labour and imperialism ★ Chris Bambery: Marx and Engels and the unions ★ Sue Cockerill: The municipal road to socialism ★ Norah Carlin: Is the family part of the superstructure? ★ Kieran Allen: James Connolly and the 1916 rebellion ★

International Socialism 2:18 Winter 1983
Donny Gluckstein: Workers' councils in Western Europe ★ Jane Ure Smith: The early Communist press in Britain ★ John Newsinger: The Bolivian Revolution ★ Andy Durgan: Largo Caballero and Spanish socialism ★ M Barker and A Beezer: Scarman and the language of racism ★

International Socialism 2:14 Winter 1981
Chris Harman: The riots of 1981 ★ Dave Beecham: Class struggle under the Tories ★ Tony Cliff: Alexandra Kollontai ★ L James and A Paczuska: Socialism needs feminism ★ reply to Cliff on Zetkin ★ Feminists In the labour movement ★